The Temple of the Jaguar

THE
TEMPLE
OF THE
JAGUAR

Travels in the Yucatán

Donald G. Schueler

SIERRA CLUB BOOKS
SAN FRANCISCO

The Sierra Club, founded in 1892 by John Muir, has devoted itself to the study and protection of the earth's scenic and ecological resources—mountains, wetlands, woodlands, wild shores and rivers, deserts and plains. The publishing program of the Sierra Club offers books to the public as a nonprofit educational service in the hope that they may enlarge the public's understanding of the Club's basic concerns. The point of view expressed in each book, however, does not necessarily represent that of the Club. The Sierra Club has some sixty chapters coast to coast, in Canada, Hawaii, and Alaska. For information about how you may participate in its programs to preserve wilderness and the quality of life, please address inquiries to Sierra Club, 730 Polk Street, San Francisco, CA 94109.

LIBRARY OF CONGRESS CATALOGING-IN-PUBLICATION DATA
Schueler, Donald G.
    The Temple of the Jaguar / Donald G. Schueler.
      p.   cm.
    ISBN 0-87156-651-6
      1. Yucatán Peninsula—Description and travel—1981– 2. Belize—Description and travel—1981– I. Title.
    F1376.S4865 1993
    917.2'6—dc20   92-24452
                                                                          CIP

Production by Janet Vail
Jacket design by Amy Evans
Book design by Amy Evans

Printed in the United States of America on acid-free paper containing a minimum of 50% recovered waste paper of which at least 10% of the fiber content is post consumer waste.

10 9 8 7 6 5 4 3 2 1

TO BETTY WISDOM

Contents

Author's Note

I wish to thank the many persons, most of whom appear in the pages of this book, who were of help to me in one way or another during my journey through the Yucatán peninsula. To Anita Coleman, my dear friend in Campeche, I owe a special debt of gratitude. I would also like to express my appreciation to John Strand and Anne S. Bradburn for their helpful editorial advice, and to my editor, Jim Cohee, for his incredible patience.

In two or three instances, I have disguised the identity of people I met during my travels in order to protect their privacy. Also, for the sake of narrative coherence, I have rearranged the chronological order in which a couple of episodes occurred.

I should also perhaps note that the Mexican government's Secretariat of Urban Development and Ecology (SEDUE), an agency mentioned several times in this book, has been recently abolished. A newly created National Institute of Ecology (*Instituto Nacional de Ecologia*) will now be in charge of the nation's ecological resources. One can only hope that this change will result in greater protection for the marvellous wild places and wildlife that still survive in Campeche, Yucatán, and Quintana Roo.

Finally, a caveat: I hope that, in an incremental way, this book will afford the reader a good many insights into the history and ecology of the Yucatán peninsula, as well as some understanding of the diverse cultural, political, and social attitudes of its people. However, although I have certainly consulted the authorities, I do not claim to be a great authority on any of these subjects myself. First and last this narrative is simply the account of my experiences while wandering through an eccentrically beautiful, always interesting corner of the world that has become very dear to me.

Prologue

Behind the Temple of the Inscriptions at Palenque, a trail climbs the steep slope to the unreclaimed Temple of the Jaguar. If you follow it, you can pretend you are entering a serious tropical jungle—the sort of place where Tarzan or Rima the Bird Girl might swing by at any moment. The air is green and dripping wet, and the trees appear to be growing down instead of up. Their trunks flange out into swirled pleats as they swoop earthward; and when they touch ground they divide and subdivide into an elaborate network of exposed roots that forage hungrily across the sunless forest floor. Everywhere, vines thick as a freighter's mooring cables are busy tying things up. Without them, all this tangled scenery would surely fall apart.

Señor Morales says it's falling apart anyway. He is partial to apocalyptic utterances, but in this case he is probably right. The jungle on this little mountain is protected because it is part of the Palenque archaeological site, but it is only a measly fragment of the wilderness that covered most of Chiapas a couple of decades ago. Now, if you overlook the region from the air, you get an eyeful of other little mountains like this one stretching back into the Chiapas hinterlands; and on the impossibly steep slopes of almost all of them grow impossible crops of maize. Since jungles do not do well as token bits and pieces of their former selves, the long-term prospects for this small remnant are not promising.

For now, however, it not only looks like a proper jungle, it sounds like one. Evening in the tropics comes on in a hurry—one of the few things that does—and this is the favorite hour for black howler monkeys to engage in group expression. The bunch that is sounding off near me is higher up on the slope, on the other side of a ravine. Although the treetop foliage bends and sways under the considerable weight of its passage, they stay out of sight.

They are not called howler monkeys for nothing. On occasion their stupendous bellowing has been known to send unforewarned tourists running for their lives. Once one recognizes the source, however, all that hullabaloo becomes the stuff of comedy. By now I have heard this bunch hooting and hollering so often that I have decided I even know what they are saying—things like "Stop hoggin' that damn branch," or "Have any of you made up your minds where we're gonna spend the night?" They are like a large, rowdy family in a tenement flat; they learn in their mothers' arms that if you wanna be heard you gotta speak up.

For a moment I find myself wishing I were up there in the treetops with them, yelling my head off. But quickly I suppress the thought. I have become self-conscious about this little quirk I have lately acquired, this tendency to wish I were almost anyone, anything, other than myself.

Compared to the excavated ruins on the palisade below, the Temple of the Jaguar is nothing to ooh and aah about. It is no larger than some of the rich folks' mausoleums in Metairie Cemetery back home in New Orleans. The jungle has overgrown the platform on which it rests and broken open the temple tomb itself. Graffiti of roots and vines deface the carvings and glyphs on the outer walls. Originally, the interior of the shrine could boast a fine tablet depicting the nobleman who was interred here sitting on a two-headed jaguar throne. Now, however, all that is left of the tablet is the bas-relief fragment of one of the jaguar's legs. The grave of the nobleman, in a small crypt beneath the temple, was plundered long ago.

None of this disturbs me. Indeed, the unrestored condition of the site is one of the reasons I keep coming back here. Each time, I feel I am the first person to set eyes on this place since the jungle reclaimed it. I rediscover it over and over again.

The other reason is that I like the name, the Temple of the Jaguar, even if it derives from nothing more evidential than that mutilated paw and foreleg on the inner wall. What matters to me is that there really was a Jaguar God, or at any rate the Jaguar aspect of a god. The fact that this little shrine was not dedicated to him in the days of the ancient Maya does not prevent me from dedicating it to him now.

Jaguars are the most splendid of the New World predators, and everything about them is of interest to me. Señor Morales, who enjoys playing Virgil to my Dante in the Purgatory that I have managed to make even of Palenque, says that the only jaguars that survive hereabouts are the ones the Maya carved in stone. He says the last real jaguar in the archaeological park was killed twenty years ago. I hate news like that. In better days, I would have been perfectly capable of feeling depressed for no other reason than that I was in a jungle where jaguars ought to have been but weren't. As matters stand, however, I am already so thoroughly dejected that the dearth of jaguars becomes, like the Jaguar God himself, a mere aspect of a more encompassing state of mind.

In recent years archaeologists have made considerable headway in decoding ancient Maya glyphs; but they still have only the fuzziest notions about the complexities of the Maya religious universe. Certainly the worship of ancestors and an extraordinary deification of all aspects of time were central tenets of Maya theology. But the exact nature and function of most of the numerous Maya gods remain elusive. The deities in the Maya pantheon came in every imaginable shape and size; apparently a great many of them represented—somewhat like Catholicism's Blessed Trinity—phases, attributes, or aspects of other gods whose nature was too complex or too schizoid to be contained in a single persona. The Jaguar God was evidently such an aspect. He is thought to have represented the Sun God during his arduous nightly journey through the Maya underworld, where his radiance was hidden from the eyes of men. That underworld was an inhospitable and menacing place, the abode of the dreadful death gods; so by the time the Sun-God-as-Jaguar completed his dark passage from west to east, he was utterly drained, the merest skeleton of himself, in dire need of a drink of human blood to restore his solar health.

I don't like to think about that gruesome thirst; but in other respects, the Sun God's nocturnal journey appeals deeply to my imagination. It seems exactly right that in the underworld he should assume a jaguar guise. I remember that somewhere in the Maya Books of Chilam Balan—a curiously stoned-sounding collection of prophecies, folklore, and astrological references that comes down to us from colonial times— there is a pretty metaphor that compares the starry night to the pelt of *el tigre*. But if the ancient Maya had known of William Blake's famous image, I suspect they would have liked that one even more. They had, after all, anticipated it. How better to conceive of the fiercely beautiful Sun God passing through a world of death and darkness than as the Mesoamerican equivalent of a tiger burning bright in the forests of the night?

In much the same way, the jaguar passes through my thoughts now.

The howlers have shut up for a minute. As if waiting for that cue, the guards at the ruins start blowing their whistles. Closing time. Ready or not, it is time for me to make my way down to the human world below.

Señor Moisés Morales owns six hectares of land on the border of the archaeological park. His home is a sort of tree house, a small tin-roofed box on stilts set in a tropical glade. A spider monkey swings about on its belted leash. Nearby a swift clear stream hurries through a makeshift swimming pool that can be filled or emptied depending on whether the planks of a small weir are in place or not. Between house and road a larger stream serves as moat, obliging visitors, of whom Señor Morales has many, to approach his hideaway on foot. "I have this dream," he says, "to make this an ideal place. But with honest money, you under-stand, which means with hardly any money at all. I plan to die with 2,500 trees around me. I plant them all the time. I planted a tropical chestnut for each of my eleven children. I ask my friends who visit me to plant a tree so they will be with me in the form of that tree. There was a man who planted one and never came to visit it. I told him, 'I talk to your tree. It's doing its best, yet you never come to see it.' He was ashamed, and when he came, he saw that his tree was taller than he was."

Señor Morales holds forth like this whenever he gets the chance. He delights in being a sort of Mexican Thoreau, a man who has traveled widely in Palenque. He is a tourist guide at the park who knows more about local archaeology and ecology than some of the professors who come here. "They ask me where I got my degree," he beams. "I tell them, 'From the University of Hunger. The University of the Tortilla.' Which is the best degree of all!"

I am in a frame of mind to envy anyone who is not me. But even in better days, I think Señor Morales would rate an envious twinge or two. His wife and many children have all gone their separate ways but he never seems lonely. He is a confirmed malcontent who is content to plant trees and talk and talk. He takes long views of the historical past and the cheerless future, and cheerfully anticipates the downfall of practically everything. He relishes his role as apocalyptic Jeremiah to a corrupt and decaying world, yet he enjoys to the hilt his everyday life in that selfsame world. I like him very much, but it doesn't seem quite fair that he should have it both ways.

He is enjoying himself tonight. His brother owns La Canada, the comfortable motel where I am staying, and all day long Señor Morales and other members of the family and staff have been helping to transform the place's dining room, a large, thatched *palapa*, into a setting appropriate for a big fiesta. Now, the flowers have been set out, streamers and piñatas hang from the rafters, and the band is belting out a sort of rumba-rock. This is a private affair: just relatives, friends of the family, assorted local dignitaries, a few hotel guests like myself. Everyone has the party spirit. I am reminded of the Cajun *fais-do-dos* I used to attend years ago. There are no generation gaps. Everybody dances, everybody makes the rounds of the tables, pounding backs, laughing, telling jokes, and where appropriate, kissing the rouged cheeks of pretty girls. Also, almost everybody becomes at least a little crocked on the nonstop supply of rum Cokes.

Señor Morales is on the dance floor much of the time, where he cuts a dashing, silver-haired figure. Conscious that I'm a stranger here, he checks up on me during the breaks; but for now, I am doing pretty well on my own. The man across the table has a thoroughly nice, mild face, with kind, patient eyes peering out at the world through steel-rimmed glasses. He is a *justicia*—a judge—for the region. And he is a Maya. "Those two facts would have been a contradiction in terms not so long ago," he tells me. "To be an *Indio*—well, you were not expected to get ahead, you know? I have had to prove myself. I feel sometimes that I am the one on trial, you understand? But I am honest. I give fair judgments." He shakes his round head. "That's no easy thing in Chiapas. Or anywhere in Mexico."

We are just getting into the subject of local politics and prejudice when a fierce-looking person descends on the table. He has the look of a rather sinister hippie: deep-set dark eyes, long narrow chin, beaked nose, a thin clamped line of a mouth. His complexion is grayish brown. Straight black hair hangs down to the hem of his loose white shirt. He gives me a curt nod and then possesses the judge, hovering against his shoulder, talking softly but with an urgent intensity into his right ear. The judge listens noncommittally, now and then nodding. From behind his steel-rimmed glasses, he gazes past my shoulder at the blank wall.

I am straining to catch the dark man's difficult accent when Señor Morales, having decided I need rescuing, comes to collect me. "There is someone I want you to meet," he says, hauling me from the table.

"Who was that man with the long hair?"

"Him? He is the son of the chief of the Lacandón Indians."

To judge from his tone, Señor Morales might be identifying the son of a local gangster. We pause at the edge of the dance floor while he fills me in: "His people own a great forest reserve to the south, 614,000 hectares. That sounds good, eh? But the sad thing is that they are the forest's worst enemy. In Mexico, we say that the law is made of rubber. Well, believe me, my friend, these Indians know how to stretch it! Because they are 'poor Indians,' nobody can be against them, you know? So they destroy everything. They have millions in the bank from the forests they sell to the lumber companies, who pay off the politicians, including our ex-governor, so they can cut everything down in this so-called reserve. And because they are 'poor Indians' they can slaughter the beautiful birds, just so they can put the feathers in the arrows they sell at the entrance to Palenque. Now they think they have political power! Not so long ago, they broke windows in the city hall because they wanted the governor to replace the mayor! They got their way, but violence is the way to chaos. We are supposed to be a government of law—"

He seems so well launched on one of his commentaries on the Mexican condition that I am surprised when he abruptly breaks off, his expression suddenly softening. "Ah, over there. The person I want you to meet. She speaks excellent English. And she is a little lonely. Like you."

Her name is Elizabeta. She is spectacularly handsome, with large, dark eyes and perfectly shaped full lips set in a neat, oval face. In the course of introducing us, Señor Morales had said she has a graduate degree in psychology, so naturally I assume she must be neurotic. Yet whether because of this or in spite of it, she radiates a vulnerability, a melting openness, that would make even the most cowardly and/or self-centered male want to protect her from lewd comments, Hunnish hordes, the chill night air. She is that rather rare thing in Mexico: a Jew. She is also dismayingly perceptive. Right off, she has a pretty good idea what is wrong with me. Which makes us instant soulmates. We head at once for the subject that concerns us. My own sad story is a simple one, quickly told. Hers is more complex, and she wants me to know everything.

Young as she is, intelligent as she is, she is working hard at screwing up her life. She has fallen ardently in love, this Mexican Jewess, with an Iranian refugee whom she met in Israel. He had been a journalist in Teheran who rubbed the Ayatollah Khomeini the wrong way, and now he is eking out a living as a cab driver in San Francisco. He and Elizabeta have not had much time together as yet, but in a few weeks Elizabeta plans to import him to Mexico. "We will live in Jalapa, I think. Far away from my family, who of course do not approve. A nice town, and not too big. Not too hot in summer. I can teach, perhaps. And he will learn Spanish. He can perhaps write. And he can cook." Pathetically she insists, "He loves to cook!"

Her beautiful eyes read the expression in mine. She places her fingertips lightly on my hand. "When two people truly love each other, that's all that matters. Nothing can put them apart, not even death. You know that. I know you do. Believe me, he is the great love of my life. He and I will manage somehow." She withdraws her fingertips, leans back, sighs. "Love is always enough."

Obviously, no one can protect this glamorous, uncontrollably romantic creature from herself. I agree with her that love is enough.

The party, however, is no longer enough. Not even Elizabeta is enough. With a couple of quarts of rum Coke sloshing around in the emptiness inside me, I bid her and Señor Morales goodnight and goodbye. I will be leaving early in the morning. "You'll see," Elizabeta calls tenderly from the table. "Someday, the memories of your love will comfort you."

Señor Morales insists on walking me to my cottage. "My friend," he says, "you should stay longer in Palenque. Because of the lovely ruins, it has become a crossroads of the world. Myself, I feel privileged to live here. Yucatán has important ruins, but nothing like so beautiful. And there is not the cosmopolitan atmosphere we have here. You'll see. Of course I can tell that something is bothering you. But for that very reason, you need to relax, try to enjoy yourself. Stay here a while, and maybe I will ask you to plant a tree."

Dawn is breaking over the rolling pastureland when I reach the highway. East to Campeche and the Yucatán, west to Veracruz, Tampico,

Brownsville, New Orleans. The rum is still rumba-ing in my head. I pull the Toyota van over to the shoulderless edge of the road and for half an hour sit behind the wheel staring at two gaunt cows nibbling at what little grass they can find in an overgrazed pasture.

I have an assignment. I am supposed to explore the Yucatán peninsula—Campeche, Yucatán, Quintana Roo, maybe Belize. But I am in a bad way, frightened and depressed. My lover of twenty years is eight months dead of AIDS. For me, the "love that is always enough" has been reduced to a few handfuls of ash and gravelly bone reposing in a lacquered box on a shelf in my New Orleans home. And, whatever Elizabeta may say about "someday," right now the memories are tearing me apart.

I don't want to go on to the Yucatán; but I don't want to go back home either.

What I want is just to sit here indefinitely at this meaningless crossroads in my journey. But the two gaunt cows have come up to the fence now, and they are giving me funny looks. Reluctantly, I turn on the ignition. Very well, I tell myself; what I'll do is keep going as far as Campeche. If things don't get better by then, I'll give up and head for home.

ONE

Campeche

At Campeche, things do get better.

On my second day in the city, a decrepit truck had bashed in the rear of my van. And because of this fortunate misfortune, Anita and her family have temporarily adopted me. Anita applies herself to my rehabilitation, her nephew Jorge to the van's. Jorge's father, Lupe, though more reserved than his sister and son, placidly accepts me as part of the household for the indefinite future. Even his little dogs eventually quit yapping at me. As for Alfonso, Anita's older brother, he has never been quite right since his mistress, with the help of a shaman, tried to poison him years ago; but at least he is no more indifferent to me than to everyone and everything else.

Anita and I had hit it off even before the accident occurred. I had installed myself for a night or two in her orchard of orange trees, which doubles as the Samula Trailer Parque whenever a customer shows up. Under the ramón trees lining the front fence, a few parking places are equipped with electrical outlets. These are used, if at all, by the occasional adventurous older couple traveling in a full-fledged RV. But most of the people who find their way here are either driving rented Volkswagens with tents stowed under the hoods, or, like me, vans pinch-hitting as campers. A few of these freelance tourists are from Central Mexico, but the majority are American, French, or Scandinavian, traveling in mixed pairs. They park in the orchard under trees with whitewashed trunks. The air is scented with green oranges. Since the tourists are young and adaptable, and the rates are dirt cheap, they put up with the trickling cold showers and spastic toilets in the cinder block outhouse. There would be no point in complaining anyway. Most have already had a quick look at Campeche's forts and churches before arriving at the trailer park, and at dawn they will be up and gone. Poor Campeche, which yearns to be a tourist mecca, is for most travelers just a road stop on the way to either Mérida or Palenque.

That first evening I was Anita's only customer. Which was about par. If Campeche is off the beaten tourist track, Samula, a ragtag barrio at the city's southern boundary, is the place that is next farthest off after that. Only budget-conscious campers who can ask directions in Spanish wind up here, or people who don't know what they're doing or where they're going.

Anita's plain two-storied house sits on a limestone shelf overlooking the orchard. Behind it are a couple of water towers, assorted chickens, a pair of tethered turkeys, and clothes hung out to dry. Lizards scurry along the cracked edge of the derelict swimming pool.

Anita has a slight limp. Long ago the metatarsal bones in her right foot were crushed by one of the heavy stone laundry sinks that can be seen in all Samula backyards, every one of them insecurely perched, as hers still is, on a tottering stack of cement blocks. The bones had never mended properly, so she was watching her step as she came down the limestone slope. But even at a hobble, she radiated curiosity and restless energy. Anita is in her early sixties, but looks and acts much younger than that. She is short and trim. Bright red is her color: red blouse, red-hennaed hair, red-rouged cheeks in a round, smiling face. "Your name Don, hah? No good to sit down here by yourself. You come up to the house, okay? You like the Nescafe or the juice?" Her voice was pert and high-pitched; her eyes, behind the red-rimmed glasses, were bird-bright and friendly. "My English is not so good no more since my husband is dead. We talk in English, okay? so I get practice. Come on, come on!"

When the cups of hot water, the jar of Nescafe, and a box of saltine crackers had been set out, she joined me at the table. Above a cement block room divider, a bare bulb threw light into both the tiny kitchen and the living room where her brother Lupe watched television, possessively guarded by his three little dogs. The older brother, Alfonso, came in the front door. He looked fey, like a little old owl who knows something the rest of us don't. He plucked a couple of tortillas from a plate beside me and wandered out again, half humming, half singing a popular song. Pepe, an insomniac rooster, also wandered in and out, clucking moodily.

Anita turned out to be a cheerful, relentless inquisitor: Where was I from? New Orleans, hah? Did I like it there? How did I make a living? Did I travel much? Did I like to travel? And how did I like Mexico?

Campeche? I liked them, hah? Did I have a wife? children? No! Well, I was still young enough, I had to have someone, right?

It was impossible to take offense at this friendly prying, and besides, I was glad enough to have a little sympathy with the Nescafe. So I gave her, as I had Elizabeta, a bare-bones version of what had happened.

"Ah," she exclaimed, "*¡Qué lástima!* A pity! to die so young! And now you lonely, hah? But is no good for you to be, how you say in English? *amargado.*"

"Bitter?"

"That's right. You must not be that. Is no good. When I lose my husband, for six months I am like this—," she gave me a droll grimace that signified weeping—"But then I say, 'Anita, what use you crying? You strong. You got to go on living.' And that's what I do. Same for you. Sometimes I miss him, Mr. Coleman. We do all this together." She waved a hand around the little kitchen. "Hard, hard work together. And at night is not the same when there is no one in the bed to talk with you, hah? But I not, how you say, bitter. No sireee. I go on! You too. You don't give up! You got to go on."

Right there, Anita set the tone. During the days and weeks that followed, I would, in any case, feel grateful to her for taking me in. But from the first, there was more to it than that: I looked to her for encouragement. And I admired her. Anita was La Pasionaria on the barricades of life. No matter what the setbacks—and she certainly had had her share—she really believed, "You got to go on."

Conveniently enough, however, the accident next day relieved me, for a while, of the need to make a decision about either going on or going back. When nephew Jorge and I returned from the doleful business of getting the van to a mechanic's shop and then trying, with no success, to corner the elusive Sanborn Insurance agent, Anita—who would rather wield a rake than a broom—was doing her best to straighten out the room that would be mine for the next three weeks. "Shoo, shoo," she cried as we entered. It took us a startled second to realize she was addressing, not us, but a large tree frog with lovely chocolate markings on gray-white skin that she had unceremoniously swept into the pile of dust, pulverized stucco, and dead roaches collecting in the middle of the floor. While Anita watched bemused, I picked the creature up and set it on a vine that was trying to climb through the windows. Understandably upset, the frog left a slimy little something on my hand.

The room, long unused, encompassed the whole second story of Anita's house with the exception of one partitioned corner that contained everything necessary to a bathroom except running water. The cement walls were of various shades of blue, depending on where the paint had run out or simply faded. Furnishings were sparse: a rickety chair and table, and two beds. Above the larger bed a pair of crinolined plastic dolls—Anita had several more on display downstairs—shared a sagging shelf with a defoliated plastic Christmas tree.

Jorge and I turned to bringing up my gear, shaking out the dusty coverlet, making up the bed. Anita critically surveyed the result. "Not fancy, maybe; but it don't cost you nothing." When I protested, she said, "No, no. You got too much bad luck already. And anyways, Jorge likes you, I like you, Lupe likes you. In Mexico we say, 'If I have something to eat, you eat; if I don't, you don't.' So! Now you rest and feel better. Soon Lupe cooks us something. He's pretty good cook. When I eat, you eat, hah? You'll see, you feel a little bit okay soon."

After she and Jorge had left I realized with a small pleasant shock that, all things considered, I was feeling a little bit okay already.

During the days that followed, Anita talked quite a bit about her dead husband, Loyal Coleman. He had shown up in Campeche in the early 1950s after what would have been, even for a man half his 70 years of age, an arduous journey from the States. It is still a rough drive to get to southern Mexico; and in those days it must have been a real axle-breaker. There was no road worthy of the name linking the Yucatán peninsula with the rest of Mexico; and the prospect of trying to get across the then untamed swamps or jungles of Tabasco in a car would have been enough to daunt even the most intrepid traveler. But you only have to look at old Loyal, staring with grim, square-jawed determination out of the wedding photograph, to know it would take more than swamps or jungles to make him change his mind or his direction.

He was a career soldier, retired. After a long first marriage, he had remarried and divorced twice in rapid succession. "They don't do nothing for him," Anita explained scornfully, "not cook, not anything. He tell me, 'I read somewheres that Mexican women make good wives.' So that's why he come here, because Mexican women make good wives."

They met at the counter of the dry goods store in Campeche where Anita was working at the time. At first she was a little intimidated by this dour gringo who had no Spanish and silently pointed out the supplies he wanted. But when, after a dozen visits to the store, he said, "I want to marry *con usted*," she accepted him. An elderly Yankee, albeit well preserved, might not be a señorita's dream of the ideal catch, but Anita was no longer young by Mexican standards and she was tired of trying to go it alone.

The going had always been rough. Anita's earliest memories were of a plague of locusts that for four years devastated the region around Umán, near Mérida, where she was born. "Oh, it was something," she recalled. "Those naughty what-you-call-thems, like bad butterflies. They were so bad I can't tell you! They eat everything, the maize, the beans, even the thatched roofs on people's houses."

Near famine impelled her family to move to Lerma, a tiny fishing village on the coast south of Campeche. There, in short order, her mestizo father and the oldest of her seven brothers died of pneumonia. Her mother made a subsistence living by selling fruits and vegetables in the streets. She was an "Arab," the offspring of one of the many Lebanese traders who emigrated to Yucatán at the turn of the century when the state was riding the crest of a boom in henequen fiber. From what Anita and Lupe say of her, she must have been one tough and bitter lady. *Muy amargada.* Even when her sons were grown and married, she would fly at them with a hammock rope if they dared to cross her. As for poor Anita, her mother kept her in a purdah that made the Hispanic way of chaperoning young girls seem downright permissive by comparison.

Anita was in her early teens when the family moved to nearby Campeche, but even in the larger town she had few opportunities to meet other young people. Her mother relentlessly discouraged would-be boyfriends who came to call. One of them, however, a fellow named Ruiz, was so stubbornly persistent that Anita's mother finally said that if he still wanted Anita after two years, during which he mustn't court her, he could have her.

When the two years were up, he showed up. Anita, then 18, accepted him just to get away from her tyrannical mother.

It was not a marriage made in heaven. "I hate him!" Anita recalls, eyes flashing. "All he want to do is hunt and sit around. He no drink, he no smoke, he no *work!* And always he want to"—here she grinds her thumb against the table top—"to keep me down!"

She stuck with him for fifteen years because there was no place else to go. She was the breadwinner, taking care of the invalid wife of a Chinese-Lebanese merchant who owned a dry goods store in Campeche. But almost from the first, she stubbornly refused to share her husband's bed. "I say to him, 'Listen, I work for you, cook for you, but you don't come near me. You no work, I not your wife!' He try to beat me, but I tell him, 'My mother beat me, but not you. What! I earn money for you and you beat me too! No sireee.'"

Over the years, however, Ruiz became increasingly unstable, and Anita did become afraid of him. If she returned home a little late from her job, he would threaten her with a pistol he now carried everywhere. The final break came one evening when she went to a party for a couple of hours with her youngest brother Lupe. When she got home, Ruiz was "all crazy in the head." That night he circled her hammock, pistol cocked, threatening to shoot her. Luckily, Lupe showed up, and when he challenged his brother-in-law, Ruiz stormed out to the back of the house and shot himself instead. He botched the job, though. The bullet passed through his cheek instead of his brain.

While Ruiz was in the hospital, Anita sold her sewing machine and bought a bus ticket to Mexico City. There she lived for two years, working in a laundry, boarding with the sister of one of her former neighbors. She never saw Ruiz again. When she returned to Campeche, she learned that he had died alone in a shabby rented room. His body lay there for three days before it was discovered.

For a while Anita and young Lupe lived with their older brother Alfonso, the same who is now an abstracted, elderly boarder in Anita's home. But the arrangement didn't work out. "He different now. After his girlfriend hire that man to try to poison him, he like a dog—how you say?—with his tail down. He say he have nervous trouble, so I let him stay here. But back then he want me always to stay home, take care of him. Like my mother! Like my husband! So I tell him, 'No sireee.'"

Anita, with kid brother Lupe still in tow, went back to work and live in the household of Señor Ham, the Chinese-Lebanese merchant whose dying wife she had once nursed. She was restocking the shelves behind the counter of his dry goods store when Loyal Coleman came in one day, shopping for groceries and a good Mexican wife.

In the mid-1950s, when Coleman and Anita first settled in Samula, it was an uncrowded place, a few thatch-roofed *chozas*—huts—and stucco houses set among brush-covered hills. They built their no-frills house themselves. Coleman could turn his hand to anything, even installing the electricity when they finally got a line through. "We work in the hot sun, 'til we see stars in front of our eyes," Anita reminisces. "We clear away all the naughty trees that give you stings, and plant the lemons and oranges. We work and work and work. Other people when they see our place, they say, 'Oh, what a nice place you got here.' Okay, it was nice—because we made it nice. Most of them that move here after us don't want to work. They buy oranges from me because they too lazy to grow their own."

Listening to Anita when she holds forth on the work ethic, I can almost hear the voices of her Lebanese mother, her Yankee husband, still grouching from the grave.

Loyal Coleman died at the ripe old age of 90. A retired American couple, the Youngs, who rent a pleasant bungalow on a hillside near the trailer park, knew Anita and Loyal during their last years together. "Those two made a good pair," says Mr. Young. "They each provided something the other needed. Loyal was the best kind of American, steady and dependable, just like his name; but he was serious to a fault. It was Anita who made things bright and lively."

Anita still misses him, but from a distance of twelve years, she can be dispassionate. "Mr. Coleman is pretty good. A little strong"—by which she means short-tempered—"but pretty good. Different."

She would have picked up the phrase, "pretty good," from him. He was the sort of man who would have considered "pretty good" to be high praise.

During my three weeks in Campeche, I settle quickly into the routine of Anita's household. Pepe the rooster functions as my deranged alarm clock. He awakens me two or three times during the night and always at an appallingly early hour in the morning with his disconsolate, geriatric crowing. A younger cock has long since displaced him as sultan of Anita's flock, but Pepe lives on, in part because he is too old and stringy to be worth killing, in part because Anita is casually fond of him. He roosts on the rickety steps leading to my room, ogling his former wives as they stroll in and out the back door.

After a breakfast of tortillas and juice and maybe an egg, I help Anita and Lupe clean the outhouse, rake the orchard, and pick the oranges, which must be harvested as soon as the first faint yellow flush begins to suffuse their green skins. To wait longer is to invite trouble from flocks of melodious blackbirds who are under the impression that the orchard belongs to them. Lupe occasionally knocks one of them off with his man-sized slingshot. But collectively the birds don't take these assaults as seriously as they should.

The big meal, the only real meal, is at midday, and Lupe almost always cooks it: usually it is a cold fish soup, seasoned like almost everything else in this area with a lot of lime. There may also be *empanadas*—beans, onions, fish, whatever, fried in a wrapping of lime-soaked dough. Or *pan de cazón*, which is ground-up dogfish plus beans and tomato sauce, wrapped in a tortilla. Or fried pork rinds, *chicharrones*, in a salad with, among other things, onions, tomatoes, peppers, and sour orange.

In mid-afternoon, when the siesta is over, if I don't feel like hiking into Campeche, I prowl around the neighborhood. I like Samula, although there is no denying it is a scruffy little place. Squatters' shacks perch atop the arid hills, where water must be trucked to them. In the narrow valley below, most of the more substantial dwellings and the few shops line the only paved street. But the largest and certainly the strangest-looking structure in the barrio is on the dirt lane leading to the trailer park. It is a featureless high-walled enclosure that looks like a gigantic cinder block with a gate in it. At one time it had a surprising function, given the neighborhood in which it is located. On weekends, a fashionably dressed clientele would arrive from as far away as Mérida to see drag shows here. The transvestite entertainers came by bus, giving the locals an eyeful when they disembarked. Eventually the place was shut down. People live there now, but no one seems to know much about them.

The walls around a few houses are topped with jagged glass; but unlike an equivalent neighborhood in the United States, there is little theft here, and no sense of danger at all, even after dark. In the streets, kids grin impishly at the tall gringo, and I grin back at them. In the yards, chickens peck and scratch around the perilous washtubs. A coati-mundi on a leash limps on its crippled paw among cast-off tires and plastic bottles. In the dirt side lanes, aged cars bake in the warm winter sun, señoras rest their brown elbows on the sills of screenless windows, gray hogs loll in mud holes left by a recent rain. As everywhere in Mexico, there are plenty of scabby, starved-looking street dogs in view. Lupe's little mutts, allowed indoors where they grow fat on a generous if risky diet of fish heads, are the *crème de la crème* of Samula's canine society.

It is three o'clock. Up rolls the metal shutter on the small cement box that is the barrio's grocery store. The cheery-looking proprietor hurries behind the counter to get out of the way of the surging crowd of customers, which consists of me and an ancient lady in a shawl who needs an earache remedy. I buy the usual necessities for life on the road: toilet paper, Carta Blanca beer, cigarettes, Oreo cookies. Also a large jar of Nescafe and a box of saltines to replenish Anita's stock.

Back on the street, the sound of children singing lures me to the crest of a bleak hill. There, the state secondary school is opening for the evening session. Maybe a hundred youngsters are mustered in the quadrangle, boys in spotless khaki, girls in gleaming white blouses and blue skirts. The broad-beamed principal and his matronly teaching staff are leading them through the not very stirring stanzas of Mexico's national anthem. Afterward, an honor guard of high-stepping girls parades the flag. Everyone stands at attention and gives the arm-across-the-chest salute. The children, with their shiny black hair, large, dark eyes, and lively expressions are a very appealing lot. By U.S. standards, most are *under*-underprivileged. But they are cheerful-looking and beautifully behaved. Remembering the near chaos I've observed at some public school assemblies in my own country, I wish the educational system in Samula would export whatever it is that it is doing right.

Evenings, I sometimes wander through the handsome streets of Campeche's old quarter or along the battlements of the city walls. In the anteroom of the governor's office at the state office building hang a number of old sepia photographs of the city, probably taken in the late nineteenth century. Nothing much has changed. The churches, the arcaded shops, the elegantly severe colonial dwellings with their wrought iron grills are all still present and accounted for, and they look hardly more weathered now than they did then.

"*Muy tranquilo*" is the way the Campechanos invariably describe their city. And indeed, traffic aside, it is a quiet place now. But the fortifications remind one that at times in the past it was anything but. Two-thirds of the massive walls that once surrounded the city have been torn down, as well as some of the forts; yet there are probably still more old fortifications—*baluartes*—intact here than can be found in any other colonial city in the New World.

The sad thing is the harbor. About thirty years ago it was subjected to the sort of vandalism that bureaucrats and city fathers so often inflict on their own history and tradition when they start getting progress-minded. For no very good reason, they decided to fill the whole thing in. Now, when you stand at the ramparts of the great fortress that once guarded Campeche's sea gate, all you get to see, instead of quays and bright fleets of fishing boats, are a couple of Hotels Anywhere, a tacky Tourist Information Center, and acres of parking lot.

But I tell myself, never mind. There is still so much of the past left that I can transfer myself back into it with no trouble at all: I throw a switch, the little time machine in my head goes into reverse, and presto! I am a young *hacendado*—a landowner—fearful but also excited, pacing this same baluarte three hundred years ago. The bells in the churches of San Francisquito and San José are sounding the alarm. Behind me, in what is now Calle 8, merchants close down their shops. Their customers run for home. The hometown militia, some in uniform, most not, hurry up the fortress ramps to man the cannons that are now aimed at a sea of parked cars. Far out on the languid Gulf, I can see the dreaded sails of the pirate ships, their Jolly Rogers flapping in the breeze. . . .

The good old swashbuckling days were in the seventeenth century, when Campeche was the poor little rich girl of the southern Gulf. Rich because she exported logwood, a tree from whose heartwood a fixing agent for dye was extracted that brought fabulous prices in Europe; poor, because so many of the notable pirates who sailed the Spanish Main had their wicked way with her at one time or another.

Objectively I know what a scurvy, unromantic lot those *bucaneros* were. But there's no denying that they gave life along this coast its figurative as well as literal cutting edge. There was, for example, the ingrate Cuban Diego el Mulatto, who ravaged Campeche unmercifully even though, as a boy, he was supposedly adopted and raised by one of its citizens. And there was William Parker, an Englishman, who took the city by surprise with the aid of a traitor (subsequently tortured and put to death) within its walls. Best of all, among the city's tormentors was a real, live pirate who, before I came to Campeche, I had supposed lived only in Robert Louis Stevenson's imagination, namely, Pie de Palo—old Pegleg himself.

Some of these outlaws were originally sponsored by England during its ongoing wars with Spain. Toward the end of the seventeenth century, however, when the two countries were temporarily at peace, they cooperated in making piracy so unremunerative in the Caribbean that anyone determined to pursue that line of work found it safer to move to a new hideout on the Gulf side of the Yucatán, conveniently located between the rich coastal cities of Veracruz and Campeche. This was the mangrove-choked fastness of Isla del Carmen, then known as Isla de Tris. Having spent some time in that area, I can understand how pirates got to be so mean. Never mind such minor nuisances as jaguars, venomous snakes, jungle rot, and belligerent Indians. The mosquito, then as now, would have been reason enough to account for—and almost excuse—the behavior of even the most despicable buccaneers. I can attest on the basis of personal experience that any poor cutthroat who dared leave the smudginess of his coconut shell fire long enough to pee would have had a cloud of the whining horrors recharging his case of malaria, while simultaneously draining him of a few pints of blood, before he even got his fly open. After a couple of weeks holed up in a place like that, the prospect of a little pillage and mayhem in Campeche would have seemed like a holiday outing.

Discomforts notwithstanding, just about anyone who was anyone in the pirate world hid out at Isla de Tris at one time or another: Captain Cook, Lewis Scott, Barbillas (named for his ferocious moustachio), the Dutchman Lauren de Graff, and the wily Frenchman L'Olonois, just to name a few. L'Olonois serves as a fair example of the stuff out of which pirate yarns are made. He is said to have raided Campeche so regularly that he kept a mistress in the town to soothe his jangled nerves after the rigors of each assault. On one of these periodic visitations, he had the misfortune to be shipwrecked on the city's doorstep when a bad storm came up. Most of his crew were killed or captured, but resourceful L'Olonois escaped the vengeance of the Campechanos by playing dead. Later, when things had settled down, he disguised himself and, with the help of slaves whom he promised to liberate, skipped town in a stolen boat. However, justice will be served. Soon after, while looking for trouble on the other side of the Yucatán peninsula, he fell into the hands of some Carib Indians, who forthwith made a meal of him.

Of the whole swashbuckling lot, though, de Graff, otherwise known as Lorencillo or Little Lauren, probably gave Campeche the worst time of all, if only because he made himself so much at home there. When he took the city in 1685, he was commanding a fleet of thirty-eight assorted vessels, loaded to the gunwales with as international a set of pirates as ever sailed the Spanish Main. Even by the demanding standards of that dastardly crowd, his two lieutenants, a fellow ironically named "El Caballero"—the gentleman—Grammont, and a Dutchman, Van Horn, were considered exceptionally villainous. They blockaded the port, overwhelmed its three hundred militiamen, and settled down to a prolonged spree of murder, arson, Jolly Rogering, looting, and whatever else pirates do. When not working the town itself, they raided inland for miles around and even undertook an expedition against Mérida. An army from that city finally succeeded in turning them back, whereupon Lorencillo concluded that he and his fellows had overstayed their welcome in Yucatán. When they sailed away, they took everything with them that wasn't nailed down, and a lot that had been. But we all know what the wages of sin are. Sure enough, the rich booty occasioned a falling-out among thieves that ended up with Little Lauren the loser, done in by the snicker-snee of greedy Van Horn.

There was a subplot to this lurid story that bequeathed to Campeche a legacy that would outlive the memory of the main event. It seems that just as the city was being overrun by Lorencillo's forces, one of the defenders, a captain named Lázaro Canto, led his handful of surviving men to the principal parish church (later the site of Campeche's handsome cathedral). There they made a stand, holding off the pirates for several days. Then, just when it looked as though the jig was up, one of Canto's men discovered a subterranean passageway below the church.

By means of it, the cornered men were able to escape to the hills outside the walls.

It was almost certainly this oft-told tale, no doubt promoted by some long-ago Chamber of Commerce, that spawned the later popular stories of Campeche's fabulous labyrinth of tunnels. At any rate, until very recently, Campechanos and *turistas* alike have believed—no one more willingly than I—that a whole network of natural and man-made passages honeycombed the limestone rock on which the city is built. First used by the Maya as a place of refuge, the tunnels—so the story went—had been extended and enlarged during colonial days to enable the inhabitants to hide from the ravening buccaneers. Some of those underground corridors, long since blocked off, were said to link the fortresses and many of the grander homes to a principal exit under the main altar of the cathedral. Last time I checked, even good old reliable *Fodor's* was scolding the city fathers for not opening some of the secret passageways as a tourist attraction.

Alas for all those generations of Campechano youngsters and all those gullible visitors, myself included, who have fondly envisioned the trembling coveys of large-eyed señoritas, the praying priests, the brave but frightened mamas with babes in arms, the mantilla-clad dowagers clutching jewelry boxes and gold crucifixes, all fleeing through torchlit corridors in the limestone rock, while overhead the cannon boomed. Alas for one more charming legend, slain by that peglegged pirate, Truth. The city fathers cannot open passageways that do not exist.

I might have preserved my own blessed state of ignorance if only Anita's nephew, Jorge, knowing of my interest in pirates, had not introduced me to a knowledgeable friend of his who works at the School of Adult Education. In a matter of minutes, this pleasant young man stripped me of my cherished faith in the romantic yarn, even lending me a couple of learned articles to drive home his killjoy assurances that the tunnel network had never existed. Oh, there are "tunnels," all right. Indeed, in the past, a chunk of street occasionally fell into one. But the system belongs to nature, not man. As in southern Florida, the porous limestone shelf of which the Yucatán peninsula is composed is riddled with caverns, a vast aquifer for a land whose rivers flow underground rather than at the surface. It may even be true that here and there someone's cellar once tapped into one of those dark chambers.

But there never was a network of bat-fretted, torchlit passageways link-ing homes, forts, churches, as I fondly believed.

Never mind, I tell myself. At least the pirates were real enough. The church bells really did ring their warnings, the local militia did once load all those now rusted cannons, the dreaded Lorencillo and Pegleg and L'Olonois did come ashore at what is now the municipal parking lot. Most indisputably real of all are the blunt gray-black walls and tur-rets of Campeche's fortifications, guarding, for want of anything else, the stirring past. The sight of those rising walls discouraged the depre-dations of the buccaneers long before their construction, which took generations, was finally completed. But for more than a century after-ward, they proved to be a sound investment, variously holding at bay troops from the antagonistic "city-state" of Mérida, government troops from Central Mexico, and rampaging Maya during the great uprising known as the War of the Castes.

Of all Campeche's forts, the Baluarte San Miguel is my favorite. It is a child's dream of everything that a fort should be. Four-square, intact, restored, it perches high on a hill south of the city. It is encircled by a dry moat, once filled not only with water but, so goes the tale, with Mo-relet's crocodiles. The little gunners' turrets were designed for eigh-teenth-century Yucatecans, who were apparently even smaller than their modern counterparts. Squeezing into one of them, I can look south to where the Melacón, the old highway, winds between the tidal flats of the coast and the dry gray-green lift of the Puuc hills, or north to the rooftops and spires of Campeche. Mostly, though, the view is of sky and Gulf. Far out in that infinity of blues and lavender grays, a few *lanchas* and shrimp boats head for the shore. For my benefit, they ami-ably pretend they are an approaching fleet of pirate ships.

The downtown office of Señor José "Pepe" Sansores could easily pass for, well, not a dungeon, perhaps, but certainly a guard room in one of the fortresses I have been exploring. Señor Sansores is a very successful businessman, but to his credit he does not go in for office chic. The limestone walls surrounding him are cindery black, the high, narrow ceiling is spanned by thick wooden beams, the board shutters of the arched doorway are shut against sunlight and heat. In thin picture frames, grinning hunters and fishermen hold out strings of red snapper, snook, duck, snipe, and a limp ocelot for me to look at.

Among other enterprises, Señor Sansores owns a cattle ranch, the Hotel Castlemar across the street, the Snook Inn in Champotón, and a flourishing guide service for hunters and deep-sea fishermen that is managed by one of his sons. He is one of the only two operators in the state of Campeche who, until recently, were licensed to take hunters into the jungle to kill jaguars and pumas. It is on that count that I am here. Not to kill jaguars and pumas, but to visit the jungles where they still survive.

Anita is a little miffed that I have approached Señor Sansores. The other operator, Señor William Ham Gunam, is a relative of the kindly Chinese-Lebanese merchant who befriended her and gave her employment when she was living with Ruiz. So she would like to do Señor Ham a favor by sending a little business his way. She herself had gone along on one of his hunting expeditions many years ago. "Is lots of fun. We shoot lots of things. One of the men shoots a big jaguar. Just the one eye shines in the dark, see? and bang, he shoots him. But then the ants come where we are sleeping. Shoo, shoo! They hurt. I no like that. But I like to hunt. You naughty not to go with Señor Ham. He is nice boy."

I had met him once at Anita's house. The "nice boy" did not at all fit the stereotype of a macho big game guide. A frail-looking, sad-eyed man with a quiet, gentle voice and a smile to match, he looked like someone who would rather play the cello or write poetry than preside at the slaughter of wild beasts. I liked him, and for that very reason, as well as the fact that he is Anita's friend, I had decided against going into the jungle with him. I would be taking notes, after all; and during our conversation, Señor Ham had not exactly come across as an authority on wildlife law. True, he had expressed sincere sentiments about the need to conserve Mexican wildlife, but he had also assured me that it was perfectly legal to hunt jaguars in Campeche, even though the state had recently passed a law forbidding all sport hunting of the animals. As for the U.S. ban on the importation of the hides of spotted cats, well—he had shrugged his thin shoulders—none of his American clients had ever had a problem.

All things considered, I concluded that I might be doing Señor Ham a bigger favor if I didn't tag along on one of his hunting expeditions than if I did.

So here I am, being interviewed by Señor Sansores. He is somewhere in his sixties, alert, canny, cool, with a still handsome square face that, in repose, becomes a little grim around the mouth and chin. One of his former wives belonged to the world of the hacendados, the landed gentry, but his own origins are relatively modest; his family began making money only after the Revolution of 1910. Nevertheless, Don José is every inch the *patrón*. Even parked behind his old desk in walking shorts and undershirt, he radiates toughness and authority. I have the impression that if one lived in Campeche, this is not a man one would want to cross.

He can change styles, depending on circumstances, with an alarming suddenness. With me he is the affable businessman and courteous host, intrigued by the fact that I am a writer who just might be helpful in expanding his safari business to include bird and monkey watchers. He is prepared to offer me a generous reduction in price if I desire, as indeed I do, to come along on one of the expeditions headed by his son, Jorge.

It is when the phone rings—and it rings all the time—that, playing himself, he plays many roles. One of the callers is an employee at Champotón who must account for a piece of equipment that is missing. Don José is not satisfied with the explanation, and there ensues a long-distance tongue-lashing during which Don José turns quite red and jams the receiver so close to his mouth that I fear he may chip a tooth. Yet a moment later, when one of his granddaughters calls, he is all tenderness with the little girl, cooing and clucking, grinning broadly at the wall, coaxing her, at the conclusion of the conversation, to say good-bye to him in English. When she does, he signs off with a loud string of smacking kisses. A minute later, during a third call from someone who is obviously a business associate, he jokes and is grave by turns. When he hangs up, he shakes his head, frowning.

His wife calls him. It seems there has been a minor domestic crisis. Like many older men, Don José has need of a diuretic. The doctors have advised him that his condition can be relieved by the consumption of large quantities of coconut milk. An old *campesino* delivers a supply of coconuts to his home every week. But this week the coconuts had mysteriously gone astray. Don José had given the old man hell, only to discover later that Señora Sansores, perhaps tired of having her home cluttered with piles of coconuts, had had them delivered to her husband's office. Don José is at first cranky with his wife, but quickly shifts to a more satirical mode: "How do you think I would know where the coconuts are? Did you think they would all bounce up and down in their baskets yelling, 'Here we are, Don José, we are hiding over here!'?'" His voice becomes falsetto, the high-pitched voice of an anxious coconut. Enchanted by the notion of the lost little coconuts calling attention to themselves, he roars with sudden laughter and stamps his feet under the desk. While all this is going on, one of the men who hang about the bleak little waiting room up front has brought me a Coke. From behind Don José, he rolls his eyes and indulgently grins. But the grin vanishes when Don José pauses in mid-laugh. Don José holds the receiver away from him, staring at it in surprise.

In English he says, "She hung up." He looks at me as though I might know the reason why. Then he gives me a shrug and a bemused smile. "The womens," he sighs. "Ah, the womens!"

Having delivered himself of this insight, he takes up where he had left off, the courteous businessman discussing the details of my trip into the jungle. He manages two or three more sentences before the phone rings again.

TWO

Cibalito

Getting into the Petén, the once near-to-endless jungle that stretches along the Mexico-Guatemala border, is not a casual undertaking. Even in the Sansores jeeps, the forty-mile journey from the Escárcega-Chetumal highway to the camp takes more than seven hours. Much of the year, the road is wholly impassable. Although this is the dry season, an eccentric little rainstorm has made huge, rutted quagmires of every low spot in the road. No ordinary car could get through.

But in Mexico, as in all the rest of the Third World, the same rule obtains: bulldoze a road, no matter how pitted and ill-maintained, through any pristine wilderness, no matter how unsuitable for human development, and people will settle along its route.

I have observed this syndrome often enough, in enough different places, to become sadly used to it. But even so, Concepción comes as a shock. Once we have gotten clear of the slash-and-burn maize operations near the highway, I begin to hope that this rough track may be an exception to the rule. It is chewed up by the wheels of loggers' trucks, but for some miles it has been leading us through what seems to be a more-or-less intact wilderness. The aspect of the forest changes as we move south, from what the botanists fetchingly call "semi-deciduous" to "semi-evergreen" to "evergreen seasonal." Meaning that, as we advance deeper and deeper into the Petén, exchanging a rather arid climate for a wetter one, the forest becomes taller, more layered, more broad-leaved, in short, more jungly. This part of Campeche never makes it to the true rain forest stage, but by the time we have put twenty-five miles between ourselves and the highway, the vegetation should be looking tropically lush enough to satisfy all but the most finicky jungle lovers.

Should be, but isn't, because suddenly the forest isn't there. Instead, there is Concepción. My guide, Ramón, says the place isn't even an *ejido*, an authorized agricultural cooperative. On paper, this entire area is supposed to be managed exclusively for timber. "Squatters," says Ramón contemptuously, "not even Campechanos. They come from some

other part of Mexico, or maybe Guatemala. Lots of refugees from Guatemala in Campeche now."

As we pass the thatched chozas along the road, Concepción's inhabitants watch us from the doorless doorways, the adults expressionless,
the barefooted children with shy smiles.

What gets me is the sheer scope of the environmental damage. There
can't be more than two hundred people in this tiny isolated hamlet. It
didn't even exist a few years earlier. But already thousands of the surrounding acres have been cut, burned, cleared—with machetes and fire
as the only tools. My driver, Manuel, explains that the squatters don't
just grow maize for their own needs; they also sell it in Escárcega and
other highway towns, competing with the native campesinos. When I
ask why the government doesn't move them out, Ramón says sourly,
"Now you'd have to shoot them to get rid of them. Anyway, the politicians are afraid. There are so many outsiders in Campeche now, so
many squatters. And more come all the time. They swarm over everything. Like rats."

When the jungle—"evergreen seasonal"—finally does close in on us,
the darkness does so too. By the time we reach Esperanza, we have only
our headlights and the rising moon to see by. Esperanza consists of a
rambling thatch-and-stucco caretaker's house, a cleared space where
helicopters occasionally deposit some of Jorge Sansores's more affluent
hunter clients, and a large, rickety shed where a number of loggers'
trucks, loaded with timber, are parked for the night. Unprepossessing
as it is, the place has an air of belonging, as well as a history, both of
which Concepción glaringly lacks. It was once a rendezvous point for
the *chicleros*, a few of whom still tap the forest's chicle trees, supplying
the needs of gourmand masticators who refuse to settle for synthetic
chewing gum. For some time after that, it served as a logging camp.
Then, about twenty-five years ago, it became an army post during an
unfriendly period in Mexican-Guatemalan relations. Currently, in the
dry season, it is a logging camp again. The truck drivers have settled in
the rickety shed for the night. Cigarettes glow like fireflies. A female
voice on a battery radio sings mournfully of love.

Now that we are about to enter the really serious jungle on this last
lap to the camp, everyone is very intent about the business at hand.
From now on, day or night, the guides will be on the alert, the hunters

ready to take a shot at anything that crosses in front of them. Wind-shields are removed, and cushions are tied to the dashboards of the jeeps as gunrests. Even I have one, on the chance that I might eventually be persuaded to try my luck at shooting something.

The jeeps are reshuffled. We are a small party, only two clients other than myself. The American, Kenneth, and his driver will go first, with Jorge, Señor Sansores's son, perched on an uncomfortable but higher seat behind them, acting as Kenneth's guide. At a respectful distance, my jeep will follow. The Spanish businessman, José, has elected to wait twenty or thirty minutes before bringing up the rear, since by then any game spooked by our passage will have resumed its nocturnal rounds.

The guns are loaded by flashlight. "Double O shot," says Jorge softly. "We go for big game."

"Oh, good," Kenneth croons. "That's just what I wanted to hear."

A mile or so into the jungle, the brake lights on the lead jeep signal a sudden stop. Then all its lights switch off. Manuel brings us to a stop too, and turns off the ignition and headlights. A three-quarter moon is visible through the canopy above, but down where we are it is black as the inside of a stone. A brief interlude of suspenseful waiting. Then the beams of three flashlights drill into the undergrowth or zap up into the trees. After quite a bit of this, one of the flashlights points at us and blinks. Ramón grunts, "Whatever it was, it got away." Manuel turns the ignition and lights back on and moves us forward.

When we pull up behind the first jeep, Jorge Sansores is sighing, "It was a good size."

"It was my fault, Señor Sansores," Kenneth moans. "A clear shot. If I hadn't turned just then to say something to you—"

"No, no," Jorge consoles, "it was moving pretty fast. A jaguar would have stopped and looked at you. But not an ocelot. Please call me George."

An ocelot. For the first time it is beginning to sink in. I am in an honest-to-God real jungle. With ocelots. And jaguars. And people who want to shoot them.

Jorge Sansores patiently explains to me that a cat will never come to the bait the first night if a hunter is posted on the stand. "Then his senses are alert, you understand? The cat thinks, 'I am stealing this goat from man, so I must be very, very careful.' It's no good to wait for him then. But once he makes the kill, he says, 'Now this meat is mine!' So when he comes back the next night to finish eating what he left, he isn't careful anymore. Ninety-nine percent of the cats we shoot are killed on that second night, in the first four hours after dark. If they don't show up then, they have either been warned or they have made another kill."

It is seven-thirty in the evening of the fourth day. The previous afternoon, four goats had been staked out at suitable places in the jungle, and a puma had made a meal of one of them during the night. The Spaniard, José, had had the luck of the draw and is at this minute perched in a tree some miles distant, waiting for the cat to come back for leftovers. Kenneth, the American, must make do with cruising the logging roads with his driver and guide, hoping to pick up something in the headlights' bright glare. Or so I have been told.

Baiting time in the jungle is bated breath time at the camp. As long as the two hunters are out there in all that vegetal darkness, there is not much for Jorge and me to do but sit under the generator-powered light bulb at the mess table, sipping drinks and trying to make conversation while we wait and listen. The stands are too far off for us to hear the killing shots if there are any. But tradition requires successful hunters to announce themselves as they approach the camp: one shotgun blast for an ocelot, two for a puma, three for a jaguar. For a supposedly detached observer, I am pretty keyed up, expectant. But Jorge is out-and-out nervous. He sighs a lot, shifts his big body in the camp chair, mops his brow and upper lip with a handkerchief.

Something is wrong. Jorge has been through this sort of waiting many times before; he has said himself that it doesn't bother him, and I believe him. I am certain he isn't thinking about José and his puma at all. It is something else that makes him edgy. Something he wants to ask me. Or tell me. But he can't get it out.

Jorge has named the camp Cibalito after the tall dense stands of cibal grass that grow in the nearby *laguna*. There are three large tin-roofed sheds in the clearing. The one for the mess is open except for the partition separating eating and cooking areas. The other two, for sleeping, have hula-skirted walls of palm thatch. There is a bucket shower and mosquito netting for the cots and outhouse. At a little distance, in among the trees, are quarters for the crew. Here the sacrificial goats had been keep tactfully out of sight until their date with destiny. No hunter wants some sullen goat throwing him a dirty look.

A narrow band of powdery insecticide outlines the camp's perimeter.

Until six years ago, Jorge's base of operations was at Aguada Seca, further to the west and only a few kilometers from the Escárcega-Chetumal highway. But the invasion of new people had wiped out the jungle in those parts, and the wildlife with it. "Push back, push back," Jorge laments. "Especially the cats; and that is what my hunters come to hunt. Not all my hunters can do as much damage in a year as one cleared cattle pasture in a week. Kill the land and you kill the game. And that's what these people do with their burning and clearing, their *milpa*—they kill the land! Push back, push back. Now I must go in six or seven hours from the highway to find the cats."

At Cibalito the daily routine is always the same, at least until one or more of the goat baits is taken. The hunters, with their guides and drivers, head out each morning after early breakfast, patrolling the endless maze of logging tracks that extend southward to the Guatemalan border. On these long morning runs, the likely targets are the spectacular Central American game birds: curassow, ocellated turkey, crested guan, and, in the laguna, migrant ducks or resident muscovies. There is always the chance of a shot at a javelina or whitetail, or one of the tiny brocket deer that make their home only in deep forest; but the chances of killing one of these animals, or one of the cats, increase greatly on the evening run, which begins about 4 P.M. and goes on well into the night. In the afternoon, after a substantial lunch, some clients settle for a siesta while others try a little still hunting. A few, like Kenneth, bring along tapes of shrieking foxes or rabbits that are intended to lure predators into range.

Once a cat has killed a goat, however, the atmosphere becomes more charged, the hunt itself more focused. The client who has drawn the stand at which the kill occurred lives now in a state of excited expectancy. José has spent the afternoon preparing for his rendezvous with a puma by alternately meditating and practicing, under Jorge's direction, the downward shot he will take if the cat returns to the bait. His guide and Jorge treat him solicitously, intensifying his perception that he is about to undergo some powerful test, an almost religious rite of passage. Ordinarily open and friendly, he becomes nervously quiet, withdrawn.

"It always happens that way," Jorge had exclaimed to Kenneth on the third morning, his tone nicely balanced between amusement and annoyance. "The man that doesn't have the gun, he is the one who sees the game."

Ramón had just reported to him that we had seen, among other things, a jaguarundi. The sighting really was something pretty special. The jaguarundi is the least spectacular but most peculiar of the three smaller feline species that share the Petén with jaguars and pumas. Instead of the splendid spotted fur worn by the ocelot and the rare, arboreal margay, it makes do with a demure little coat of brown, gray, or black. With its flat head, rather short legs, and elongated body, it looks like a miniature puma that something rather large has stepped on. It is rarely seen, and hardly anything is known about its habits. But my jaguarundi had not been particularly shy. It had trotted into the road in front of the jeep, and paused long enough to allow me a good, long look at it before disappearing behind the splayed roots of a sapodilla tree. The driver, Manuel, had growled, "You could have had him. An easy shot!"

Now Kenneth piously observes, "Even if a jaguarundi did show itself to me, Señor Sansores, I would not think of killing it. The species is protected in Campeche."

Jorge cannot suppress an "oh, come off it!" roll of the eyes, but all he says is, "Ah, yes, of course. Please call me George."

I am pretty sure that Kenneth's remark is actually aimed at me. He knows I am a writer and a conservationist. He also knows that he makes me and everyone else a bit uncomfortable. He is as correct and unknowable as an English butler. Even out here, where he can be just one of the boys, he would no more think of letting down his guard than of taking off his toupee. He is excruciatingly polite, always saying "Good morning, sir," or "Excuse me, sir." When he occasionally tries to unbend, it's even worse. He comes across like Uriah Heep.

As a hunter, he is not so much enthusiastic as methodical. But he wants me to understand that he is a sportsman. On our first day in camp, he gave me a little sermon on blood sports: "You must understand, sir, that there are different types of hunters. There are the primitive types who aren't happy unless they come back with their hands full. And there are the civilized people. With them it's the hunt that counts. When I kill, I feel disappointed." He gave me a disappointed-looking smile. "It's all over. The hunt is ended. Therefore I'm actually happy when I don't see anything."

Kenneth makes me a generous offer. Knowing that I plan a return trip to Africa before long, he tells me that I may have the rent-free use of a bungalow he leases in Zimbabwe, where he sometimes goes to hunt. I blame myself for not being more affected by this generous overture. But, somehow, I can't take the invitation at face value.

I *have* been lucky. By the third day, the two hunters have only one cadaver to show between them, a muscovy duck shot by Kenneth. Whereas I have seen not just a jaguarundi but a fair sampling of other wildlife, shootable and otherwise. I am easy to please. A family of spider monkeys threading their way through the treetops, keel-billed toucans grunting like frogs, a flock of white-fronted parrots gobbling wild fruit— these delight me as much as the more edible ocellated turkeys and several pairs of very beautiful and very large crested guan and great curassow that perch in trees beside the trail, fairly begging to be shot.

Much of my luck goes by the name of Ramón. The guide has the eyes of a forest falcon. Trying to spot wildlife in a Central American jungle is a far cry from going on a game drive in East Africa. And not just because the year-round leafiness obscures the view. Acre for acre, the animate biomass in this tropical forest is undoubtedly greater than that of the Serengeti, if you count everything that runs, flies, or crawls. But most of that everything is smallish, antisocial, and camouflaged to a fault. Time after time Ramón spends two or three minutes directing me and my binoculars to some particular tree limb where a coatimundi or a collared aracari is quietly posing. When I finally pick it out, he rewards me with a patient smile.

Our drives sometimes bring us close to the shore of El Teniente, a laguna that extends from the campsite eastward for several miles. Presumably it was named after some lieutenant stationed at Esperanza during the troubles with Guatemala. Maybe he went swimming there. Maybe he drowned. No one seems to know.

The laguna is not really a lagoon in the dictionary sense. It is a sizable inland marsh fed by subterranean water welling upward through several large *cenotes*. In the Yucatán peninsula, cenotes punctuate the surface everywhere, marking places where the porous limestone crust has collapsed into the underground aquifer. On higher ground, they show themselves as vertical-sided natural wells, often very deep, at the bottom of which lie pools of clear black water. But near the coast, or in low-lying inland areas of the Petén, they function more or less as springs, overflowing shallow depressions to form marshy lakes such as El Teniente.

From one point on the logging road, it is possible to walk to a cenote located at the very edge of the laguna. On high ground or low, cenotes are always beautiful and mysterious, and also a little spooky. This one is no exception to the rule. One blunders through yellow marsh grass six feet tall until one reaches a patch of open water that one might reasonably expect to be shallow, murky, and algae-stained. Instead, one looks down into a depthless well of water as transparently clear as air. "No bottom," says Ramón. No sides either, from the look of it. All around the pool, the mud- and reed-covered limestone ledge on which we are standing extends like a layer of gray ice over an infinite watery emptiness. Way, way down, a few little fish flicker in the last of the afternoon's sunlight.

One reason we have come to El Teniente is to look for tracks. Here the logging road traverses soggy ground. Whitetails, javelina, and brocket deer leave the signs of their passage in the muddy ruts. The big cats also. Even with the jeep in motion, Ramón can spot a set of pug marks and casually pronounce "*puma*" or "*el tigre*" on the basis of small differences in the width and depth of the animals' heel pads.

Unlike me, Ramón takes even the jaguar sign in stride. But one morning, with an unusual show of excited interest, he tells Manuel to stop the jeep. He and I climb out to examine a set of huge splayed tracks that we haven't come on before. Some are four-toed, others three, depending on whether the fore or hind feet had left the prints.

"*Tapir*," Ramón murmurs. "*Muy raro.*" Then he points to a nearby set of the same tracks in miniature. "*Un bebé*," he grins.

I stare at those fresh, wet tracks, and for a long, welcome moment, nothing in the world exists for me except the animals that have made them.

This empathy, mysterious even to myself, usually makes itself felt when I am in touch, in some tangible way, with one of those rare hold-out creatures that embody whatever is still uncorrupted in a particular wild place. Traveling about over the years, I have compiled a private bestiary of such totem animals. The panther in south Florida. The grizzly, the wolverine, the wolf in the northern Rockies. The wild dog and the greater kudu in East Africa. I have become something of a purist regarding their selection. Rarity is not the only consideration. Rather, the special trait of all these chosen beasts is that they authenticate—to my satisfaction, at any rate—the integrity of the environment they must have to survive. Without their presence, the landscapes in which they were meant to exist are like houses that have been abandoned by their owners.

Here in the Yucatán peninsula, the jaguar inevitably looms in my imagination as the *sine qua non* of beasts epitomizing what is left of the region's wilderness. Indeed, more than once since I left Palenque, *el tigre* has slouched moodily through my dreams, the object of a half-acknowledged quest that, like all true quests, is also an escape. Nowadays, it is true I am afraid to hope for anything at all. Yet even if I were capable of a more optimistic frame of mind, I would not hope to see a jaguar. I know the odds against that happening—without benefit of a bait, that is. But that's all right. It is enough of an escape just to be, some part of the time, in places where jaguars are.

Or tapirs. My private list, exclusive though it is, can accommodate more than one premier species in a given setting. Gazing at the tracks Ramón has shown me, I need no reminding that a tapir is as emblematic of the tropical wilds as the great cat that sometimes preys upon it.

Tapirs are classified as distant relatives of the horse and rhinoceros, although their arched, tapering snouts suggest they might once have toyed with the idea of evolving into elephants. That would have been a long time ago, however. Tapirs are conservative animals. Judging from the fossil remains, they have not changed their shape at all during the millennia when rhinos and especially horses were changing theirs. Some people think they resemble pigs, and they do have a piggy passion for wallowing in mud. But basically, tapirs don't look like anything except other tapirs.

They are frantically shy animals, as well they might be. They will use their teeth if they are cornered, but their chief defenses against their enemies are their sheer bulk and thick hides, and a knack for swimming underwater. Indeed, they are most apt to thrive in areas where water is dependably at hand, which explains the proximity of this mother and her "bebé" to El Teniente. They also need to be left alone by people, which they seldom are. I have been told that tapir steak is unpleasantly greasy to the human palate, if not a jaguar's; but whether that is true or not, the animal makes too impressively large a target for any campesino with a gun to pass it up. Even more than my totem jaguar, the tapir is what scientists call an "indicator species." Wherever the human presence is heavily felt, it is the first of the jungle animals to call it quits. Its disappearance in what is now the state of Yucatán, long before the arrival of the Spaniards, is probable evidence of the overexploitation the ancient Maya were imposing on their environment way back when. And the species has been losing ground ever since. In Campeche, the Laguna el Teniente is one of only a few locales where this marvelous species still survives.

For a longish while I contemplate the baby tapir's tracks. I can see him trotting along on his stubby legs, keeping up with his huge chocolate-colored mother. Unlike her, he is sporty as a fawn, tricked out in a bright coat of stripes and spots. I want to believe that, when and if he grows up, the wilderness hereabouts will still be intact enough to shelter him. The odds are against him, but maybe, just maybe, the cancer of Concepción won't spread this far to the southeast.

It is a little after eight. Jorge asks me if I want to go ahead and eat dinner now, but I tell him no, I'll wait until José and Kenneth get back to camp.

Jorge is still ill at ease. Sporadically, he tells me about other hunts here at Cibalito. The large herd of white-lipped peccary (much rarer than their cousins, the collared peccary) that practically ran through the camp, the fine jaguar his pretty wife killed on a "vacation" hunt, the hunter who tried to call up some turkeys and got an ocelot instead. On a more typical expedition, Jorge would have seven or eight clients spending almost two weeks in the jungle. On average, two or three of them would score with a jaguar, a puma, or an ocelot. On the hunt preceding this one, four hunters had killed four cats all in the same night.

When I ask if the jaguar in particular can stand that kind of pressure, he says, "Let's put it this way. Maybe fifty jaguars are killed in the state in a year. Between Señor Ham and me, our hunters kill perhaps eight or ten. All the rest are killed by people who are out to shoot anything, who don't pay for the license, who don't bring money into the country." Then, reverting to a favorite theme, he adds, "But even all those others don't do as much damage as the ones who clear the land, the ones who push back, push back all the game."

He is right, of course. But still, in a diminishing habitat, even legal hunting pressure is bound to affect a jaguar population that, on the basis of territorial requirements alone, cannot add up to much more than a couple of hundred animals in all of Campeche. Somewhat gingerly, I broach the subject that both of us have been wanting to talk about.

"You must know, Jorge, hunting jaguars in Campeche is illegal now."

Jorge wipes his brow, shifts his large bulk in his creaking chair. "That law," he scoffs. "What good does it do? I tell you, my hunters are not the problem. Next year, you wait and see, we are going to get that law changed!"

"But what about now? What if a jaguar had come to José's bait instead of a puma? Hunters pay big money to come out here. And the jaguar is the top of the line. Would you tell him no, he can't shoot it?"

Jorge is suddenly calm, if not relaxed. He looks at me steadily for the first time that evening. "Would you write about it, if . . . something like that came up?"

I tell him, yes. "But what I don't understand, Jorge, is why you agreed to take me along in the first place. You knew where my own bias lies."

He shrugs, sighs. "This is a shorter hunt than usual. Only two clients. We brought along only four goats. The odds . . ."

The implications of the situation are only now dawning on me. Suddenly I feel like the bastard at the family reunion. I tell him, "Look, Jorge, I don't know what's up; but the best thing is for me to clear out first thing in the morning. Manuel or somebody can get me as far as Escárcega—"

A silence lies between us. Then, just as Jorge is about to say something, two shots smash into the darkness nearby. We both jump.

"He got him."

"Yes," says Jorge. "The puma."

He walks out of the mess and stands in the headlight glare of the approaching jeep, wearing the congratulatory smile the occasion calls for.

The puma is a husky adult male, a little smaller than his counterpart in the U.S. West. Ramón, Manuel, and some of the other men give José's driver and guide a hand hauling the body to the mess, where it is strung up to a roof beam by one of its forepaws. As it twists, the beautiful feline face comes round to stare at me. Jorge had once spoken of the "power" in the eyes of even a dying cat. The eyes of this dead one are still liquid and bright, but serenely calm. The final pain and fury have drained out of them.

I feel a bit schizzy. Throughout the evening I had been silently hoping the puma would not return to the bait. But now that the thing is done, it would be churlish to begrudge José his prize. He is a thoroughly nice, easygoing fellow from the Basque country, a contractor who specializes in the construction of small shopping centers. At 45 he still looks like one of those blandly handsome college seniors who cannot help but be popular. Toward everyone he projects the unaffected friendliness of a man who justifiably likes himself and assumes that everyone else likes him too. Including God, who has set him up with a puma on short notice and against the odds.

Usually he is placidly calm, but right now, the camp generator could run on the excited energy he gives off. Once the picture taking is over, he wastes no time telling us how he got his cat.

At four o'clock, he and his guide had arranged themselves in a tree above the remains of the bait. Instead of a platform, hammocks supported them, hung at an angle that enabled them to sit upright. They waited. And waited. No smoking, no talking, no moving about. José was in a state of almost unbearable suspense. "I was thinking all sorts of things," he says. "Wondering if the cat would come back, if I would make a clean kill . . . I thought about my two sons, about how I would someday bring them to this place. But the excitement! Well, it affects different people in different ways—"

"Oh, that is true!" Jorge interjects. "I remember one client, an older man. We were on a night drive, and this huge jaguar comes out on the road right ahead of us. The jaguar practically poses for him. He raises his gun, but nothing happens. 'Shoot him,' I whisper. '*Shooot* him!' But he can't. He freezes, you know? He says, 'Take me back to camp right away.' And then I realize the poor man has shit in his pants."

José laughs. "In my case it was not like that. After three hours of waiting, I fell asleep!" The next thing he knew, his guide, who had already turned on the powerful floodlight, was urgently shaking his shoulder. José awoke to see the puma standing over the bait.

Reliving all of this, José jumps from his chair and aims an imaginary shotgun. "Right away I was wide awake. Bang! I hit him in the back. He clawed at himself"—José claws the air—"but then he got up, badly hurt, and made for the woods. I shot three more times, bang, bang, bang, and would you believe it, I missed every time!" José laughs at himself. "My guide was hissing, 'Kill him! Kill him!' but then he realized I was out of shells and gave me one. This time I hit the cat in the side, in a wide pattern, and that finished him."

Jorge, caught up in José's account, had put aside some of his earlier uneasiness. But now he abruptly turns toward the night outside and frowns.

José and I hear it too, the approach of Kenneth's jeep. But no shots are fired. A second later, the headlights are beaming through the trees.

Jorge strides outside, putting his back to us so abruptly that José and I realize we are not invited to follow him. Out there at the edge of the darkness, he and Kenneth converse for some time. When they come into the mess, they are both wearing smiles that seem a little strained. Kenneth does not look at me. Politely he congratulates José on his good fortune.

Finally, the cook is able to serve the long-delayed dinner. While we eat, some of the staff take the puma away. They will work late tonight, skinning it and boiling the flesh from its skull.

When the meal is over, Jorge clears his throat. He addresses José. "Would you mind, my friend, if we return to Campeche earlier than we had planned? In fact, tomorrow? Kenneth has decided—"

Kenneth still does not look at me. He says to José, "Señor Sansores and I have talked the matter over. I think we are done with the hunting here. Anyway, there are some things I need to take care of. I want to spend a little time in Mérida."

Well, I think, so much for the free lodgings in Zimbabwe.

The change in plans suits José fine. He has what he came for, and now there will be time for a little deep-sea fishing at Cancún before he heads back to Spain. Still, he looks pained. He realizes that Kenneth has not had a chance to get what he wanted, and that I am somehow to blame.

"So," Jorge sighs, "that is settled." He gets up heavily from the table. "It has been a long day, my friends; so now, if you will all excuse me, I think I will go to bed."

That night I lie awake a long time, listening to the mosquitoes whining outside the net. It is almost a relief, to feel depressed, for a change, about something as manageable and immediate as being a spoilsport. But that isn't what keeps me awake. I am thinking of my hypothetical jaguar. I will never know for sure if he has already helped himself to one of Kenneth's baits. But it doesn't matter. The important thing is that he is out there prowling the jungle night, with his spotted hide still intact. Rather than hanging by a paw while Jorge takes a picture of Kenneth posing with him. With Kenneth, of course, looking disappointed because it's all over. Because the hunt is ended.

THREE

Ticul

A couple of days after my return from the hunting trip, it is time to say goodbye to my Campechano family. Anita has given me a place that I can properly start out from, so now I got to go on, right?

Anita's eyes are a little damp. So are mine. Still she manages that bright indomitable smile of hers. "We good friends now, hah? We don't say goodbye for good!" Jorge and his parents stand a little to the side, looking solemn. I promise that, most certainly, I will return when my travels in the Yucatán peninsula are ended. I am so busy waving as I drive off that I almost run into a ramón tree at the entrance to the trailer park. A shrink might say that I wanted to. But then, finally, I am on my way. Goodbye, Anita, Jorge, Lupe. And tranquil Campeche. Goodbye, also, to the idea of turning back.

Now, a couple of hours later, on my way to Ticul, I say hello to Sayil.

It is, I suppose, a juvenile strategy, but I have found that a good way to escape depression is to make believe. And Sayil is the perfect place to make believe one is an ancient Maya prince. It is also very good for bird-watching.

Nowadays it is bad form for Americans to be judgmental about past and present cultures—other than their own, that is. But at the risk of getting poison pen letters from archaeologists and anthropologists with politically correct views, I'm bound to say that a great deal of what we call ancient Mesoamerican culture, including Maya culture, gives me the creeps. That doesn't mean I'm not impressed—as one is meant to be impressed—by the incredible feats of architectural engineering, the brilliant artistry, the elaborate calendars, the complex social structure, all that—especially since it was produced by a Stone Age civilization. But—I'm sorry—whenever I visit the really big ceremonial sites where a lot of restoration has been done, I am more than a little bit repelled by all those daunting pyramids, those skull-engraved altars, those monstrous faces of bloodthirsty gods. I especially feel this way at Uxmal and

Chichén Itzá and Kabah, probably because of their overlay of Toltec-Itzá influences. But at almost any large site in Maya domains, I can't shake the thought that, to an extent probably unmatched by any other civilization (except other Mesoamerican ones), the *Zeitgeist* behind all that architectural grandeur was necromantic in its spiritual conception, totalitarian in its intention, dehumanizing in its execution, and, in the most literal sense, bloodthirsty in its religious function. Some sites, notably Palenque and Tikal, manage to be more beautiful than oppressive because the jungle setting (which wasn't there when those places were at their zenith) softens everything and at the same time serves as the Central American equivalent of Shelley's lone and level sands, reminding us of the transience of megalomaniacal ambitions in particular and worldly glory in general. But it's still there: a soullessness, an indifference to everything that is humane and individualistic in the life of our species.

Considering the foregoing, it might seem inconsistent to say that I am fond of Sayil. It was, after all, part of the same culture, a satellite metropolis in what was probably a shaky confederation of dominant and dependent "city-states" in the northeastern sector of the Yucatán peninsula during the Late Classic period (A.D. 700–900). But anyone who visits the place will instantly see and feel the difference. It isn't just that it is out of the way and not too overrun by tourists. The same can be said of next-door Labná and Xlapac. What matters is that, as it survives today, the architectural presence that dominates Sayil is not a temple but a palace.

I call it a palace. Everybody calls it a palace. What it really was is anybody's guess. Admittedly, there is nothing in this rambling pile of stone that would pass as an audience hall. Much less a ballroom. And the apartments are small and disconnected. Some archaeologists theorize that it and other places like it might have served as administration centers, or maybe "monasteries" for priests, or condos for cults of warriors. But in the absence of any real evidence one way or the other, I can believe it's a palace if I want to.

From the outside, it certainly has the look of a nice, comfy palace, unlike most other Maya structures that bear that name. As palaces ought to be, this one is a bit pretentious. Yet, it is built to the human scale. Reiterations of the snouted face of the Rain God Chac—grotesque but not as frightening as those of most other Maya gods—embellish and enliven the cornices. Clusters of Puuc half-columns, ranked in groups, soften the façade. Most pleasing of all, galleries of rounded columns create an airy openness that is absent in most Maya structures. Along with the broad terraces that set each story back from the one below it, they give the place a horizontal, lounging look that is more welcoming than awesome. Almost Mediterranean.

Late afternoon, and the few other tourists have gone away. I sit in the doorway of one of the chambers on the top terrace, drinking in the warm golden light. From here and there behind me comes a scaly, scraping sound. I have been motionless for so long that the resident iguanas are emerging cautiously from their niches to join me in a little sun worship. The poor creatures have good reason to be wary. The gatekeeper and his family will make a meal of any they can catch.

So would I, if I were really the Maya prince I am pretending to be.

I am pretending to be a Maya noble—both prince and priest—on his day off. No sacrificial ceremonies, audiences, battles, or hallucinogenic enemas are on the schedule, so I am free to take my ease, perched comfortably on the doorstep of my palace apartment, smoking a very strong cigar made from wild tobacco plants. I am dressed in an unceremonial tunic of thin cotton and my bottom reposes on a mat made of kapok, the cottony fiber of the sacred ceiba tree. Whatever Ludwig of Bavaria, or some modern archaeologists, might say about it, I consider the rather small chamber behind me to be just the right size to shelter a noble personage such as myself, along with my wives and assorted children. In fact it is just the right fit for any Maya family, no matter what its rank. Even now, the Maya are not fond of privacy or large interior spaces; and back in the spirit-infested nights of a thousand years ago, I would surely have felt that the family that huddled together stayed together.

The grassy open space below the palace is no longer grassy nor particularly open-looking. It is, in fact, a plaza paved with lime and mortar, its surface gradually sloped to carry rain runoff to the nearest *chultún*. There are many of these cisterns at Sayil. Between them, they can hold enough water to carry the entire community, almost three thousand people, through the long dry season.

It is the dry season now. According to the senior priests, the Corn

God has accepted the serfs and captives sacrificed to him this year, so the rains will arrive on schedule. On this market day, the plaza is reassuringly crowded. Thatched sunshades cover the raised permanent stalls. The choice locations are held in lease, like almost everything else at Sayil, by the same families from one generation to the next. Below them, less privileged vendors have spread their wares on mats. In this last quarter of the afternoon, both buyers and sellers bestir themselves for a final round of bargaining and barter. There is no lack of produce to choose from: huge woven baskets of beans, chilies, squash, and maize; neatly laid out arrangements of finely chipped celts, spear heads, blades; stacks of ceramic bowls, jugs, and funerary vases for which the Puuc region has become famed; bolts of cotton cloth, some exquisitely woven and dyed; piles of furs and bouquets of feathers for ceremonial costumes; jars of honey; wicker cages containing turkeys, parrots, monkeys. Beneath the thatched roof of one of the permanent stalls, half a dozen captives from the recently defunct city-state of Río Azul crouch passively side by side between hanging quarters of deer, javelina, dogs. One of the wives of a jaguar warrior is exchanging a long bolt of cotton cloth for a young boy. When he has been fattened and purified, he will serve as a sacrifice substitute for the warrior's son.

Along with the locals, itinerant peddlers hawk their special wares: Campeche salt; cacao beans from Becán; necklaces, bracelets, funerary masks and figurines finely carved of albite, chrysoprase, and precious jade from abandoned, oft-looted centers such as Tikal in the lowlands far to the south. It disturbs me a little that a good half of the traders, and those the most prosperous, are either Mexicans deriving from Tula and other Toltec regions, or else Mexicanized Maya from the western frontier. Such peoples have been doing business with us for a long time, but now, well, they seem to be getting a bit above themselves. The Mexicans have even been allowed to establish their own enclave at Uxmal, erecting their own stelae, marrying into the best families. One hardly knows where it will end.

Notwithstanding these xenophobic qualms, and my well-bred distaste for trade, I take a certain satisfaction in the prosperity implicit in the vulgar buying and selling that is going on below, indeed, in all the prospect that lies before me. Much of Sayil is in sight, including the city's most notable temple tombs, glowing blood red in the late afternoon sun. Though not as imposing as the grandest pyramids at the mother city of Uxmal, a couple of them would not be out of place there. Smaller temple tombs and the raised compound residences of lesser lords and priests are gathered in clusters, the former grouped around open plazas, the latter around private courtyards. There are main avenues, but no grids of streets, and the scattered thatched chozas of slaves and bonded serfs merge randomly with the agricultural operations on which the life of Sayil depends.

In the early tenth century, as in the twentieth, these operations are based on the slash-and-burn principle known as *milpa*. Although the prince I am would be horrified to see the present-day condition of Sayil, it would be a mistake to suppose, as some artists' renderings of other Maya centers suggest, that in its heyday the dry, thorny forest roundabout was utterly cleared away. Milpa is a successional system: for every patch of land growing rows of beans and maize that are barely visible among the sheltering weeds, four or five others would be at various stages of reverting to scrubby forest. The point of all this was (and still is) to allow the impossibly thin soils of the region several years in which to regenerate, through the reaccumulation of leafy humus, to the point where they could sustain a couple of years of renewed cultivation. When a given tract reached that stage, its second-growth forest was cut and burned, and the cycle begun again.

The arrangement was sensible, even environmentally sound, as long as the cycle was sufficiently extended to permit the necessary rebuilding of soils. Unfortunately, in the Sayil over which my imagination presides, the warning signs of excessive exploitation are already present. For miles and miles around, right up to the border shared with Labná, the rotational cycle has been sharply reduced. Since Sayil, like all Maya centers, is a necropolis as well as a living city, an ever-expanding work force, much of it forcibly imported from conquered city-states in the Maya lowlands, has been needed to build more and more temples and tombs; and the demanding priestly castes who propitiate the ancestral dead have greatly increased as well. There are more mouths to feed, less to feed them with. During the last decade, there have been three years of famine. And the other city-states roundabout are no better off. Disputes have arisen over borderlands where the soils are not as exhausted as they are closer to the ceremonial centers.

Luckily for me, I cannot know that within two generations, the Puuc dynasty to which my own noble family belongs will be overthrown by that of the Itzá, the Toltec-Maya usurpers who will ensconce themselves at Chichén Itzá. Or that, after a brief, grandiose flurry of self-glorification, enslavements, and enforced cultural assimilation, these new rulers will preside over the beginning of the end of Maya civilization in the northern Yucatán. Already, although neither I nor the prophet priests nor anyone else is aware of it, Sayil, like Uxmal and Kabah, has seen its best days. Before very long, it will suffer the fate that has already overtaken the great Maya centers to the south: it will become a hollow shell of its still flourishing self—its ruling classes exterminated, its artisans scattered, its iconography and complex religious rituals debased by an ignorant, disbanding peasantry. Long before the Spanish arrive, bats and iguanas will be the only inhabitants of this sunny palace.

That, however, is not my worry. Right now, which is to say, in the early tenth century, I am enjoying myself. So I push my luck. I invent for myself a senior wife. She is down there in the plaza, still a fine-looking woman at 25: Her nose is curved and shapely; her brow (like mine) is fashionably sloped by the strapped boards that, in infancy, reshaped her head. Her front teeth are inset with jade, her forearms painted with red cinnabar. While a servant holds a parasol above her head, her maid bargains on her behalf with a trader from the coast near Edzná. She has bought a pair of carved ear flares made of sea shells—all well and good. But what is that the maid is now holding out toward her while she nods her approval? A handful of sanctified stingray spines! Oh, Lords of Darkness! I had forgotten! The Feast of Ek Chuah, God of War, draws nigh. My wife will allot a barbed spine to herself and each of my two younger wives. At the forthcoming ceremony, they will draw them back and forth through their tongues, thereby inducing a hallucinatory transport during which the spirits of the honored ancestors will make an appearance, disgorged from the dreadful jaws of the Earth God Serpent to sample the taste of noble blood.

But she has also purchased a fourth spine, and that one, as I know only too well, is reserved for me. I too will be required to display the proper spiritual fervor. Except that, in my case, it will be the penis, not the tongue, that the spine will pierce.

That does it. With a shrinking in the loins, I scurry back to the twentieth century as fast as I can.

It's too bad; but that's the way it goes whenever I play my time machine game with the ancient Maya. Something gruesome always turns up. Even at Sayil.

The path to "Temple Two" winds among mounds of overgrown rubble, all that remains of the residences and shrines I have been rebuilding in my mind. The dry forest, dominated by many species of acacia, makes up in density for what it lacks in height. In fact, it is all but impenetrable. It is a great advantage to the Maya that they are a small people. They need to be, just to get through this stuff.

There is still a little sunlight left. During a half a mile's walk, I spot several Montezuma oropendolas, as well as their hanging basket-stocking nests. Also Yucatán jays, as loudmouthed as all other members of the tribe, a lineated woodpecker, a barred antshrike in its jailbird outfit, a noisy flock of Aztec parakeets, and a covey of demure little Maya quail scooting in and out among the rocks. Best of all, though, I get a fine view of a turquoise-browed motmot sitting in a thorn tree.

In their glowing shades of blue and green and rufous red, motmots are pretty all over, but no more so than a hundred other tropical species. What makes me so partial to them are their enchantingly eccentric tails: Just where most birds' tails end, the tails of motmots sprout two very long feathers as a flamboyant afterthought. But that's not all. The birds themselves are not content to leave well enough alone. They neatly strip the upper part of these extravagant plumes so that the brilliant blue tips, edged in black, are transformed into fairytale flowers drooping downward from black stems. When in an exhibitionist mood (and motmots often are), they swing these gorgeous pinnulae from side to side, as my bird is doing, catching the light, flashing out an iridescent semaphore through the dull green acacia foliage.

Another nice thing about motmots: their name is fun to say. As this one flies away, I call after it, "Goodbye, motmot; nice to have seen you, motmot."

I should have known better, of course. If there is one thing certain in life it is that if you start talking to motmots, someone besides a motmot is bound to overhear you. In this case there are two someones coming around a bend in the trail ahead of me. A man and a little boy. They are campesinos, dressed in the usual white shirts, and the man is carrying the usual machete. They stop dead in their tracks to stare at the goofy gringo.

"*Buenos,*" I say.

"*Buenos,*" the father answers, glancing warily into the impenetrable thickets, not really wanting to discover whatever it was I was talking to.

His profile, dressed up in some stylized feathers, would be right at home on an ancient stela. The little boy, too, has the Maya look: beautiful, far-apart eyes and an owl beak nose in a broad, flat face.

I engage the father in conversation about the local wildlife, trying not to act like someone who might actually talk to it. I remark that the woods look like a good place for deer, turkey, javelina. Are there any around?

The man points behind me and shakes his head. "The road," he says. Although this says it all, he politely elaborates on the subject. Since the road to Oxkutzcab was paved, the animals have "moved away." There are still some deer a few kilometers back from the ruins. The javelina, though, are gone. Three years ago someone shot a jaguar. None have been seen since. Nowadays the hunters can get to all the cenotes in the area, and during the dry season the animals must come to the cenotes to drink. He shrugs ruefully. He himself hunts, he explains. It is too bad that now the game is becoming scarce.

I thank him for the information. "*De nada,*" he says, carefully stepping past me, the boy following. But when they are at a little distance, they both turn around for another look at me.

"Excuse me, Señor," the father says in Maya-accented Spanish. "You are alone?"

I come clean. "I saw a motmot, *un momoto.* I called its name."

He smiles with sudden, friendly understanding. "Ah, *momoto.* It brings good luck. In Maya, it is called *toh.*"

"Toh," I repeat.

He gives me a grin and makes a little joke that is not perhaps altogether a joke. "I thought maybe it was one of the *yuntzil.*"

"Yuntzil?"

He searches for a word. "*Un duende. De la selva.*" A ghost. A spirit of the woods.

"No. Only a toh."

"Ah," he says, and nods. "Well, go with God."

The little boy bestows on me a brief, brilliant smile before he follows his father's retreating back. The light is fading. The man is hurrying now along the path that leads to the palace and the road. Soon he and his son are white shadows, weaving their way swiftly through the shambles of tree-covered mounds that were once the homes and tombs of their ancestors. Whether I was talking to one or not, the man knows that the yuntzil are apt to lurk in a place like this.

The ghost that I converse with cannot be left behind at Sayil, even if I wanted that. Still, I decide that I had better be heading back to the road too.

When the explorer-archaeologist John L. Stephens arrived in Ticul a century and a half ago, the town struck him as "the perfect picture of stillness and repose." So he wrote in *Incidents of Travel in the Yucatan* (1843). Around the plaza and along the adjoining streets stood sturdy stone houses, *casas de piedras,* with "flat roofs and high garden walls, above which orange, lemon, and plantain trees were growing." Round about them, extending for a mile in any direction, "were the huts of the Indians . . . generally plastered, enclosed by stone fences, and embowered among trees, or rather, overgrown and concealed by weeds. . . . Altogether, for appearance, society, and conveniences of living, it is perhaps the best village in Yucatán, and famous for its bullfights and the beauty of its Mestiza women."

Prescient as he sometimes was, Stephens could not know when he wrote those lines that only a few years later, in 1848, the "stillness and repose" enveloping Ticul would be of a very different order. The town, attacked and overwhelmed during the great Maya uprising known as the War of the Castes, would be only a gutted shell of its former self, its stone houses roofless and abandoned, its pretty mestiza women, along with all the other inhabitants, either slain or dispersed. It would be years before the survivors would dare to return and rebuild.

"And yet, you know," says George Cobb, "after all that, Stephens' description still holds wonderfully true. The town really hasn't changed that much."

I remind him of El Zapato, and we both laugh. "I can't imagine," says George, "what Stephens would have had to say about *that!*"

El Zapato is the centerpiece of the little *glorieta* round which traffic circles at the east end of town, not far from the home of George and Janet Cobb. Glorietas are an intermittent feature on the main avenues of every sizable Mexican town. As a rule, the monuments that adorn them—usually honoring some revolutionary hero or Mexican mother-hood—are so ugly in their "modernist" way that visually discriminating people squint their eyes getting around them, thereby sometimes caus-ing accidents. But the one at Ticul makes you smile rather than wince. It is a replica of a two-toned shoe—a woman's shoe—of a style that, when I was a boy, was described as "sensible" and was still worn by cer-tain elderly, tight-lipped lady schoolteachers. This one, however, is the size of a rowboat. It has a thick, slightly elevated heel and bulbous toe, and is painted chocolate brown and black.

"Of course," George explains, "shoemaking is a big thing here in Ti-cul, but Oxkutzcab, down the road a bit, is really to blame. It's a quite prosperous agricultural center, you know, and there's a certain amount of rivalry between the two towns. So when Oxkutzcab's city fathers de-cided to put up a huge, very *orange* orange in their glorieta to celebrate their citrus industry, people here had to do something to top them, now didn't they? The result, as you see, is our Giant Shoe."

The Cobbs and I are sitting, somewhat islanded, in the immense space that is the living room of their home, the Quinta San Benito. George describes a *quinta* as "a type of colonial farmhouse." If that is so, the farmers who built this one must have been pretty well off. True, the place is not quite as showy as a hacienda's *casa grande,* but it's no one's idea of a modest homeplace either. The design is chastely simple: a long central area fronted by a gallery, bracketed at either end by rooms that extend forward to form a U-shaped floor plan. But the proportions are palatial. Without crowding, the central room could accommodate the entire herd of elephants in the African Hall of New York City's Museum of Natural History; and several hippopotami could fit comfortably into the kitchen wing. In that sort of vertical as well as horizontal space— the beamed ceilings are twenty feet high—the Cobb's modest furnish-ings, and indeed the Cobbs themselves, get a little lost-looking, like Pi-nocchio and his boat in the belly of the whale. By comparison, the wing containing the sleeping quarters is almost cozy. It has been divided into two rooms that are merely very large rather than cavernous. In the first of these, George has his bed, and Janet her hammock. I am installed in the second. To my relief, my room is furnished only with a bed. I love the idea of hammocks: they are compact and easily transportable; and, best of all, you don't have to make them up in the morning. But in practice, I don't do well in them because I sleep on my stomach, a posture they don't allow for. It wouldn't matter so much if I could just accept my limitations, and the hammock's, and let it go at that; but whenever I am exposed to one of the things, I can't resist giving it another try, and I always end up in the morning with my spine bent out of shape.

I can hardly believe my luck in discovering the Cobbs. They are kind, hospitable people who, in their diffident English way, have offered me room and board at a very reasonable rate. Their beautiful house is the perfect base from which to explore the roads around Ticul. And best of all, they themselves know everything there is to know about this part of Yucatán and are eager to share their knowledge with me.

This evening, for example, we talk about the local shaman. My lament about not being able to survive a night in a hammock without a backache reminds George of the time he had a problem with his lower back. "There's a fellow here—lives on a back street—who laid me on the floor on a sack and bent my arms behind me until I couldn't stand it. But it absolutely cured it."

Janet has also had back trouble. "In my case, he used a salve and said a lot of prayers. He insisted on massaging my front as well as my back because he felt that the problem was actually in my stomach." She sighs. "It did help. But then he borrowed some money and we've had an awful time getting it back. Fifty thousand pesos! He said he'd repay us in three days. That was eight months ago. We finally got it back last week. Said he owed someone else first so he couldn't pay us."

"Still, he's an awfully interesting fellow," says George. "Name's Don Diego. Not an old man by any means. He's one of the Pech dynasty, you know. His ancestral grandfather was a Maya high priest. He claims to go back forty-five generations. Anyway, it's fascinating, the remedies he knows. Some of them really work. The *zabila*, now—or *Aloe vera*, as we know it—it looks a bit like henequen, with a yellow flower on a long stem—"

"Birds love them," says Janet.

"—Right. Well, the Mayas make a sort of jelly of the leaves. It's absolutely wonderful for sunburn. And wounds."

"I use it as a face cream," Janet says.

I remark that, these days, so do a lot of Americans.

"Oh, it's been around a long time," says George. "There are biblical references to a related plant. But the interesting thing is the way they regard it here. To the shamans, it's sacred. Don Diego has seen the little fairies that live in it. You can't just cut the leaves, you know. You'd be assassinating them. First you have to water them and recite a prayer: 'I believe in the god of Cristo Cosmos'—something like that."

Dusk is coming on. Two parrots, whom the Cobbs regard as members of the family, start screaming at each other from their respective cages. Janet eyes them fondly. "Pancho is so much more cranky since we got Joey. He's jealous of him."

"According to Don Diego," George continues, "the little people have yellow tunics and completely blond hair that reaches to their feet. And around their necks hang pendants in a design of the sun and its rays, with the zabila in the center." He pauses, then adds, "You can make a cocktail with the inner part of the leaf, you know. Mix it with orange juice. It purifies the blood and stimulates the stomach. Really seems to work."

While we sip more conventional cocktails in the enormous central room, and a Schubert symphony that George has taped from the short wave competes with the arguing parrots, the talk drifts, with little sense of transition, from Maya shamans to Christian missionaries. George is very down on the fundamentalist groups that have made themselves ubiquitous throughout the Yucatán. The Jehovah's Witnesses are one of his pet peeves: "You can't stop them, of course, because of freedom of religion and all that. But they're worse than the Catholics ever were for destroying Maya customs. They even tell their congregations how to vote. And they use the local campesinos to go door to door, proselytizing, which gives them the edge on the Mormons and some of the other denominations that have Americans or Mexicans going around wearing ties. . . . Of course, the Roman Church is partly to blame. They charge for baptisms and funerals, you know; even for the electricity for evening weddings."

"All our neighbors feel sorry for us," Janet smiles, "because our church—we're Anglicans—isn't here."

George and Janet Cobb are the only English-speaking foreigners resident in Ticul. He is very distinguished-looking, with his even features and neat gray beard. She is a little wisp of a woman, with a vague, melancholy air about her. Born in England, they have spent most of their lives in Canada, where they raised a family and George did pretty well in the newspaper advertising business. In their demeanor (amiable but mildly reserved) and attitudes (well informed and temperamentally conservative), they resolutely reflect their English middle-class heritage; yet, like a good many others of their nationality and class, they possess a taste for geographic if not metaphysical adventuring in which practicality and romanticism are beguilingly combined. It is the sort of temper, I suspect, that accounted for the long success of English colonialism. Indeed, I can easily picture the Cobbs as middle-ranking members of the Raj in nineteenth-century India, or maybe operating a coffee plantation in Kenya during the 1920s. Even in a contemporary foreign setting, there is much about their lives that recalls bits and pieces of Somerset Maugham's short stories.

After George's retirement, the aforementioned mix of pragmatism and adventurous enterprise landed them in Yucatán in the early 1970s, when the area was far less developed than it is now. Not for them the American Way to Senility—the ranchette in Phoenix or the condo in Florida. Yucatán was affordable and winter-free, considerations with which any retiree might empathize; but it was also unfamiliar, exotically remote from anything in their experience, and lacking a good many of the amenities they were used to. In short, it was a challenge.

They lived for a couple of years in the interior, "surrounded by cowboys, cattle, and scrub," before finally settling in Ticul. But even after twenty years of expatriate life, and notwithstanding their interest in local culture and their addictions to *Aloe vera*, parrots, and siestas, they are not about to go native. George must have his soft-boiled eggs each morning, read the out-of-date *Manchester Guardian*, and religiously listen to short-wave news from faraway London. Janet is devoted to her flowers and classical music. Together they go birding, explore nearby ruins, attend to the extensive garden that surrounds the quinta, read anything in English they can get their hands on, and make a weekly shopping trip to Mérida. Their neighbors, who accept them precisely because they are imperturbably themselves, sometimes invite them to their children's christenings and birthdays. On the basis of this casual fraternizing, George has become something of a social observer. Unlike many of the townspeople themselves, he feels that, locally at least, the standard of living has definitely improved in recent years. "Oh, yes," he says, "if you went to a birthday party five years ago, there'd be a filthy yard, bottles of soda pop for the kids, and no tables or chairs to sit on. Nowadays there's a huge two-tiered cake from the *panadería,* rented tables and chairs, and a photographer; and the daughters hand round beers with a glass atop each. The food is the same, though: two sandwiches and a plate of salad. And a piece of cake, of course." In a more general way, he notes that "the first priority of a Maya family is to have a sewing machine. Next is a bicycle, and then a radio. Nowadays quite a few of them have all those things. And nearly everyone has electricity."

The Cobbs, in their unassimilated way, are comfortably at home in Ticul. But the town is off the beaten tourist track, and I have the impression that their isolation sometimes weighs heavily on them. Luckily, they get on well together, as people who have survived each other for decades quite often do. They occasionally bicker, and Janet can put George down with considerable asperity if he intrudes too carelessly on her areas of authority. But they share their interests, and invariably use the pronoun "we" even when speaking of their separate activities. The problem, I suspect, is that, in the way of all adventures, theirs has run its course. They have "settled" Ticul, and although they still like to bird-watch and explore, they have seen all the local ruins and festivals and caves and birds there are to see. They don't really want to start all over again, but even if they did, it wouldn't be easily done. For reasons that have something to do with the exchange rate, their income is presently much reduced, so they are stuck with their beautiful quinta and sleepy Ticul. Not the worst of all possible situations by a long shot, but they seem a bit bored and stranded, even perhaps lonely.

Which may explain the idea they have come up with. It is a measure of the importance they place on it that they have brought it up at all. Ordinarily the Cobbs keep their private affairs private, as do I when I am with them. This is not, after all, a household like Anita's. These good people would be, above all, embarrassed, if I were to bring up a subject as personal as grief. Of course, their momentous idea isn't anything like that private; but even so, George broaches it to me rather shyly: "Do you suppose," he asks, "that other people might like to stay here? You know, as paying guests, with breakfast and perhaps dinner included? Nice, quiet people, of course. Bird-watchers, that sort of thing." Clearing his throat, he proposes a very reasonable daily rate for my consideration. Janet looks pained. I can imagine how they feel. On the one hand, they want the stimulus of meeting new people and undertaking a new enterprise; and as George says, they could use "a few extra pesos." But they are an intensely private pair, and the idea of using their home as a guest house takes some getting used to. So when I express my enthusiasm for their plan, they look relieved; and when I further promise that, once back home, I will tell all my friends about the Quinta San Benito, they seem really pleased.

Meantime, I afford them a useful test case to practice on and am treated accordingly. I must see everything there is to see within a thirty-mile radius. So, armed with their instructions, injunctions, and hand-drawn maps, I set out next morning to explore the roads around Ticul.

Xul is not really in the middle of nowhere. Hunto Chac, an even smaller hamlet that lies a rocky twenty miles further south, on the Yucatán-Campeche border, is that. But Xul is certainly halfway to the middle of nowhere, which is far enough to go on an afternoon's drive. There are a couple of unexcavated Maya ruins nearby, but if an outsider visits the place at all—and not many do—it is usually for the same reason that the bear went over the mountain: just to see what he can see. The drive south from Loltún is a pleasant roller coaster ride over the toes of the foothills of the Puuc Hills, through a landscape noticeably greener than the one just a little further to the north. Along the way I take note of a migrant kestrel sitting on a pole—a rare sight nowadays, according to George—and a flight of Aztec parakeets passing noisily overhead. Also my first grisson, a large sort of weasel, dead, alas, on the narrow road.

Unlike the bear that went over the mountain, I do in fact have a special reason for visiting Xul. When I had mentioned my interest in the War of the Castes to George Cobb, he had advised that if I wanted to get an intimate, hands-on sense of that long ago rebellion, Xul would be the place to do it.

Until I came here, it had not occurred to me that most of the historic ruins through which sightseers wander with their guidebooks have arrived at their present desolate state by way of a more-or-less gradual process of abandonment and decay. When you think about it, ruins that are the result of a sudden, violent catastrophe—Pompeii, for example—are pretty rare. Ordinarily when a town or city is destroyed in the course of a war or a natural disaster, people eventually rebuild on the site, in the process either restoring or leveling what was there before. When the Maya rebellion eventually subsided, that was what happened at Ticul, Valladolid, Izamal, Peto, and many other Yucatecan towns that had been looted and burned.

But that did not happen here at Xul. The little settlement was too far out in the bush, where marauding Chenes Maya were still at large decades after the War of the Castes had officially ended. Simple fear kept any of the surviving white or mestizo inhabitants from returning to their former homes.

As a result, the unprepossessing shells of the town's church and monastery and its dozen-odd stone houses still stand emptily around a weedy space that was once a busy market square, occupied, until recently, only by iguanas, rattlesnakes, and the shadows of a long-ago terror. Even the knowledgeable Cobbs hadn't been able to tell me exactly what happened when the Maya took this particular town. It was just one among so many, and there was no major battle fought here. The skirmishing, or whatever did take place, probably was over quickly. It would have been different from the Indian fighting in the American West, because here the Maya had been subjugated for generations before the uprising occurred. Possibly the handful of resident whites and mestizos—the *dzul,* as the Maya called them—were able to organize a retreat to Tekax or Peto, soon destined to fall themselves. More probably, though, they were murdered in their beds or dragged outside and cut to pieces by Indians they had seen the previous day at Mass, or in the marketplace bartering venison for bullets.

I can think about all that. I can guess about what happened here. But for some reason my time machine isn't working today. I can't imaginatively enter that long-ago scene. I feel a bit let down. Even the ghosts seem to have departed from these gray broken buildings.

Perhaps the reason is that, although the ruins are as abandoned as ever, the site of Xul is not. A number of little huts indifferently share the square with what is left of the nineteenth-century dwellings. One of them actually sits within the roofless shell of one of the old buildings, using its walls as a sort of compound. The scene could serve as a set for a futurist movie: aboriginal survivors of some nuclear holocaust living in squalor among the ruins of a culture that had become too advanced for its own good, etc., etc. Certainly the people living here now must be having a hard-scrabble time of it from the look of things. The few that are in sight are raggedly dressed. Their features are more mestizo than Maya. I wonder if they are squatters from Mexico or Guatemala, like the ones at Concepción. But of course I can't ask them that. What I do ask a barefoot youngster who has emerged from the village store is whether the settlement is an ejido—a farm co-op—or not. He shakes his head uncertainly, giving me a wondering look. Then I point to the nearest ruins and ask him if he knows anything about their history. "No sé," he says, and hurries off.

The *tienda* is a tiny shed, the roof so low that I can barely stand up straight in it. Most of the interior is taken up by a battered counter, a cooler containing beer and soft drinks, and two or three shelves scantily furnished with canned goods, coffee, sugar, a selection of cookies and candies in plastic wrappers, and a box containing a few packs of cigarettes. What little standing room there is is mostly occupied by seven or eight women and children standing around an electric grinder, into which the proprietor is carefully pouring a sack of shucked maize. While everyone watches raptly, the machine roars and chomps like a garbage disposal, dispensing at its nether end the makings of tomorrow's tortillas.

When the last of the maize is ground up, the proprietor turns to me, affable, but a little surprised to find a gringo in his store. The women and children eye me with interest too, not budging even though their business is apparently concluded.

I order a beer, and then, remembering I am out of smokes, take my wallet out again and buy a pack of cigarettes. Now that I have established myself as a customer, I feel entitled to ask the room at large the same questions I had asked the youth outside. As to whether modern-day Xul is an ejido or not, there seems to be some disagreement. One of the women nods, a girl shakes her head, the others look puzzled, and the proprietor replies that *"la gente aquí son milperos"*—the people here are milpa farmers. I want to tell him I already know *that*. As for the history question, everyone knows they don't know the answer, except for the proprietor. He beams at me and says authoritatively, *"Ah, las ruinas! ¡Las ruinas son muy antiguas!"* I smile politely, thinking, Thanks a lot. Finally I ask them a question about the local wildlife. Are there many deer or javelina in the area? *"Sí, sí,"* says the proprietor. But one woman shakes her head, another says, *"Un poco,"* and a third, less guarded than the others, says there are still a few deer around, but no one has killed a javelina in a long time.

"Ah," I say, as though I have somehow been enlightened, when in fact I feel exasperated. Hell, these people don't know anything about anything. Their lack of curiosity about their own surroundings—or maybe it's just plain uncommunicativeness—annoys and depresses me. I can see how they might be tight-lipped about the wildlife if they're hunting it illegally, which of course they are. But the other questions had been harmless enough. I can't help experiencing a small rush of contempt. If *I* lived here, by God, I would at least want to find out what those ruins were all about!

With everyone's eyes following me, I step outside, take a last look at past and present Xul—neither very appealing to the eye—and get in the van. I am already pulling away when I hear what sounds like a shriek, then another. A little unnerved, I look into the side-view mirror. Everyone who was in the store has rushed out. They are chasing after me, waving their arms, yelling and screaming their heads off! For a stupid split second, I know how a dzul must have felt a hundred and fifty years ago. What have I done? I don't know, but I am tempted to take off.

That wouldn't do, of course, so I come to a stop instead. Immediately they crowd up at the open front windows. They are all laughing and shouting at once. I am so flustered that at first I don't understand what they are yelling. Then I do. *"¡Su billetera, su billetera!"* they exclaim. Even when I see a young girl waving the wallet at me, I automatically touch my hip pocket, unable to believe I could have done anything so stupid as to leave it on the counter. It had a lot of money in it, my tourist card, ID, everything!

With a large grin, the proprietor explains that he didn't notice the wallet because it was blocked from his view by a box of candies. It was a lucky thing, eh? that young María had seen it as she turned to leave. If she hadn't, I would have had to drive all the way back from wherever I was staying when I discovered it was missing.

María, a girl about 16 years old, reaches the wallet to me. She is gig-gling and laughing like everyone else, but when I have said thank you about twenty times, and extended a bill to her—"*un regalo,*" a gift—she glances uncertainly at one of the women, presumably her mother. The woman, smiling, gives her a nod, and with a shy little "*gracias*" she takes the money. Then more thanks on my part, more smiles all around, a handshake with the proprietor, an extra wave to María, and I am on my way.

I drive back to Ticul in a contradictory mood. I am ashamed, of course, of the ungenerous sentiments I had showered, in the privacy of my thoughts, on the poor but honest people of modern-day Xul. At the same time, though, I am suffused with a rare, ephemeral rush of good feeling that encompasses not just them but everything that is decent in human nature. The girl, María, and all the others at the grungy little tienda—poor as they were—hadn't even *thought* about keeping the wal-let. Their first and only impulse had been to get it back to me. I feel more than just grateful to them. In a nice, impersonal way, I love them all.

This is not a sentiment I normally entertain when I think of human-kind in a collective way. Philosophically I am a born-again misan-thrope—have been since long before my personal life went bad on me. Given the hard evidence of what we've done to ourselves, each other, the whole living world, I don't see how any thinking person, least of all an environmentalist, can truly love his fellow man in this Iron Age. I make no apologies for this jaundiced but principled view, and I am cer-tainly not going to change it just because some smiling campesinos re-turned my wallet to me.

And yet, and yet—this sudden friendly feeling that I harbor for my irredeemable species becomes, if anything, stronger with every passing mile. As though, just for an hour or two, I and the whole human race were crowded around a piano bar, a little tight, arms on each other's shoulders, singing old college songs.

I'm not big on caves as a rule. Certainly, I would never make it as a ge-ologist. Rocks leave me unmoved. And concepts of geological time, the eons it takes for mountains to rise and caves to become caves, defeat me. Nevertheless, the Cobbs told me I must go the the caves at Loltún, and so I went.

I attached myself to a tour group that had come over from Uxmal. They had their own guide with them, and when I asked his permission to tag along, he referred the question to them. Of course I could, they said. They were a friendly, high-spirited bunch of middle-aged Californians in search of novelty; the sort of sight-seeing people who can with perfect honesty write "Having wonderful time" on the postcards they send home. Some of them forgot to take their sunglasses off until we were almost through Loltún's sunless underworld, but they were well behaved and interested in everything. The guide was a small, stocky fellow, with aggressive-looking mustaches and rather pudgy Hispanic features. He was very good at his job. Of course everybody tittered when, at the Grotto of Tetas and the stalagmite "statue" of the Very Well Endowed Man, he made the obvious little jokes. But he really seemed to care about Maya and pre-Maya culture—more, I was glad to note, than geology—and we all listened raptly when he held forth about it. Apparently Loltún, which means Sunless Flower, was being occupied by indigenous peoples thousands of years before the birth of Christ, and the guide had a lot of interesting things to say about the accomplishments of those ancient people, the pictographs they had left behind and the excavations where they had dug out clay for pottery. He would begin every other sentence by saying, "Think of it!" And in fact, I could almost see those long-ago people, hunched over, working the shallow pits by the spooky light of flickering torches, or praying perhaps to their cave-dwelling rain gods. I could imagine *them:* but how could they have ever imagined *us,* this little party of sun-tanned folk in flowered shirts and blouses, meandering through a stone labyrinth that glowed, beyond their shamans' wildest dreams of magic possibilities, with mauve, pink, and yellow lights?

"Where're you from, hon?" one of the women asked as our guide led us to the next Point of Interest. When I told her, she exclaimed, "Oh, I just adore New Orleans! My husband and I were there for Mardi Gras three years ago. We had such a good time. You folks certainly know how to throw a party."

I am used to this sort of reaction when I am away from home; and I like hearing nice things said about my city. But now I had forgotten all the usual responses. Except for the hunter, Kenneth, I hadn't been within speaking distance of any of my countrymen for a month and a half—it seemed more like half a year—and suddenly I was tongue-tied. I said something lifeless, like being glad she'd had a nice time. The woman was no dummy. She realized I didn't want to talk. As quickly as she could, she rejoined a couple of the other women in her group, and started telling them about the wonderful time she and her husband had had at Mardi Gras.

The guide had not forewarned us that the best was saved until last. He had led us down yet another passageway of melted-looking stone that debouched suddenly into an underground chamber much larger by far than any other at Loltún. The Californians emitted subdued ohs and aahs and Well-I'll-be-damneds. I guess I did too.

The place was unlike anything I had ever seen. Where we had entered it, its ceiling rose maybe fifty or sixty feet above our heads. Halfway across, however, a worn limestone terrace, bearing pictograph traces of the ancient people who had worked and worshipped here, reduced the height of the vault by ten or fifteen feet. Still, the spaciousness of this underground cavern was breathtaking, and to come on it so unexpectedly was something of a jolt.

Yet the scale was the least of it. What gave the place its special character were two large openings at the apex of its dome. There, where the cavern, like an enormous air pocket, pressed closest to the surface of the earth, the thin limestone ceiling had collapsed, allowing natural light to enter what would otherwise have been a black void.

The effects created by this trespassing light from the outside world were absolutely magical. The light itself was that. Golden bright high up at the gaping openings, it became as milky in its descent as sunlight filtering through water, finally falling on the cavern's floor like a luteous snow. Directly beneath the larger of the openings, where the terrace reached its highest, most jumbled elevation, two or three slender trees, fallen as seeds from the world above, had taken root and made of themselves a sort of underworld glade in which some Maya Eurydice might have languished. Their attenuated trunks and limbs were utterly focused on reaching up to the light that was reaching down to them. One of them had even succeeded in extending its thin canopy through the broken roof, bypassing the tangles of vines and roots that the outer-

world forest had lowered into the cavern like nets. It was the most sur-
real and fantastic sight, those slender subterranean trees, the invasive
light dissolving in the gloom, the perplexed roots and vines groping for
a hold on empty space. And as though to link all this together, hundreds of swallows, swirling around the rims of the jagged openings,
where light and dark, leaf and root, the over- and underworlds con-
verged, showered their faint, twittering voices down on us like the tin-
kling, glassy sound that sunlight might make breaking into a darkness
that was never meant to be disturbed.

I stayed behind while the others followed the guide through an opening at the side of the cavern and climbed the outside slope to the road
where their tour bus waited. But in a few moments the guide came back
for me, saying that visitors weren't allowed to linger in the caves alone.
He was very nice, though, about the extra trouble I had caused him. "Is
very beautiful, yes?" he said, joining me for a minute in taking in the
scene. "Oh, yes," I agreed. But it was something more than the under-
the-earth beauty of the place that made me reluctant to leave. Something that had to do with the way I felt about everything. I just wasn't
very eager to return to the surface of the world.

Uayalceh, Mucuyche, Tibech, San Bernardo, Santa María . . . with
the Cobbs' directions to guide me, I spent a couple of days easing the
van and myself over the stony back roads around Ticul, touring the casa
grandes—the "haciendas"—that once housed, at least for a few weeks
each year, the owners of the region's henequen plantations. The oldest
of the haciendas, with their long, cool galleries and Moorish arches,
were stopovers for Stephens and his companions, Dr. Cabot and the artist Frederick Catherwood, on their journey from Mérida to Uxmal. At
Mucuyche, I took a dip in the cenote where the men had bathed, and
admired the fine Moorish gate where the doctor had shot a circling
hawk "to the astonishment of the gaping natives." But most of the haciendas were of more recent vintage, impressive beaux arts villas with
wide stairways and towering façades, built by nouveau riche hacendados
during the great henequen boom at the turn of the century. Although
two or three of these grand dwellings have been restored by private owners, and a few others are minimally maintained as schools by the ejidos
that have replaced the old plantations, most are abandoned and in

ruins. In their weedy courtyards I parked the van, then prowled their gutted interiors, meditating on the transitoriness of it all under the suspicious eyes of browsing goats. Even in their fallen state, these buildings could be dauntingly impressive—Ozymandian monuments to the vision and the vanity of the hacendados who had built them.

Yet, imposing as they were, I finally decided that none of the ruins I visited in the vicinity of Ticul could quite match those of Uayamón, far to the south in Campeche.

No rain had fallen during my northward journey, so the window of my van's rebuilt hatch door still carried on its dusty surface three full sets of smeary handprints and two half-sets. I had only to glance at them in my rearview mirror to remember the excursion to Uayamón, and Anita and her family. And the strange little adventure that had befallen me when, alone, I had revisited the great hacienda by moonlight.

Actually, none of the prints on the glass were Anita's. The three complete sets belonged to her sister-in-law, Lupe's wife, and two young, buxomly attractive nieces from Escárcega who were visiting her at the time. The half prints at the corners of the van were mine and her nephew Jorge's. Anita, who had problems with her back as well as her foot, had appointed herself rear guard, carrying the girls' white high-heeled shoes and emitting empathic little grunts and gasps as we pushed the van slowly onward.

We had been returning from the picnic excursion in my van, which I had just reclaimed from the mechanic's shop, when a light on the dashboard flashed on, warning us of what proved to be a slow leak in the oil tank. I, like a fool, hadn't stocked a reserve can of oil, so there was nothing for it but to stop and switch the engine off. The track we were traveling was barely wide enough to allow for the passage of a single vehicle, so if another car came along—which might happen five or six times in a day—it would have been effectively blocked.

I felt awful. Up until now, we had had a pleasant time of it, exploring the ruins of the hacienda, eating oranges and cookies on the weed-choked grand stairway, and taking each other's pictures in the gallery. (Anita, a natural ham, had posed dramatically against one of the columns with her arms outflung, like the heroine in some lurid costume drama, and when I exclaimed, "¡Ah, la actriz!" her nieces had screamed with laughter.) And so, because the preceding hours had passed so agreeably, it seemed that much more a rotten shame that I should have stranded these good people in the middle of nowhere, with night coming on.

Wonderfully, however, Anita and her family had reacted to the situation with far more grace than I did. They treated the whole thing as something of a lark. The women, all in their white Sunday finery (except Anita, in blazing red), piled out of the van, took off their shoes, and, laughing and joking, joined Jorge and me in pushing the van forward along the stony track, while up front, short-legged Lupe both pushed and steered. By sheer luck, our strength had lasted long enough to get the van to one of the road's infrequent wide spots, where a byway led to a deserted milpa.

I decided not to take the chance of leaving the van unguarded through the night. Anita had fretted about *bandidos* and Jorge had offered to stay with me; but I eventually convinced them all that they must try to reach the paved road, a good two miles away, before darkness fell. Lupe said that he and Jorge would return with a wrecker first thing in the morning. Then, with many waves and backward looks, they finally left me.

Which is how I got to see Uayamón by moonlight.

I had come ill prepared for this misadventure. Normally, the van would have been adequately stocked with vodka, cigarettes, and Off!; but this was supposed to have been an afternoon's jaunt, not a camping-out. An orange, a roll of toilet paper, and three cigarettes remaining in the pack were the only necessities aboard. It was hot—impossible to shut the windows—and by midnight, what with a swarm of tormenting memories stirring in my mind, and bloodthirsty mosquitoes humming in my ears, I had had it. The way I was feeling, if bandidos wanted to steal the damned van they were welcome to it. Provisioned with the still uneaten orange and my lone surviving cigarette, I headed back along the moonlit track to Uayamón, serenaded along the way by the voices of a million tree frogs.

In due course, I passed the landmarks we had driven by in blazing daylight, now appropriately spectral and bleached-looking, every moon-washed masonry plane a bluish white, everything else a bluish black. First came an impressive private railroad station set beside the narrow-gauge tracks on which miniature trains once carried both

freight and people, the only automated means of travel in this part of
the Yucatán until not so long ago.

Beyond the tracks, barely visible in the heavy shadows of the trees
that crowded in on them, were the shells of several stone and stucco
outbuildings, not as large as quintas, but well proportioned and still
handsome despite their gutted state. Anita had said that these were
once the quarters of the *"esclavos,"* the slaves. But she was surely wrong
about that. Such substantial dwellings would have housed the hacienda's overseers and factory foremen. The Maya workers would have lived
in stucco shanties and thatched chozas—as they still do. To me, for
whom the preservation of fine old buildings seems almost as worthy a
cause as the preservation of wildlife, it was a difficult thing to understand: how at Uayamón and most of the other ejidos that were once haciendas, the workers, who could have easily made the outbuildings, if
not the great houses themselves, comfortably habitable, had chosen not
to do so.

That afternoon, when we overshot the overgrown side lane leading
to the hacienda, we had inadvertently ended up at the hamlet where
the ejido workers lived. It was mid-afternoon, and the settlement lay in
a somnolent trance. It was a dreary-looking place, the small huts baking
in the sun around a large communal square-*cum*-grazing ground. The
only inhabitants in view were two short, brown, weathered-looking
women standing in the middle of the shadeless dusty square, wearing
white cotton *huipiles* and brown *rebozos*. Anita had acknowledged their
existence just sufficiently to ask directions to the casa grande. They had
acknowledged hers just barely enough to point us back the way we had
come.

It was weird, that minimal exchange, and the way everyone else in
the van fell silent and kept their eyes averted from the ejido and its
women, as though they were embarrassed by the sight of them. This was
my first small experience, though it would hardly be my last, of a cultural separation that still exists in Mexico, not so much between Indians
and mestizos, although there is enough of that too, as between the urban middle class and the rural workers. Actually, the distinction is a little more complicated than the obvious one between city mouse and
country mouse. There are gradations, of course, as the studies of a number of social anthropologists have made painstakingly clear. But the basic demarcation is between those who feel at ease in the twentieth

century—that is, the modern technological world—and those who do not. In the States, where even people who live on remote farms and ranches are, in effect, exurban residents of an urban hi-tech world, this particular type of class apartheid has pretty much faded out. But in Mexico, where the impact of technology-and-all-that-goes-with-it is still a recent phenomenon concentrated largely in the cities, the effect has been the opposite: it has tended to intensify the traditional differ- ences, especially marked in Hispanic countries, between cosmopolitan town and backward country. I doubt that those differences were con- sciously present in the thoughts of Anita and her family; but they were there. On this easygoing picnic afternoon, with a *norteamericano* in their company, they just didn't want to be reminded that the place where we had dead-ended—these thatched hovels and these Indian women with their impassive faces—represented everything that they regarded as still benighted in their country. Not to mention, of course, everything from which they, thanks to Anita and Lupe's fierce Lebanese mother, had escaped.

They were glad to escape now. As soon as the ejido community was out of sight, everybody fell to talking and laughing at once. I too put the strained awkwardness of the moment out of my mind—until that midnight, when I retraced my way to Uayamón. Then I remembered the distancing, impersonal look the two Indian women had given Anita and the rest of us, denying us every bit as much as my friends had denied them, and it occurred to me that this habit of rejection, long ingrained in the conservative minds of rural people, might at least partly explain why the ejido workers refused to inhabit those roomy satellite dwellings at Uayamón, much less the casa grande itself. They allowed the build- ings to decay for the same reasons that they had allowed the jungle to dismantle the great palaces and temples of their own vanished priests and kings a thousand years ago: because these marvelous structures, which they had given their lives and labor to build, represented a state of civilized consciousness that had been systematically denied to them. Ancient and modern, the cultural trappings that had once set their masters' lives apart were still beyond reach of their aspirations or even their envy. Even derelict, the hacienda and all its trappings rejects the humble campesinos. They sense this, I think; they know they could never be at home where they were never welcome.

At Uayamón, however, there is one exception to the general state of not-so-benign neglect. During the afternoon visit, I had noticed that the chapel at the right side of the grand staircase was the one part of the casa grande that the people of the ejido had, after a fashion, maintained. The bell was missing from the small belfry arch, but the facing wall was freshly painted. The door was locked, but peering through the window grill, we had been able to see most of the stark, shadowy interior. A plastic crucifix and a faded picture of the Cristo in a brown wood frame hung behind a simple altar table. There were a few chairs, and the floor had been recently swept. The one cheery touch was a strand of gilded tinsel wrapped around the iron frame of the ceiling lamp. Otherwise, the effect of the place was to project the impression that if God dwelled here, He was under house arrest.

I could understand the way a campesino might feel about Uayamón, but there was no way I could share that feeling myself. Certainly not now on this beautifully luminous night. The raised central building was a chiaroscuro masterpiece of light and shadow: the three huge Palladian arches and their supporting columns reflected the moon's reflected radiance as though they were its source; while behind them the gallery hoarded darkness as a miser hoards gold. The wide, grassy quadrangle below the central stairway was drenched in an almost phosphorescent light. On one side it was flanked by the remains of the huge plantation factory and storehouse, and on the other by a long, narrow building that had perhaps been used as carriage house and stables. But notwithstanding their utilitarian functions, these buildings had been ambitiously built to conform to the grandiose effect of the *tout ensemble*. As I advanced from the *entrada,* the details of their façades—archways, lintels, cornices, steps—stood out in bold moonlit relief against the yawning openings that had once been wide doors and windows. Only at the corner of the quadrangle where the casa grande and the factory were almost joined was this symmetrical etching of skeletal white on black interrupted by a total darkness—the shadowy mass of a huge ceiba tree billowing upward into the clear sky like a thunderhead.

Viewed from the near distance, the hacienda appeared to be spookily deserted but intact, the very sort of place that some well-bred Hispanic vampire might have chosen for a good day's sleep. But I knew from the afternoon's explorations that there was no way he would have got one. Uayamón was gutted: the sun had barged brutally through doorless doorways wide enough to admit a sixteen-wheeler; through gaping holes in the walls that sprouted gardens of ferns; through the shredded plaster still clinging to ceilings twenty-five feet high.

I had fretted about all that while the sunlight was busily ransacking the place. But now the decay seemed natural and inevitable. I fit into it comfortably, like a figure introduced into a Piranesi drawing to indicate the scale. Moonlight and desolation were the perfect match for my present mood.

Even back when I had enjoyed a healthier frame of mind than any I had experienced lately, I had always been romantically susceptible to *Gone with the Wind* syndromes. As a small boy, I had fought back tears when Vivien Leigh had to eat raw turnips because the Yankees had looted Tara. In college I was the one who sympathized more with the *Cherry Orchard's* evicted aristocrats than with the old servant they absentmindedly left behind. And now, here I was, smoking my last cigarette on the rubble-strewn gallery of moonlit Uayamón in the middle of the froggy, bug-ridden night, getting into it again, bestowing on this lovely, lizard-haunted wreck, as might Prince Charming if he had kissed a really dead princess by mistake, an imagined but almost palpable sense of the decorous life it once harbored, the pleasant family gatherings, the house parties and fiestas, the flirtations and small domestic dramas that, according to Señor Sansores, had still been enacted here only fifteen or twenty years earlier.

I welcomed this hazy communion with a sadly but safely vanquished world. It was somehow comforting to indulge a painless nostalgia for the loss of something that had never been mine to lose.

So then: this was the otherwhere in which my mind was roaming when the girl materialized from out of the shadow of the ceiba tree.

The ceiba was that something extra; the perfect prop to set the scene. The tree was sacred to the ancient Maya—it was the central support holding up the world's sky-roof—and out here in the country, some of their descendants still believe it possesses magical properties. One such belief holds that it is the dwelling place of the *x-tabai*, a sort of Maya Lorelei who destroys unwary mortals. Anita, when we had passed under the tree that afternoon, had excitedly revived some of her half-forgotten childhood fears: "At Umán, when I was little, oh, I was afraid the—how you say? witch?—would come down from the branches at

night and get hold of me." She had grabbed her elbows and hugged herself nervously. "I no like that! No sireee."

I, of course, was not afraid of the x-tabai. I knew perfectly well that
there was a real girl down there. She was wearing a white dress and cra-
dling something flat and silver-tinted in her arms. But her sudden appearance was so melodramatically improbable that, for as long as it took
me to stop blinking my eyes and holding my breath, I couldn't help but
wonder if she might be real to me the way the wife of an octogenarian
friend of mine was real to him. The woman had been dead for almost
ten years, but when he was in one of his fugue states, he still held the
door for her whenever the three of us went out for a little walk.

By the time I had gotten over that sort of uncertainty, the girl—I was
sure she was young, even though her face was shadowed—had come forward, moving toward the right side of the central stairway. There, the
roof line of the chapel blocked my view, but I knew she had slipped inside it. I was surprised at how quickly she accomplished this. There was
no rattling of a key, no sound of squeaking hinges. Evidently the door,
locked that afternoon, had been unlatched by someone before she
arrived.

I sat up there on the gallery for what seemed a long time—ten minutes, maybe—being careful to brush the mosquitoes away rather than
slap at them. I bounced the still-unpeeled orange in my hand, and listened to the heartbroken, thrice-paired cry of the tinamou, a rather
large but demure bird that I had never heard calling except at dawn or
dusk. All the while, the curiosity that had killed the cat was killing me;
and finally I gave into it. Helped by the brilliant moon, I picked my way
down the steps, maneuvering them a good deal more quietly than I had
on the way up. When I touched ground, I moved out a considerable way
into the quadrangle, not wanting my shadow to fall across the open
chapel doorway, then circled around to the large, grated window
through which I had peeped that afternoon.

I'm not sure what I expected. An assignation? Or maybe some sort of
secret rite? After all, ever since the days of Bishop Landa, Catholic authorities have been scolding Mexican Indians for not keeping their pa-
gan superstitions and the true faith as separate as they should.

As it turned out, the reality was somewhere in between: an assignation of a sort, and a secret rite as well; but orthodox enough in its

intense, off-hour way. The girl was kneeling on a white handkerchief she had spread on the tiled floor. Two large votive candles, of a sort commonly available in Mexican churches, burned on the altar. Also on the altar was a silver-tinted picture frame, faced toward the picture of Jesus on the wall above. The girl's face was tilted in the same direction. Jesus was calmly gesturing toward his bleeding, thorn-encircled heart, exposed against his breast as though an ancient Maya priest had had a go at it.

I assumed she must have come from the ejido settlement; but although I could see no more of her face than the left ear and an angled view of her cheek and chin, she didn't seem the type of a campesino's child. She was very slender, long-necked, and, as best I could judge, fairly tall; and her hair, under a small, lacy, white cap, was short and waved, maybe even permed.

Whoever she was, there could be no doubt about the intensity of her devotions. Her attention was absolutely fixed on the picture of Christ. Her hands, hanging limply at her sides rather than lifted in prayer, suggested, not laxity or just plain tiredness, but a touching defenselessness; as though to signify that she were quite at the Savior's mercy.

It was this vulnerability, not meant for me to see, that made me realize I was doing something wrong. Until I reached the chapel window, it had seemed a natural-enough impulse to want to know what the girl was up to; and it had been exciting and suspenseful, sneaking up on her as I had done. But now I felt guiltily conscious of being an emotional voyeur, spying on someone who had innocently bared her heart just as Jesus had bared his. Chastened, I made haste to slink away; but before I did, acting on some obscure, propitiatory impulse, I left the orange on the windowsill—although I knew she would almost certainly not notice it.

I passed under the ceiba tree and then kept close to the walls of the old factory until I was clear of the quadrangle. At the entrada, I broke into a run, and kept on running until I reached the van.

For what was left of the night I slept soundly, awakening only when the wrecker showed up soon after first light, with Lupe and Jorge aboard. Even before it came to a full stop they had jumped out, grinning, the one waving a thermos of coffee, the other a pack of cigarettes.

Occasionally I still think about the girl. I hadn't needed to see the face in the turned-away photo to guess what she was praying for. The problem must certainly have been serious to warrant the absolute privacy of that late-night rendezvous with Jesus. Perhaps the fellow didn't love her as much as she did him, or maybe the parents were objecting to the match. But whatever the obstacle, I want to believe that Jesus of the Bleeding Heart answered her prayer. How could he not? How could he not have been charmed and touched, and perhaps a little amused, by someone who had brought him her beloved's picture just to make sure there wouldn't be any mix-ups when he granted her her wish?

FOUR

Celestún

On an impulse, I decide to travel to Celestún by way of a back country lane that crosses the coastal savannah northwest of Halacho. It turns out to be a good idea, a pleasant drive, despite the hardship inflicted on my poor van, which has to shake, rattle, and roll its way like some epileptic robot over thirty miles of quaternary road. Beyond Halacho, large fields of henequen—better known as sisal outside Mexico—dominate a landscape otherwise given over to citrus orchards and the usual milpa mix of scrub and unweeded rows of maize.

It gives me the willies, henequen does. No crop grown by man is more bizarre and savage-looking. It is a sharply spiked agave, and when it is collectively lined up in neat rows, it looks like nothing so much as a mutant army from some war-loving vegetable planet, ready to take over our little earth. I wonder if the campesinos, who must amputate the stiff, pointed lower leaves with their machetes, ever have nightmares in which they are turned loose blindfolded in a field of these homicidal-looking plants. In the course of a working day, they must always risk the chance of stumbling—the fields are full of stones—and impaling themselves on the stiff leaf-blades.

Right now, all I know about henequen, other than that I don't trust it for a minute, is that it was once to Yucatán what King Cotton was to the antebellum South. Its fibers provided baling twine for markets abroad while vastly enriching the landowning gentry here at home. However, as in the case of cotton, social upheaval and the advent of synthetic substitutes eventually put an end to the boom. The henequen I've seen growing today is only a small fraction of what was once planted in these parts.

Wherever there was henequen, there were once haciendas. In this area, however, only two or three of the old casa grandes are still intact enough to serve as reminders of the good old days when caballeros were caballeros, and campesinos knew their place. One of these is located at

Chunchumil, where it sits far enough back from the road to be easily missed by all but the most practiced hacienda-spotters, among whom I now count myself. It is not as sprawlingly palatial as Uayalceh, or as poetically glamorous as Uayamón, or as old as Mucuyche, but it is, nevertheless, a real gem, flawlessly proportioned in its Palladian way: the angled corners and the height of the arches, in relation to the width of the façade, create an effect of verticality that is unusual in hacienda architecture, even in the case of buildings that are larger and that have more elevation. At the same time, the next-door chapel, taller and much more narrowly fronted than the main house, deliberately throws off balance a symmetrical effect that might otherwise seem excessive.

I pull over to take a long, comfortable look at its faded grandeur. The double row of small buildings that form its approach is all there is to the ejido of Chunchumil. Judging from the look of things, the place is not exactly in flourishing shape. But that is hardly surprising. For some time, the country I've been driving through has become increasingly dry and brittle-looking. I can't imagine what could flourish hereabouts other than scrub and subsidized henequen.

The minute I get out of the van to take a picture, however, I learn what else: Children, of course! Mexico's most bountiful crop. I am so suddenly surrounded by them that I feel rather like the Pied Piper without the pipe. Which I don't need anyway. In this outback Hamelin, where probably nothing much changes except the time of day, a very tall gringo turista with a camera, a sunburned nose, *and* a Toyota van, is a sight worth looking at. For my part, the children are a sight worth looking at too. I don't know what it is about these mostly indio youngsters. When they grow up, they won't possess what passes on television (including Mexican television) for good looks; but while their childhood lasts, not all the cherubim in all the Renaissance churches in Rome can match their beauty. They smile radiantly, with their whole faces—shy, bold, expectant all at once. And they retain, even into early adolescence, a lovely, authentic naïveté that most American kids seem to lose even before they graduate from *Winnie the Pooh* to "Miami Vice."

"Aw, Meester," they cry, "Señor! where are you going to?" "What kind of car is that?" "Take me with you!" "How tall are you?" "You must be American, yes?"

There are about twelve or fourteen of them. I tell them to line up in front of the hacienda so I can take their picture. They noisily oblige, giggling, jostling, yelling at each other to get down in front. After the third shot, I am about to disband them when a voice says, "Would you like me to take your picture with them, Señor?"

A plump middle-aged man, wearing a somewhat pained smile, has come up behind me, apparently materializing from one of the nearby doorways. I tell him that I would like that very much indeed. So, it seems, would the children. They mug it up unmercifully, grabbing my hands, hanging on my shoulders, arms, legs as though I were monkey bars.

When we have all been immortalized by my Kodak, and while the children mill about, I thank the man. He wears a spotless white city shirt, laced city shoes, and a neat mustache which he often smooths with his forefinger. In his different way, he looks almost as out of place here as I do. I wonder, without being pushy enough to ask, if he might be a schoolteacher or a government official of some sort. But he is evidently not the latter. When I remark on the architectural beauty of the hacienda, and express concern at its apparent neglect, he makes a little grimace of distaste. "It probably belonged to one of the Peón family," he says scornfully. "At one time they owned most of the land around here. But whoever owned it, you can be sure they built it just to keep up with their rich neighbors. People like that, they were too good to live in the country and get their hands dirty. They deserved to lose it." He is so ready with this sociological commentary that I have the curious feeling he has been waiting all day, perhaps all week, for someone like me to come along so he can get it off his chest. He leans closer, speaks more confidentially, as though the children might overhear and report him. "The sad thing, the tragic thing, is that it is not any better now that they are gone. Not so long ago, the hacendados were the oppressors. Now it's the government. And if you want to know the truth, I'm not so sure the government isn't the worse master of the two. It subsidizes the henequen, it tries to run things; but it doesn't know what it's doing. And the corruption! Whatever else, the hacendados—their overseers, anyway—knew what they were about. I don't like them—¡La casta divina!—they exploited their workers. They kept them in debt, you know, so they couldn't leave the land. But what good does it do them, now that they can leave, eh? They might as well be poor in the country as poor in Mérida."

One little boy, about 5 or 6, is tugging at my hand. "You want to give me a ride in your car, Señor?" he says with a wide, pleading smile.

"But these kids," I say, "surely it must be better for them. They get a better education, now. They have more opportunities."

The man's already discontented grin becomes so pained at this remark that he looks like he is baring his teeth. "You don't understand," he says. "More education, yes. More opportunities, no. There aren't enough jobs for people now, especially not for the educated ones. Look at me! I cannot live on what I earn. So what will happen to these young ones? What will they do when they grow up?" He shakes his head. "I think sometimes they would be happier if they were cutting henequen instead of learning how to read."

I suspect that for this man life's glass is always half empty. But that doesn't mean his pessimism is unjustified. One doesn't have to spend a great deal of time in Mexico before one realizes that the country's problems are intractable enough to make a cynic of Pollyanna. So I give him a commiserating shrug and say the first thing that comes to mind: "I really wish I were the Pied Piper. I'd tuck all these kids in my van and carry them off."

The man gives me a funny look, no doubt wondering if the Pied Piper might be some notorious gringo child molester. But then he decides that I have made a joke of some kind and chuckles knowingly. We both chuckle. But I hadn't meant to be funny. Whimsical, maybe, but not funny. When I was myself a child, I had made up my own story about what the Pied Piper did with all those never-to-be-seen-again youngsters of Hamelin: he had led them off to a wonderful secret place where they never had to worry about what they would *be* when they grew up.

I thank the man for the picture taking and the informative chat, distribute Oreos to the children, and retreat to the van without ever having had the long, appreciative look at the hacienda that I had promised myself. As I drive off, waving back at the waving kids, I make a mental note to expand my interest in haciendas to include the landed class that once owned them. From what the man had said, there should still be some specimens of the type around.

Beyond Chunchumil, the road is totally empty of traffic, a straight line bisecting a landscape of waterlogged savannahs and acacia woods that puts me in mind of the East African bush during rainy season. Yellow warblers flicker in and out of the roadside thickets. The late afternoon sun paves the way with golden light; and Bach and Handel, taking turns on the cassette player, distill and concentrate that same light in their music. In me, too.

To give some point to a sudden, unexpected rush of well-being, I remind myself of why I am going to Celestún. There are flamingos there. In the life I lead now, there can be no better reason to go anywhere than to have a look at some flamingos.

"It stinks," is what a visiting friend told Barbara Sheffer, a field assistant at Celestún's Centro de Investigación de Aves Acuáticas. It wasn't a value judgment. The friend was just stating the literal truth. Like most any other fishing village in Mexico, Celestún fairly blooms with the aroma of decaying shrimp tails and shark guts. The aroma saturates the lovely beaches and coconut groves that front the town, eddies down the half-dozen sandy streets, fills the grubby square, reaches even to the biological research station on the bank of the estuary where Barbara and her boyfriend, John Thompson, live and work. One soon becomes used to it, but still, it is always present, an olfactory leit motif reminding the one of our senses we can't ever turn off that Celestún depends for its life on the sea.

Stink and all, I like it here. Except for American bird watchers and budget-conscious French couples—the latter wearing bikinis and the usual disdainful expressions they assume when traveling abroad—few tourists find their way to this isolated community on Yucatán's northwestern coast. Fishy aromas aside, it has some other minor drawbacks that are apt to put off the sun-'n'-fun set. The accommodations are spartan, the water too shallow for swimming or surfing, and the three or four fly-blown little restaurants best cherished for the freshness rather than the preparation of their seafood.

Also, the nightlife is nil. True, a lot of drinking goes on here. For some reason—maybe it's just being out on the salty sea so much of the time—Mexican fishermen are particularly susceptible to boozing. Sober, they are the nicest, friendliest people you would want to meet; but give them a few shots of tequila and they will walk into moving cars or beat their wives or pass out standing up. Their wives know all this from hard experience. When the fishing boats pull in, they are right there on the quay to collect the money from the sale of the catch. But the men must manage to get hold of some of it, because there are always a few of them lying passed out on doorsteps or the beach. That, of course, doesn't count as nightlife. The nightlife, as I say, is nil.

Despite such minor shortcomings, Celestún is an attractive, restful place to be. Mornings, I walk three or four miles along the empty, un-spoiled beach, one ear tuned to the slip-slap of tame wavelets lapping at the berm, the other to the wind rattling the palms. Once out of reach of town, there is no footprint in the sand to remind me that I am not alone in the world. But there are other signs and portents: engraved and polished shells, shorebirds and tricolored herons posed silently on rip-pled sandbars, grave pelicans, mysterious whorls and traceries in the sand, the desiccated remains of dolphins and groupers and, once, a large shark spotted with bird droppings, its toothy mouth curved in a half-smile.

One evening I decide to drive north along a washboard sand track that follows the coastal ridge. It takes an hour and a half to cover the eighteen miles to my destination: a lighthouse tall and slender as a min-aret. This side of an airplane, the lighthouse offers the only available overview of the land-and-seascape along this coast. The technicolor panorama of the Gulf at sunset is in itself worth the dizzying climb; but what really holds my interest is the country behind the barrier ridge, the no-man's-land of bleached sand flats and mangrove swamp and salty shallows that stretches north and south as far as eye can see. A black hawk sails by below me, and, lower still, a homing flight of egrets. But as usual when I am in a place that humans haven't overrun, I find myself thinking about what I can't see more than what I can. I know there are deer down there; they've left their tracks in the marl, abraded at the edges by some sort of invisible sand beetle or worm that, for reasons mysterious to me, is excited into activity whenever man or beast in-dents the surface of its underground landscape. Inevitably, I wonder whether a few jaguar might not be hanging on down there too, hemmed in between the Gulf and the inland ejidos. Bob Singleton, the amiable manager of the research station, has heard no reports of any in the area;

and when I asked them, the fishermen lounging on the concrete porch outside the lighthouse had said, *"Muy raro."* This, I have learned during a good many years of asking questions in out-of-the-way places, is a judgment local people usually make on the status of a species only after the said species has totally disappeared from their area. So I ruefully conclude that my totem beast has become extinct in these parts.

But I am wrong. There is certainly at least one jaguar down there, prowling the long, narrow mangrove wilderness that the lighthouse overlooks. I will find out a year later, because by then, according to a report in a Mérida newspaper, a local cattleman will have proved its existence by shooting it.

It is, as social events go around here, a great occasion: Emilio Rangel is taking Bob Singleton and the four graduate students at the Research Center out to a fish and beer lunch at the most adequate of Celestún's restaurants; and since I am on the premises, I have been invited along too.

Emilio Rangel has the official title of Director of Research and Conservation for DUMAC, the Mexican division of Ducks Unlimited. Unofficially, Bob Singleton tells me, he is known as Mexico's "Mr. Wildlife." Privately I think of him as Mr. Dynamo—the sort of man whose main function in life is to provide disorganized people like me with a model we can't live up to. He is an absolute whirlwind of constructive energy, "always on the run" just as Bob admiringly claims. Two days ago he was flying about in the Sierra Madre, helping in a control effort to reduce coyote numbers so that the region's whitetail deer can make a comeback; yesterday he was attending a DUMAC board meeting in Mexico City; this morning, he has descended on Celestún—the recently opened research station is one of DUMAC's projects—just long enough to check things out and treat the staff (and me) to a lunch. By this evening, he will be in Mérida, officiating at a fund-raising auction. And tomorrow morning he will be up north again, trying to persuade representatives of The Nature Conservancy to bankroll an effort to save the last viable population of black bears in Mexico.

He makes me feel like a slug with a bad self-image, but I like and admire him all the same. Animated, which it almost always is, his face is brashly handsome and boyish-looking; but when he isn't smiling or talking, the tiredness shows through and he ages ten years. His conversation, like his itinerary, touches a variety of bases, and covers a lot of ground. His primary responsibility is the management of the diminishing but still huge flocks of migrant waterfowl that breed in the United States and Canada, and winter in Mexico. However, his interest in wildlife is eclectic, as well as necessarily pragmatic. He says the decision to establish a research station here (there are two others in northern Mexico) was based in part on the Celestún estuary's importance as the southernmost major wintering ground for waterfowl on Mexico's east coast; but he admits that governmental preference had something to do with the decision. The estuary is vital both to Yucatán's flamingo—a "tourist bird" which the government is interested in protecting—and to the area's vital fishing industry. In future, researchers at the station here will study not just ducks, but the total environmental picture, which includes, of course, flamingos and fish. In Mexico, private conservation organizations must walk softly when dealing with government bureaucracies, which have the final say about everything and are very jealous of their prerogatives. "We have a kind of mutual admiration society," says Emilio, a little dryly, of this relationship. "DUMAC will do its best to protect this area for the benefit of the country, and the government, we hope, will support our aims."

Like most of the handful of Mexican professionals in his field, Emilio received his education in the States. He deplores the dearth of wildlife management schools in his own country. There are only a couple, recently founded and ill funded. Which partially explains why there are so few trained wildlife specialists on the government payroll. In Mexico, even more than in the United States, the government's swollen bureaucracies seem to exist to provide people with jobs—and politicians with loyal supporters. SEDUE (Secretariat of Urban Development and Ecology), which is chiefly responsible for the administration of wildlife resources in Mexico, is no exception to the rule. The agency is grossly overstaffed and underfunded. But the saddest thing of all is that most of its employees are untrained and unmotivated. And even if a division chief tries to hire a biologist instead of some other bureaucrat's second cousin, qualified applicants are hard to find.

In rapid succession, Emilio expresses concern that the government is "dumping a hell of a lot of landfill garbage into the marsh" at Progreso,

Yucatán's port city; warns that if Yucatán's once abundant deer population is ever to make a comeback, it will have to pay its way as protein
("In northern Mexico, American hunters pay a thousand dollars for tro-
phy bucks, but here the deer are too small"); and musingly complains
that officials in neighboring Belize have not responded to DUMAC's offer of a warden's salary for that country's new jaguar preserve—which I
hope eventually to visit.

While he pauses to eat a bite of overgrilled redfish, I jump in to ask
him how Mexico's own jaguars are faring. He gives me a mischievous
grin. "You know where they are doing well? In the mountains of northwest Mexico, that's where. And you know why? Because of the marijuana growers. Up there, if you're in camouflage, the soldiers shoot you.
If you have a gun, the growers shoot you. So it's not a very good place
to hunt. Or live, for that matter."

Later on, talking to other people, I will learn that Emilio is not ex-
aggerating about this vaguely symbiotic relationship between hunted
men and hunted beasts. In Nicaragua, Guatemala, Colombia, the story
is the same: One of the best places for a jaguar to live nowadays is in an
area where an impartial jungle shelters people who are doing something
illegal on a large scale, like raising weed or coke or a guerrilla army. Because then, of course, other people daren't move in and cut the jungle
down.

I am a better, more invigorated person for having been exposed to
Emilio Rangel; and tomorrow, or, for certain, the day after, I will defi-
nitely start organizing my life in a more orderly way. For now, however,
I am relieved that Emilio has jumped into his rented car and headed for
Mérida. For this is Barbara Sheffer and John Thompson's day out of the
blinds, and I want to spend as much time with them as I can.

Early this morning, I had accompanied them and Bob Singleton on
a tour of the estuary in a motorized skiff. Specifically we were searching
for a particular boat-billed heron that was known to haunt a particular
mangrove slough; but the others also wanted to give me a look at the
flamingos and ducks and herons that make this place a birder's paradise.

The boat-bill did not cooperate, which is not surprising, given his
appearance and character. He resembles our black-crowned night
heron—only with a bill that looks like it has been run over by a truck.
He wears conservative black and buffy brown plumage that is hard to

see, goes about his business mostly at night, lives only in places where there are a lot of mosquitoes, and is temperamentally reclusive and unsociable.

With the flamingos, it is altogether different. They obviously understand that they were meant to be shown off, and as long as you don't crowd them, they seem to enjoy being looked at.

They are outrageous, of course. They mass themselves on the black surface of Estero Celestún as though for no other purpose than to create one of the most unnatural-looking sights the natural world has to offer us. As a general rule, Nature feels the same way about shocking pink vertebrates that a Baptist matron feels about punk hair styles. So she was obviously in one of her what-the-hell moods when she created the flamingo. But it isn't just the color she used that is in questionable taste. She also made the bird's skinny neck and spindly legs way too long in relation to its body, and its tail much too short; and, for good measure, she screwed its funny little head on upside down. No wonder the flamingo's plaster effigy—once the ultimate expression of suburban tackiness—is now an artifact much sought after by devotees of High Camp.

And yet, you know, when we are done having our fun at its expense, the flamingo has the last laugh—or, more exactly, the last inverted smile. Perhaps more than any other creature on this still teeming, lovely planet, it is living proof that Nature can accomplish the impossible: namely, make masterpieces of bad art. Seen in its natural setting and in large numbers, as I saw it that morning at Celestún, the grotesque ungainly bird becomes the animate equivalent of some luridly gorgeous aquatic flower repeating itself and its reflection over and over again as though there were no way the world could get enough of it. The spectacle literally takes one's breath away.

It would have been, for me, an unusual experience if only because the esthetic impression—one that ignored all the esthetic rules—totally overshadowed my usual pleasure in seeing, or just being in close proximity to, creatures in the wild. Beauty, in itself, is not normally a consideration. I would as gladly look at an "ugly" alligator as a pretty, dappled fawn. Or—if I only could!—a chunky tapir as joyfully (well, almost as joyfully) as a jaguar.

But just for a moment there, I forgot that flamingos are a species of wildlife. I was seeing them as though they had been roses painted on black velvet. The effect should have been bordello tawdry. But it wasn't.

Barbara Sheffer unintentionally routed me from my esthetic trance. During an earlier conversation, she had made it clear that she is easily upset by manifestations of machismo wherever she finds them; and in Mexico she had found plenty. "I mean, look at Fernando (a Mexican research student at the station). His wife fixes his breakfast every morning, and then he sits down, eats it in a hurry, and leaves without having said a word to her!" An exasperated sigh. "I guess I'm not as forgiving as I thought I could be. I feel frustrated with Mexican culture. For instance, the way the mestizos treat the Maya. And I can't relate to the women's role at all!"

Now it turned out that even the Mexican flamingos had been testing her capacity for forgivingness. Bob Singleton had turned off the boat's motor, and at a distance of twenty yards, we drifted past a great pink cloud of the birds wading in the shallows, gabbling at each other like geese. From behind me came Barbara's voice: "I remember the first time John and I saw the flamingos having sex. What with their long legs, it was awfully acrobatic. But what got me was how terribly *rude* the males were! They just climbed up on the females' backs; and then, when it was all over—it's very quick, of course—they just slid down in front and pushed the females' heads into the mud. I mean, really, thanks a lot!"

Singleton and I chuckled, no doubt reinforcing Barbara's view of the universality of male coarseness. But there was not a peep out of John. I hadn't expected there would be. By this time I knew him well enough to realize he would never allow himself to be amused at Barbara's expense.

The flamingos, those that have reached their fifth birthday, may have sex at Celestún, but it is the sort of carrying on that must presumably count as foreplay. Until Hurricane Gilberto tore up the coast of Yucatán subsequent to my stay, thereby revitalizing the coastal marshes and opening up another breeding site for the birds, they had only one nesting area in all the peninsula. This was in the sodium-rich lagoon at Río Lagartos on the northeast coast. Even now that Gilberto has provided them with an alternative site, most adults still raise their families there, one chick per couple, hatching them on mud platforms in the tepid shallows of the estuary. Celestún is strictly a feeding ground, where fledged birds mature to breeding age, and many adults, attracted by the estuary's high sodium content and rich organic brew, come to fatten up—to the extent that a flamingo can be said to fatten up—for next year's mating season. During much of their stay, they feed, in their own peculiar way, from morning to night, using their seinelike beaks to filter out all sorts of tiny edibles—algae, brinefly pupae, transparent little fish—from mouthfuls of mud; which explains why they are forever swinging their heads around underwater like vacuum cleaners. By late winter, however—if they haven't been too harassed by guides who run their motorboats at them so the tourists can photograph them in flight—they take time out to prune and preen, ogle each other, and, eventually, perform the sexual acrobatics that Barbara and John observed.

The flamingos were by no means the whole show. I had already been impressed to see wood ibis, a threatened species in the States, poking phlegmatically about within yards of the research station as we embarked. And now we passed rafts of ducks and coots, large numbers of tricolor, night, and great blue herons, a black hawk, egrets, brown pelicans, ospreys, and—to make up for the uncooperative boat-bill—a beautiful bare-throated tiger heron posing atop a mangrove. Its throat *is* bare, though not in an unattractive sort of way, the skin being shaded a nice chartreuse; but even if it were a little on the raw-looking side it would hardly matter, since the blemish would be so totally overshadowed by the wonderful plumaged neck that gives the bird the rest of its name. It is striped, though in fact not tigerishly; the feathering looks like a fine linear petit point done in striking shades of creamy white and black. To make sure we got the full effect, the tiger heron turned its head this way and that, meanwhile croaking like a frog.

It was Bob's idea to visit the *ojo de agua*. We had just seen what was, for my companions, an exciting "first"—a snow goose paddling about close to the mangrove banks. The species does not winter at Celestún, and this lone bird could not tell us how it came to be here. But in drawing as close to it as we could, we had also come close to what Bob remembered as "a pretty spot."

Indeed it was. Bob had eased the skiff a short distance into the mangroves, grabbing the looping roots to pull the boat forward. Then, suddenly, we were in a sort of watery glade, where the mangroves soared upward to become towering trees, their thick roots arching well above

our heads. All around us, tall ferns grew on mud hillocks. The water was
clear as window glass. A terrific silence enclosed us. And in the center
of it, surging upward in a swirling current, was the underwater spring,
the "eye of water" that accounted for this weird and lovely place.

An "ojo de agua" is not an underwater cenote like the one I had seen
at that tapir-haunted lagoon in the jungles of Campeche. It is a true
spring, fed, as best anyone can tell, by underground seepage from the
Puuc Hills further south along the coast. There are a great many of these
springs in this part of Yucatán. Some, welling to the surface on seasonally dry land, bear a resemblance to Everglades hammocks, although
they are not the same thing. From the air they can be readily spotted:
dark green islands surrounding gleaming pools in the long coastal expanse of mangrove and khaki bush. But at ground level, travelers on the
roads are unaware of their existence, and even the local people have a
hard time getting to many of them afoot or by boat. For this reason, they
are havens where wildlife can find fresh water and, further inland, a bit
of dry ground during rainy season. Troops of spider monkeys still inhabit
some of them—which seems to me amazing, since their next-nearest
kin live far away in Quintana Roo and Campeche, separated from these
isolated colonies by miles of milpa and dry acacia scrub.

We got out of the boat, and for a while scrambled about on the network of roots. I don't know what the others were pretending to be, if
anything, but I was a spider monkey who could have used a spider monkey's prehensile tail. A couple of times, doing a balancing act, I almost
took a spill. Not that I would have cared if I had fallen in. The morning
was warm, and if I had been alone, I would have been skinny-dipping
in that clear, mysteriously welling water in no time at all. I wondered if
spider monkeys could swim.

"Look," said Bob, "a pygmy kingfisher." It zipped past us, a tiny
thing, dark green and rufous brown. It lacked the mussed-up crest that
other kingfishers wear, but there was no mistaking the family resemblance in its oversized bill and torpedo flight.

We all found comfortable roots to sit on. Barbara and John shared the
same one. Way off, through the screen of mangroves, I could see fishermen standing waist deep in the lagoon catching shrimp in small nets.
They couldn't see us. I wondered if the people around here would kill
and eat a spider monkey if they got the chance.

For some time the four of us perched companionably on our respective roosts, not saying anything, taking in this quiet, secret place. When Bob finally eased himself down into the boat, saying, "We better head back. Emilio will be getting here soon," I, like Barbara and John, followed his example. But at that moment I couldn't help resenting him and Emilio both. I would have liked to postpone becoming human again for a little while longer.

At a discreet distance, I circle round the life that Barbara Sheffer and John Thompson share, inevitably attracted by its light and warmth. I would interview them in any case; but as it works out, the questions become an excuse for hanging around.

Barbara wears her hair in pigtails, and is slim and tall, with long limbs that she flings around in an appealing, lanky way. In the bleak little kitchen of the staff quarters, she drapes an arm around John's shoulder while we talk. John is serious-minded, balding, a bit shy, and as stiff in posture as Barbara is loose and easy. They are telling me how they met at Auburn, where John was working on his M.S. degree and Barbara, also a graduate student, had just gotten a divorce from her professor husband. "When I was moving out of the house," Barbara laughs, "John was nice enough to volunteer to help, even though we hardly knew each other. While he was carrying my things, a professor passed by and told him, joking, that he better hope my husband didn't have a gun. Poor John didn't know what the man was talking about."

When John went to Syracuse to work on his doctorate, Barbara transferred there too. "We ended up here," John explains, "because my major professor was interested in waterfowl research in Mexico. It's a frontier; nothing's been done."

"The money is, well, meager," Barbara chimes in, "but it was a once-in-a-lifetime chance to experience Mexico. And, of course, I wanted to share it with John."

"Romance aside," says John sturdily, looking pleased and a little embarrassed by the presence of Barbara's encompassing arm, "you couldn't ask for a better field assistant than Barbara. This is our second winter here. Our time budget is sometimes seventeen hours of work on a good day: twelve hours in the box, then copying data sheets, going through food samples, processing ducks, stuff like that."

Twelve hours in the box sounds like what Alec Guinness got for being stubborn in *Bridge Over the River Kwai*. According to John and Barbara, it's not as bad as all that, especially since the confinement isn't solitary; but there's no question that a dedicated attitude is a prerequisite for the job.

During those twelve hours, John and Barbara watch ducks. To tens of thousands of amateur wildlife watchers, myself among them, this might sound like an agreeable way to pass the time. But let's face it; ducks are not renowned for their individualistic behavior and twelve hours in a 4- by 8-foot blind can get old pretty fast. It doesn't help that the watching is done according to a strict set of rules. John and Barbara each choose a duck to watch, keep their attention fixed on it for exactly five minutes, note its activities on a checklist, then turn to another duck, do the same thing for another five minutes—and on and on. If fishermen, or a bunch of tourists in search of the flamingos spooks a duck they've been watching for four and a half minutes, that duck doesn't count. When I ask, "Do you ever cheat, just a little?" John's eyes widen behind his glasses. "Of course not," he says stiffly. "With research, if you don't want to do it right, you shouldn't do it at all."

John can't tell me what new insights into duck behavior his research will produce, since the data haven't been analyzed yet. But the general idea is to determine what advantages certain flocks of waterfowl—mostly shovelers, pintails, and blue-winged teal—find in wintering here in southern Mexico, while the majority of these same species prefer to remain on the Gulf's more northerly coasts. There are ten to twelve thousand ducks using the Celestún estuary, and they have braved the rigors of a Gulf crossing to get here. Why? In order to answer that question, all sorts of comparative data are needed: sex ratios, the types of food consumed, weather conditions, mortality rates.

But even though John and Barbara may eventually be able to explain why certain flocks of ducks keep coming back to this remote lagoon, there is a related question—one that particularly fascinates me—that probably no one will ever be able to answer; namely, how did the ancestors of these Celestún ducks find their way here in the first place? Insufficient food in the traditional wintering grounds? A gale that blew them far off course? A flock leader with a defective internal compass? A maverick, charismatic duck with the soul of a Cortés? Only the ducks will ever know for sure.

The ducks and, perhaps, a goose. I think of that lone snow goose bobbing in the lagoon this morning. It pleases me to imagine him, in a year or two, leading a splinter flock of pioneering snow geese back to this tropical world he has discovered. Who knows? Maybe someday I will return here and find a whole gaggle of snow geese paddling about as though they own the place. In which case I will be able to boast that I was among the chosen few who encountered their leader, their Moses, when he first alighted in this tropical promised land.

"It helps to talk," John is saying. "Sometimes we play Trivia to pass the time."

"We're avid tourist watchers," says Barbara.

"It's people-watching at its best," says John. "We guess their nationalities, their relationships; and if we're really bored, we make up stories about them."

"But a lot of the time we just talk."

"We've probably gone through more conversation than most people do in a lifetime," says John proudly. "It has to be the true test of a couple, to keep on spending twelve hours a day together in a box." Barbara smiles and nods.

However, even for this compatible pair, the box has its limits. "We've found we can stand two days in there at a stretch before we absolutely lose it," John says. "Then we take one day out."

"Out but not off," says Barbara. "The best thing we can do around here is keep busy. And for John—it's his project—if he can't work, it makes him antsy. He wants to be out there collecting data all the time."

John tries to look modest but he is obviously gratified by this tribute to his industry. He explains that on the day "out," he and Barbara arise long before dawn to make the drive to the lighthouse, where they collect from hunters the specimen ducks they cannot collect themselves due to a snag in the licensing procedure. It seems they have a permit from one agency to acquire the ducks, but haven't yet received a permit from another agency that would allow them to use firearms. "They must expect us to swim underwater and grab the ducks' legs," grumps Barbara, who finds Mexico's bureaucratic red tape almost as hard to forgive as the machismo of Mexican men.

Anyway, once they have their ducks, they take them back to the station and process them, which means grinding up the entire carcass, *sans* feathers, and extracting samples for laboratory analysis from the resulting mess. "It's a really nice grinder, though," Barbara giggles. "You could set up a stand and sell duck sausages."

John smiles at her, then goes on in his businesslike way to explain that collecting ducks is just part of the "out" day's work. They also do some censusing, check out the habitats the ducks prefer, take water samples to test salinity, and collect specimens of the vegetation the ducks feed upon.

During their previous winter stint, the couple had occasionally visited Mérida, "but we burned out on it pretty quick," says John. Barbara adds, "It just isn't what we choose to do. I mean, you get carbon monoxide poisoning just walking down the streets."

What they choose to do now is draw a pretty tight circumference around their lives. They are incurious about the Yucatán outside Celestún, and even here, they keep to themselves and their work. When they do take a little time off, rather than merely "out," they explore the beach or the estuary on their own.

By now, they are preparing supper. Barbara pauses in the act of reaching toward the cupboard shelves. "We love to go to places like the spring we were at this morning. Sometimes you get desensitized, you know? We see the ducks, the flamingos, the pretty wading birds every day, but we don't really think about it. It's important to take a quiet moment sometimes to appreciate what you have around you." She sighs, takes down a can of soup. "I've come to feel that I'm a very fortunate person, to have that kind of interest. Some people have no awareness whatsoever. All they know is bars and cars and clothes. I mean, they're just not in touch with their environment at all."

John touches her arm lightly, and gives the back of her pigtailed head a loving smile. To me he says, "That kind of awareness is one of the big things that Barbara and I share. Like she says, we're fortunate people."

"You are indeed," I tell them, trying not to envy them too much. "You really are."

FIVE

Mérida

The black Labrador, Cotton, is sprawled on her back, legs indelicately spread apart, beside the couch where Joann Andrews sits. But the other dog, which doesn't quite look like a German shepherd, keeps to the far end of the long, tiled library, lying right side up, alert and wary, in a doorway that opens onto the thick tropical greenery of the garden. Out of the corner of my eye, I watch the stout Maya woman who is sweeping the tiled floor at that end of the room. As she draws close to the dog, she throws a quick glance at Joann, whose back is to her, then makes a threatening feint at the animal with her broom. In one reflexive move-ment, it is up and away, scooting into a clump of the enormous bro-meliads and orchids that climb the garden trees.

What I'd half-consciously realized all along now becomes an uttered thought: "My God, Joann. That's a wolf!"

Joann, preoccupied, looks up. "What? Oh yes. Lobita. Such a beau-tiful thing, isn't she? My Maya family are a little afraid of her, but ac-tually she's harmless enough." She gives the vanished wolf an indulgent smile. "Her great vice is stealing things. She's very clever about it. She *wants* me to know what she's up to. She dashes out to the garden with my glasses, shoes, correspondence, and waits for me to run after her. As a rule, though, people frighten her. I can touch her because I bottle-fed her when she was small—she's zoo-born, you know—but the one she really loves is Cotton. She adores her." She leans down, gives Cotton a pat, and then is back with the map again. "Come look," she says. "These are the general boundaries of Calakmul, the biosphere reserve we're so excited about. But do, please, put out your cigarette first."

I hastily obey this polite command, even fanning the air a bit to dis-perse the offending smoke. Then, careful not to impinge on her space too much, I sit down beside her.

Joann Andrews is a small, fragile-looking woman, almost anorexi-cally slim. But in fact, what there is of her is tough as seasoned leather.

She must be close to 60, but she still takes the prize for open jumping at the local riding club, plays a mean game of tennis, and thinks nothing of walking many miles through steaming jungle when, as sometimes happens, her four-wheel drive breaks down in an inconvenient place. Her very pale blue eyes regard whoever happens to engage her at the moment, in this case, me, with a lively, smiling interest; and her voice, even when she gets worked up while describing one of her current projects, retains a soft, still faintly Southern intonation. But, right off, one senses the strong will that governs her disarming social style. Clearly, she is a lady who is accustomed to having her way. I can't imagine even Lobita daring to snitch something without her tactic consent. She complains, fairly enough, of her too-crowded schedule; but, like Emilio Rangel, she always seems to know what she is doing and where she is going.

Her life has been largely self-chosen. She grew up in Virginia, where she acquired a passion for horses and horsemanship that has led her to do what everyone said was impossible, namely, breed "tall" thoroughbred jumpers in Yucatán, where the grass is brown, not blue, and horses have always been runty. After studying foreign affairs at Barnard and Johns Hopkins, she joined the Foreign Service. While most of her peers were putting in for Paris or London, she asked for, and got, Africa. She served as an economic counselor in Senegal, Cameroon, and the (then) Belgian Congo. Unlike most Americans doing duty in those parts, she "adored the Congo," and reminisces fondly about the English language classes she organized and taught by herself. "Twenty boys, no air conditioning or even fans, mimeographed sheets for texts. . . . My students spent a tenth of the money they earned on gaslight so they could do their homework. . . . One of them later became head of the country's U.N. delegation. . . . And when I left, they came to the ferry and gave me ten eggs. I'll always remember that. It was the most precious gift!"

While in Leopoldville, by the sort of seemingly destined happenstance that makes one think of first encounters in Jane Austen novels (Jane Austen would have loved Joann Andrews), she met and hit it off with an archaeologist who was visiting the area on a tour of duty with the State Department. There was no romance, but on several occasions they dined companionably together at places like the Drunken Hippopotamus, named for an alcoholic hippo that mooched drinks from customers while the proprietor kept tabs. ("Poor thing," Joann smiles sadly, "always drunk as a coot. I heard later it died of cirrhosis.")

Ten years later—it was 1964, and Joann had recently returned to the States—the archaeologist, Edward Wyllys Andrews IV, invited her to visit him in Yucatán and she accepted. He had become, by then, one of the most eminent authorities on ancient Maya sites in the peninsula. In due course, they were married and settled in Mérida, where Andrews bought and remodeled the quinta near the Paseo Colón that has been Joann's home ever since. The exterior is starkly simple compared to that of the Cobbs' quinta in Ticul, but the house itself is anything but. There are many levels and rooms, and, what with the gardens and tennis court and swimming pool, the whole establishment takes up all of a city block. In 1971, Andrews, a heavy smoker, died of lung cancer (which accounts for his widow's aversion to the habit), leaving Joann to raise the two youngest of his four sons by a previous marriage, as well as their own small son and daughter. But Joann is not the sort of person who has ever needed anyone to tell her You-Got-To-Go-On. "It was hard, of course. For a year after, my two-and-a-half-year-old son would cry, '¡Avión, avión, Papa!' every time he heard a plane. But I wasn't desolated. I had such good friends. And I had my Maya family!"

This Maya family, the Varguézes, looms large in Joann's life. Some of its members had worked for Andrews long before Joann appeared on the scene; but it was she who adopted the whole lot of them, not only as household staff but as a sort of second family-in-residence. (It was one of the daughters who had flushed poor Lobita.) "Modesta was *nana* to all the children," Joann explains, "while I became sort of the father after my husband died, the disciplinarian and all that."

I had already been introduced to Modesta, the elderly matriarch of the Varguéz clan, in the kitchen where she sat enthroned, overlooking the activities of other family members. She had turned up to me an uncompromisingly Maya-looking face, with a great beak of a nose, deep-set eyes, and flat gray cheeks that creased into a hundred papery wrinkles when she smiled. Joann "loves" her, her family, the Maya generally. "Such nice, kind, patient people—unless, of course, you push them too far. Then you get something like the Caste War in the nineteenth century." She gives me a fierce look. "If I had been around back then, I would have been right in there fighting with them."

She means what she says. I, for one, have no doubt that if the rebelling Maya had been willing to overlook the color of her skin and put her in charge of their uprising, they would have won hands down.

Environmentalists should be glad that she is in charge of the Yucatán affiliate of ProNatura, Mexico's still embryonic equivalent of the Sierra Club or Audubon Society. When the president of the organization invited her to found a more-or-less autonomous chapter in the state of Yucatán, she almost begged off, arguing that she already had too many irons in the fire. But the temptation to do something to preserve the region's marvelous, and very much threatened, flora and fauna proved irresistible. Since her girlhood days on a Virginia farm, she had been interested in nature, and her exposure to the tropical worlds of West Africa and the Yucatán had only intensified that interest. She had a particular enthusiasm for orchids; and on the many occasions when she accompanied her husband into the jungle he had taught her how to collect and catalogue them. Now—"by default," she says—she is the leading authority on the peninsula's seventy-two known orchid species, many of which she was the first to identify.

In nature study, one thing leads to another. For Joann, always the generalist, always pro nature, it was only a skip and a jump from wanting to preserve rare orchids to wanting to protect the ecosystems that harbor them.

Considering how young it is, ProNatura Peninsula de Yucatán has a lot to show for itself, most of it Joann's doing. She is at home in the world of Méridan high society, and doesn't hesitate to put the touch on her influential friends. She has variously persuaded them to buy portfolios of prints of Yucatán birds, attend benefit dinners, or turn out at a downtown cinema for the opening night showing of a film on Mexico's fauna and flora. ("Such beautiful invitations! The place was packed!") She convinced a number of local businessmen to donate the equivalent of a worker's minimum monthly wage (about $80) to the cause, and got one of them, Carlos Abram, to make his vastly popular new supermarket available for the display of an exhibit on Yucatán's wildlife.

Such efforts have paid off. ProNatura posters can be seen in dozens of downtown shops these days and the membership continues to grow. Even ordinary people in Mérida have heard of the American lady who wants to protect Yucatán's forests and wildlife. More importantly, however, the organization has made itself useful in helping to advance a number of important projects in the region. In Mexico, conservation is a low-priority budget item when government funds are being passed around. So ProNatura helps foot the bill for, among other things, a warden to patrol the northern beaches when endangered hawksbill and green turtles are nesting, a radio communication setup between Yucatán's wildlife refuges, and a variety of research projects in proposed or existing reserves. One way or another, ProNatura has been involved in almost all the conservation initiatives that have taken place in the state of Yucatán during the last few years. But even before the local organization's charter was amended to include the rest of the peninsula, Joann's interests were already crossing state lines. "Calakmul," she says, speaking the name as though it were a mantra. "If only we can make *that* work!"

Calakmul is where we came in. Joann has sketched the boundaries of the biosphere reserve—a walloping 1.8 million acres—on the map for me to look at. She explains that the original idea of setting aside a vast protected area in southeastern Campeche, not all that far to the east of Jorge Sansores's hunting camp, belonged to Dr. William Folan, director of The Center for Social Studies at the University of Campeche. He had come up with the concept while working at archaeological sites in the area. Thanks to his research, SEDUE's director in Campeche at the time had agreed to put Calakmul on his "action list."

Joann also put it on hers. When she talks about her past and future plans for the reserve, the words rush out, the pale blue eyes light up. It is bewildering fun to try to keep up with her:

"Early on, we arranged through Emilio Rangel's DUMAC for Ducks Unlimited to send an ornithologist into the area. In no time at all, he collected a basic list of 130 bird species; and it turned out that almost 70 percent of them are also found in the Petén, across the border in Guatemala. So you see, don't you? That shows how integrated the whole ecosystem is. What we're hoping for eventually is an *international* biosphere reserve! The entire area is terribly important to migratory warblers and other birds that need a tropical semi-evergreen forest. For a thousand years that area was heavily populated by the ancient Maya, you know; but by A.D. 800 it had all collapsed, very likely because they overexploited the land. And now, since 1975, the exploitation has started all over again. The government has been moving people into the region to take the pressure off Central Mexico. But the rainfall down there is terribly irregular. And you can't irrigate, you know; you'd have to go down 200 meters. What you *could* do is leave the whole area in forest. The world's supply of tropical hardwood timber is supposed to run out by 2020. So if we managed the area now, you see, the timber would be worth a lot of money by then. And there are ways the people can make a living without cutting everything down. We're going to try marketing carvings and parquetry made from discarded mahogany fragments. And the timber industry could selectively cut unexploited trees like siricote and guayacan as replacements for the vanishing stocks of mahogany and Spanish cedar. Right now, the World Bank is looking into that possibility at Calakmul. . . . The next-to-last time I went down there I took my son David. An ornate eagle—the idiot!—was rearing two young right by the road. So ProNatura gave SEDUE the money for a guard. . . . Soon after that, when I was in Illinois, I asked the Audubon chapter there for help and they gave us funds for a toucan study. We didn't know a thing about toucans. How far they fly, their seasonal food supplies, the trees they need for nesting. But the problem was finding an ornithologist. You'd be amazed—not an awful lot of people want to spend six months in the jungles at Calakmul! . . . I remember taking Dr. Marcelo Arando, the zoologist, in for four days. Both my four-wheel drives broke down. We had to walk twelve kilometers. Fortunately, Dr. Arando was a handy man with a machete. . . . We were *so* disappointed not to find jaguar tracks, but we did see a tapir, and spider and howler monkeys, some horned guan—very endangered!—and lots of javelina and—"

Joann is interrupted by her teenage daughter, Wiggie. Tomorrow night, Joann is giving a dinner party for thirty of ProNatura's strongest supporters, and Wiggie, who is helping with the preparations, wants to settle the question of which candles to use. It is a little bit odd, hearing the daughter of two very American parents speak English with a distinct Spanish accent.

While she and her mother weigh the pros and cons of green or orange or white, I weigh the pros and cons of what Joann has been telling me about Calakmul and the efforts to save the jungle there. Certainly, something of her enthusiasm has infected me. The mere thought of a biosphere reserve at the base of the Yucatán peninsula is thrilling to contemplate. But I have become thin-skinned; these days, I shy away from the possibility of even abstract disappointments. The more I think about it, the more the idea of a vast international reserve, or even a viable Mexican one, seems like a pipe dream. As Joann had said, and as I had seen for myself, more and more people are invading the jungle in southern Campeche, cutting out its heart. It is what one expects in a developing country like Mexico; even a holding action can't work for long. So I take the easy way out, sliding into a skeptical mood.

I wish I hadn't. For I could have kept the excitement and hopeful mood that I had caught from Joann, instead of merely regaining it, as I have now. Right now, as this book goes to press, the prospects for the Calakmul Biosphere Reserve are looking pretty good. The World Bank will soon join The Nature Conservancy and ProNatura in providing funds for research and administration, and the Mexican government, under Salinas, is at least sounding serious about wanting to conserve the area's wealth of natural resources. On the Guatemalan side of the border, in the Petén, an even larger "Maya Biosphere Reserve" has been set aside—though on paper only—that links up with Calakmul to the north and the Tikal National Park to the south. Finally, in northeastern Belize, the Río Bravo Management Area, some 150,000 acres contiguous to the Guatemalan reserve, has been purchased by a consortium of international organizations as a showcase for the use of tropical forest resources on a sustainable basis. Of the three tracts, only the one in Belize is presently being managed and protected in anything like an adequate way. But before long, there is a good chance that in Mexico, and even perhaps in Guatemala, the incomparable tracts of jungle wilderness that have been set aside may become reserves in more than name.

All of that, however, is future-thought. On this warm sunlit afternoon in Joann's beautiful book-lined study, I am not buying hopeful possibilities.

The question of the candles has been settled; but before leaving the room, Wiggie reminds her mother that a television crew will be arriving soon.

"Sorry," says Joann, turning back to me. "They're going to do a special program about ProNatura." But she isn't quite ready to turn me

loose. "Before you leave," she says, "you must taste this. Isn't it delicious? The flavor—and the fragrance!"

She holds out a spoon and a small jar of amber honey. After one swal-
low, I agree that it is quite possibly the most delectable honey I have
ever tasted; and certainly the most beautifully scented. "It's a combination of all those different jungle flowers, all those different kinds of
nectar," Joann beams. Of course she has a plan. She is trying to drum
up interest in marketing the honey, and she wants me to give it a plug.
(And so I shall: It is now available to specialty shops and health food
stores in the United States under the brand name *Jungle Honey.*)

As she walks me to the door, Joann is still talking about agroforestry;
she is very interested, she tells me, in the cultivation of vanilla because
it grows in forest shade. But I am not really paying attention. At the
threshold, meaning to catch her off guard, I ask her if she is really as
optimistic about all these projects as she seems to be. I half hope she'll
admit she isn't. After an afternoon's exposure to her enthusiasms, I am
feeling as burned-out as she ought to be but isn't. I also feel, in some
way, obscurely shamed.

"Optimistic?" She looks bemused, as though she had never really
thought about that. "Oh well, when you consider the inflation, and
the drop in the price of oil, I think it's quite encouraging what the
government has done. And these wonderful new measures that have
been passed, so that now ecology is being taught to children in the
schools—"

She breaks off, then gives me what I have no choice but to interpret
as a very optimistic-looking smile. "The children. We've had such
amazing luck with them! Take our turtle project, just for example. I
wish you could have been with us this summer when the baby turtles
were hatching. The children all stood in circles around the nests to keep
the gulls away. It's *so* important that they feel they're helping!"

I smile and nod. She wins. As usual. I can see those beautiful children too, laughing, shooing the gulls away.

For a fleeting second I think of the man who took my picture with
those youngsters at Chunchumil. "What will become of them?" he had
asked.

I don't know. But it would be nice to believe that at least some of

Yucatán's beautiful children, all grown up, will still be protecting—just for example—newly hatched sea turtles from the circling gulls. Thanks, in large part, to Joann and ProNatura.

I think—as I have tried until now not to do—of my own environmental commitments. How I have let them slide, like everything else.

Joann and I shake hands. "Thanks for everything," I tell her. "I've really learned a lot."

What I would like to tell her is that I wish she could put some of that enthusiasm and vitality of hers into little jars and market it like jungle honey. I would be the first customer to get in line.

The Señora does not want her name used, so we shall call her Doña Ana. She is in her seventies although no one would ever guess it. Her face is relatively unlined, her eyes and voice serenely clear, her lips rather primly pursed. She is slim, wears an expensive-looking blue silk dress, and holds herself in the sort of relentlessly erect posture that old-fashioned finishing schools were able to impose on women more effectively than military academies ever have on men.

We are sitting in the small, crowded back office of a commercial establishment located a few blocks south of Mérida's main plaza. Doña Ana is running the place in the absence of its owner, her son-in-law; and to judge from the demeanor of the salesmen and secretaries, she is very much in charge. But even immersed in the vulgar hustle of the money-making world, she never forgets she is a lady, and if you want to get on with her, you better not forget it either.

"All my aunts and uncles were sent to Europe for their education," she explains, "but my mother was educated in the United States, so that is where I went when I was a girl. I was born during the Revolution, you know, just before Alvarado came here in 1915. He closed the churches and banned the saints, and had people hanged in the square. He had the cathedral stripped of its gold, even the *retabla* was taken out." Her delicately shocked voice takes on a cynical edge as she adds, "And then he married a girl from town. I left for the United States in 1924 soon after Carrillo was killed—they blamed that on us, of course—and when I came back, Cárdenas had just come into power. They gave the Indians the land, and that was the end of—how shall we say, the Emporium of Green Gold? It didn't do the Indians much good, and as for us, we were poor as mice. By then my grandfather and father had died. Several of my aunts and uncles emigrated to Mexico City. The boys of my class had patched elbows, their collars were threadbare. That dismayed me."

Thus, in her own way, Doña Ana recalls the great social and economic upheavals that, during her youth, convulsed Yucatán and changed its face forever. By this time I have done some homework. I know that Salvador Alvarado and his much more radical successor, Felipe Carrillo Puerto, were reformist governors of Yucatán during the first phase of the revolutionary government's takeover of the region. Lázaro Cárdenas, president of Mexico from 1934 to 1940, was responsible for the land reforms that, by means of expropriation, transformed privately owned land throughout Mexico—nowhere more rigorously than in Yucatán—into ejidos.

The "emporium" of the Señora's neat cliché was Yucatán during the more than half a century (roughly 1860–1920) when it was by far the wealthiest state in Mexico. The "green gold" was henequen.

Henequen is not cotton or sugarcane or tea. I have a hard time conceptualizing the fact that a raw product used primarily to make baling twine for American wheat harvesting machines could have made this dry, rocky corner of the Yucatán peninsula one of the richest places on the planet; but it is so. It is said that at the turn of the century, provincial little Mérida could claim more millionaires in relation to its total population than most of the world's great cities, not to mention a flourishing class of bourgeois tradesmen and artisans. Out in the country, of course, it was a very different story. True, even here there was a growing demand for skilled and semiskilled labor to operate and maintain factory machinery, tramways, service shops. But the Maya campesinos who worked the fields were de facto slaves, bound to the haciendas by a system of debt servitude so inexorable that it makes the indebtedness of Appalachian coal miners to the company store seem downright benign by comparison.

"The Indians were very ignorant," Doña Ana explains, "and most didn't want to learn. Different people treated them differently, of course, but we treated them well. My grandfather used to give them *rosarios* as gifts, made of gold filigree, silver and coral. They liked the red coral very much." She smiles wryly. "Now they don't like to wear their traditional clothes, so we wear them on special occasions. . . . In those days there were two clubs you could belong to, quite competitive. Such scrumptious dances! Especially during Carnival. For the young people, at least. The mothers chaperoned, getting stiff backs sitting in the gallery until three in the morning. The president of the club would lead the march with the girl who was chosen as queen, while all the other men and boys would parade the other girls around the gallery in all their finery. . . . And the street parades, such lovely wagons. One was a peacock, another an artist's painting. . . . Now there are different clubs, of course. The dances are not the same. There is, shall we say, less refinement, less elegance."

American visitors to Yucatán at the turn of the century, as well as generations of Mexican revolutionaries and reformers, have pictured the region's ruling class—la casta divina—as a collection of cruel, bloated parasites ruthlessly indulging their luxury-loving tastes at the expense of the enslaved Indian masses. Certainly, as the Señora's reminiscences suggest, they made the most of their privileged status, living it up when they got the chance. But, in fairness, it would be a mistake to picture this elite caste as perpetually engaged in a Yucatecan version of la dolce vita. They were, in fact, a remarkably resilient, if also contentious, lot. Doña Ana herself inadvertently illustrates, in her modest supervisory way, how they could, and to some extent still can, survive all sorts of changes in the political and economic weather. The oldest families go back to the days of Spanish rule. Since then, at one time or another, they have variously declared Yucatán's independence from Mexico, feuded incessantly with rival Campeche, sought annexation by the United States, and managed to retain, until a few decades ago, their region's cultural separatism—all in the face of various takeovers by Federalists, foreign imperialists, and homegrown radicals. ("Always," says Doña Ana, "there is Yucatán, and then there is Mexico.")

Driven into the northwest section of the peninsula by the War of the Castes, the hacendados turned from ranching and sugarcane to the single-minded cultivation of henequen, developing the means of production and transportation—and the system of debt peonage—that gave Yucatán a virtual monopoly on the export of fiber for twine. As individuals, their entrepreneurial instincts and simple greed got many of them in trouble: the boom and bust cycles of a monocrop economy, as well as the growing power of a few families, notably the Molinas and the Monteses, to fix export prices (at levels acceptable to the United States's International Harvester Company), led to many bankruptcies. But as a class, the hacendados throve. Even the eruption of the Mexican Revolution in 1910 did not greatly affect their insular world at first. The violence that took hundreds of thousands of lives in northern and central Mexico scarcely touched the peninsula. When federal authority was finally imposed in 1915, and General Alvarado became governor, the takeover was relatively peaceful. If people were hanged in the square, as the Señora claims, their number was not great.

Alvarado created an urban labor movement in Mérida, and, to the consternation of the hacendados, proclaimed an end to debt peonage. He also expanded state control of the henequen industry, driving up prices in the export market (in contrast to the Molina-Montes oligarchy, which had kept prices artificially low). But he attempted only a moderate degree of land reform. The haciendas remained intact, and especially during World War I, when the international demand for hemp fiber greatly increased, the planter elite continued to prosper. After Alvarado was recalled, however, the governorship of Yucatán was won by a native Yucatecan of a far more revolutionary turn of mind. Felipe Carrillo Puerto made a systematic effort to give the Revolution a regional impetus—an approach that did not sit well with the federal government in Mexico City. He sent cadres of agricultural workers and schoolteachers into the countryside to organize the campesinos into "resistance leagues" and to preach a fiery gospel of social change emphasizing ethnic pride and hatred of *la casta divina*. But in 1924, before he could accomplish a plan to appropriate hacienda lands, he was assassinated by rebelling federal officers. As Doña Ana remarks, the hacendados were widely suspected—not without good reason—of having contracted for his death. What is certain is that during the subsequent decade, the old planter class reconsolidated its power in the Yucatán. By then, however, the impact of competition from other countries and from synthetic fibers, not to mention the worldwide depression, had made the Golden Age of Henequen considerably less golden than it used to be. It was at this critical juncture that Lázaro Cárdenas became president of Mexico, and proceeded to fatally cripple the ailing industry in the interests of socialist revolutionary theory. During the late 1930s, all privately held land was confiscated except for *pequeñas propiedades—*

small properties—which each landowner was permitted to retain. Collective farms were set up in their place, and as a consequence, henequen production radically declined. The collectivist experiment was so manifest a failure that during World War II and for a time afterward, private owners were again given control of the industry—which now included the domestic manufacture of rope and twine. For a time economic conditions in Yucatán improved. However, in the 1960s the entire industry (along with most others in Mexico) was again taken over by the government. Since then, the Green Gold has become Red Ink on government ledgers. Part of the problem has to do with continuing international competition; but these days hardly anyone except maybe some government officials would bother to deny that the well-intentioned initiatives begun by Cárdenas have led to bureaucratic mismanagement and corruption on an epic scale. The result has been that henequen production, from cultivation to finished product, is now a heavily subsidized industry that does not pay its way.

It has also forced virtually all of Yucatán's hacendados to part company, once and for all, with their landowning past, much of their wealth, and the last vestiges of their former political power. Perhaps the most regrettable consequence of this change in the social order has been the loss, in Mérida as in the countryside, of so much of Yucatán's impressive architectural inheritance. On the once splendid Paseo de Montejo, all but two or three of the great beaux arts mansions that Green Gold had built have been demolished to make way for the sort of junky arcade stores and offices that one finds in any U.S. shopping mall. In the streets near the main plaza, most of the fine old colonial town houses have been transformed into appliance stores, small hotels, or restaurants, while their former owners, in a sad parody of American white flight, have removed themselves to the city's northside suburbs.

Yet in spite of revolutions, confiscations, economic busts, and a change of address, *la casta divina* still manages to survive, chiefly by the tried and true strategy of combining old names with new wealth. Once again, Doña Ana illustrates how the system works. "My husband's family was against *Us*," she explains. "His father had very humble beginnings and worked at all kinds of jobs. But he was meritorious: he worked hard and did well. He had a cordage mill during the Second World War, and, ha! he also bought a hacienda, this man who did not like the hacendados. I must add, in fairness, that he made it profitable with his hard work. My daughter's father-in-law also owns a hacienda. Like my father-in-law, he bought it."

Her marriage and the changing times have lent a certain ambivalence to Doña Ana's attitudes. At one point she says with a flash of contempt, "After the Revolution, they called us 'la casta divina'—they used the words sarcastically, of course—but they all would have been glad to belong to that caste if they could!" Yet when the conversation takes another turn, it is a meritocracy that she supports. "I stick my nose out for the Lebanese. When they first came here they were just immigrants; they were looked down upon, like the Irish and Italians in your own country. But they are good merchants, hard-working and very united. They have bettered themselves. And they are good fathers. They want their children to prosper, not just to make money, you know, but for refinement's sake. I have concluded that there is now one Lebanese in every aristocratic family. After all, what would you want in your family? A courser for show, or a camel for work? A camel, of course! We—the old families—stick together, it is true; but if there is a worthy outsider through marriage, he is taken in." She gives me a dry, amused glance and says in a fastidious voice, "So you see, we are all mixed together after all!"

My favorite place to sit and watch Mérida go by is not the main plaza, pleasant though that is, but the charming little square just a block away to the northeast. Here the grand old Gran Hotel, once the city's finest, shares shady space with a cinema, at which the evening crowd is lining up to get an eyeful of American sex and violence, dubbed in with Spanish voices, gasps, and screams. The rest of the square is taken up by a couple of pleasant outdoor cafés, at one of which I sit, drinking tequila.

During a brief holiday visit to Mérida almost ten years earlier, we stayed at the Gran and sat at this same café. But strangely, although I am certainly haunted, this little square is not. It does not disturb my heart overmuch to be here with someone I met only an hour ago.

Armando is an interesting but moody companion. He is painfully aware that, at 30, he is still neither one thing nor the other. His father is a Yucatecan Lebanese, and his mother was born in Central Mexico. His family is by no means poor but he does not count himself among the city's moneyed elite. He is a *licenciado* in education but he wants to be an artist and a poet, not a teacher. He despises the clannishness and conservative mind-set of the moneyed establishment; but he hates even more the paternalistic socialism, not to mention the corruption, of the PRI (the entrenched political party, the Partido Revolucionario Institucional, that has ruled Mexico for more than half a century). Finally, to round out this congregation of ambivalences, he is in love but not in love enough.

But why should I tell you these things about Armando? Although his use of "they's" and "we's" gets a little confusing, he speaks very ably for himself.

"Some of them still call us *turcos* or Arabs behind our backs," he says with a frown. "But of course now it's because they envy us. My father always talks about how his grandfather came here with nothing. They all did. They were mostly peddlers. My great-grandfather too. They worked hard. They went around the little villages selling spoons and needles and thread, or they sold things in the streets."

I fleetingly glimpse Anita's bitter, driven mother selling produce in the streets of Campeche. I hear Anita's furious indictment of her first husband: "He no *work!*"

". . . They made money in all the little businesses that the Spanish couldn't be bothered with, and that the Indians were too lazy—well, let's say unenterprising—to manage. They lived in little holes above the shops they bought. And now look! We practically own Mérida. And what has happened? They were always clannish, and now they have become just as elitist as the old families. It's amusing to watch when there is a mixed gathering of some sort; they sniff around each other like dogs. And of course they had to have their own exclusive club, the Club Lebanese, since only the old names could join the Campestre. My father doesn't belong to the Club Lebanese, but he's just as bad. His only friends are Lebanese. The one time he broke the rule was to marry my mother, and she has no Mexican friends outside her family. . . . It's funny, you know; neither the Yucatecans nor the Lebanese like the Mexicans that are coming in now. They are too aggressive, they know everything. But I think they are good for us. Mérida has more going on now because of them, more places to go at night, more people interested in the arts. Yucatecans are too conservative except about government handouts. About everything else, they are always twenty years behind everywhere else. Abortions are still against the law. The only reason you can get condoms now is because of AIDS."

We order dinner, *pollo píbil* for me, a *biftek* for him. Between mouthfuls, he continues: "I don't want to be a teacher. My father said I had to have some profession if I didn't want to be a businessman. He wouldn't pay for me to go to art school! So I got my degree in education. But I will have to teach in the state schools and they don't pay anything. And you must teach just what the books say, which is what the PRI wants them to say. I wouldn't be able to speak out. Not that anyone does too much of that. Oh yes! it's true; we are just a little bit afraid here. The PRI is pretty good at that. Not big oppression. Usually just little oppression, you know? Look what happened when PAN managed to elect a mayor in Mérida a while back. [PAN is Partido de Acción Nacional, one of Mexico's token opposition parties; many Yucatecans regard it as a manifestation of their state's last-gasp resistance to total federal control.] The federal government cut off all the funds for running the city. So PAN put out donation barrels on Friday afternoons, and the people who were afraid to give donations openly just dropped money in the barrels. My father too, and he never gives away money! And they ran the city pretty well just on that. But when the mayor ran for governor, the PRI really got scared. Then we started getting federal money, you can believe that! And of course they faked the election results; they had more votes from one town than there were people living there! It's a bad joke, when you think about it. Can you think of a better oxymoron than Partido Revolucionario Institucional—the party of *institutional* revolution? *Permanent* revolution?"

Armando shakes his head. "I will probably go into business with my father after all. He says he wants 'something better' for me, just as his father wanted 'something better' for him. But of course he doesn't consider being an artist as something better."

At this moment, one of the shoeshine boys that are ubiquitous in downtown Mérida comes up to us. Unless somebody actually wants his shoes polished, natives and tourists alike—I do not exclude myself—either pretend not to hear the solicitations of these little street children, or at most shake their heads without looking up from their drinks or newspapers. But Armando is the exception. He pokes his canvas shoes out from under the table and gently explains that they do not lend themselves to polishing. The little boy—he can't be more than 9 or 10—looks at him blankly, then nods and turns away. Armando follows him with his brooding eyes. "You see that boy?" he says. "There are men here who operate gangs of these children. They take almost all the money the kids earn in exchange for giving them their food and a place to sleep. The parents come from the country, you know? They have more kids than they want." He grins sadly. "It's lucky that beans and tortillas are healthy food; otherwise a lot of people would be in a bad way around here."

We talk for a while about his painting—I gather it is impressionistic and romantic—and his poetry. He recites a short poem he has recently composed. My Spanish is not up to the task of evaluating the style, but the subject, unrequited love, is familiar enough. It is also close to Armando's heart.

"I wouldn't have met her, you know, if a friend hadn't taken me to the Cocoteros. It's a yacht club in Progreso that both the members of the Campestre and the Lebanese can belong to. She likes art, things like that." His face suddenly breaks into an unexpectedly boyish, unequivocal smile. "She thinks I am handsome," he says delightedly. I nod agreement. He is, in fact, very pleasant-looking when he smiles. But then the smile departs as quickly as it had arrived. "It's difficult, though. Her family is not rich, not anymore; but they are so proud of their old name, you know? Their so-called pure Spanish blood. My father sent me to the Universidad Nacional, but they somehow managed to send her to the Universidad del Mayab. That's the private university, the good one; it's run by the rich Spanish and Lebanese families. They even sent her and her brothers to Europe for a while. So they don't like me much. Oh, no; not because I'm Lebanese. She dates a rich Lebanese sometimes and that's all right. They want their children to marry a Lebanese as long as he's rich enough. Or at least they don't mind if their daughters do. I told her it's because in the Lebanese families all the money goes to the sons; but she says it isn't that; it's just that the Lebanese boys have the best cars and can afford to take their dates to the best places. Maybe she is right. But I am not one of the ones who can do that, you know? I could if my father would let me, but he won't." He scowls randomly at the passersby. "I don't know what her family would say about him, my father. He doesn't wear a tie even at a christening, not even at a Christmas party."

Despite his chronic discontent, Armando has a good appetite. He finishes the thin, overcooked beef steak and puts down his knife and fork. "I don't know," he says. "I think about her all the time, but if I asked her to marry me she would probably say no. Even if she said yes, what would we do? I would have to work for my father or be a poor schoolteacher for the rest of my life. I am not sure I love her that much, you know? I am not sure I want to marry at all. Sometimes I want something else. But I'm afraid, you know?" He smiles—sadly this time. "What will probably happen is that I will end up marrying some nice Lebanese girl, and work for *her* father for the rest of my life."

It is close to midnight when I wander, by a roundabout route, back to the hotel. I love the streets of Mérida late at night. What Barbara Sheffer had said is true enough of the city by day: near the plaza, the streets are full of heat and noise and black exhaust fumes from senile trucks and buses. But after ten o'clock, they are silent and empty. They are also safe, even though a large percentage of the city's population is desperately poor. I walk in the middle of the street, to have a better view of the old houses on either side. Although many buildings have been defaced to make them look more like modern stores or offices, a lot of the colonial façades are still intact; and now, in the quiet night, I am at leisure to pick out the variant details in their rather homogeneous general style: the marvelous paneled doorways, the ornamental lintels and entablatures, the molded cornices above the tall windows. After a couple of hours of listening to Armando, it is a restful way to pass some time.

So I am a little surprised to hear a sudden blare of rock music and then see a convertible, the nose of it at least, coming to a sudden halt at the intersection just ahead of me. There is no red light, no stop sign. Car doors open and slam shut. The volume of the car radio is increased to an even louder pitch. And then the convertible's occupants, two slim young girls, are out there in the middle of the intersection, under the soft street light, dancing expertly to the hard rock tune. Unaware of my presence, they go at it with a will, not touching or even looking at each other—just whipping their bodies about in perfect time with the beat. Then, in less than a minute, the song is over and the performance too.

I hear the tinkle of their laughter as they get back into the convertible. The doors slam, the engine varooms, and they are gone. Nervously, the quiet returns.

During the late 1920s and early 1930s when traveling by road and tramway had become more or less safe again, the Zapatas spent their summers with their parents at the family's vast 7,000-hectare estate near Mérida. The place was officially known as Hacienda San Domingo, but like everyone else, the Zapata children usually referred to it by its Maya name, Hunxectanan.

Now, at the other end of their lives, the Zapatas remember those lost summers as a blurred progression of golden, hazy days in which small adventures and domestic rituals were idyllically combined. The weather was usually blazingly hot despite the seasonal rains, but the casa grande was spacious and relatively cool, surrounded by well-kept orchards, banana groves, irrigation pools. The weekday routine was always much the same. The six children were awake by 7 A.M. After a breakfast of chocolate and fruit, they were free to play on the grounds. The two oldest boys, Manuel and Fernando, played American baseball with Maya boys their own age. The younger children followed the farm workers about, or climbed trees in the orchard, or played hide and seek in the stables. The boys all had horses and did a lot of riding, and when they were old enough they hunted quail with the grownups. A little before noon everyone sat down to the main meal of the day: chicken stuffed with peppers, pork or beef, salad, oranges, papaya, bananas. The tortillas, made while the dinner was being served, were eaten fresh and piping hot. Afterward the entire hacienda would fall into a siesta trance for a couple of hours. Then, while their father and uncle went off to the henequen fields, and the women sat sewing and gossiping on the gallery, the children resumed their games. At four came one of the best times of day: they were allowed to go swimming in one of three large pools that were used in the old days to catch condensed water from the steam-operated farm machines so it could be used to irrigate the orchards.

The light evening meal was served at six. The grownups, listless in the collected heat of one more long summer day, sipped chocolate and nibbled at salads and sweets; the young, less enervated, filled up on *puchero*, a sort of stew. Ordinarily there would only be electricity when

the hacienda's generator was used to run the machines that rasped henequen leaves into hemp; but when the Zapatas were in residence it was
also turned on in the evenings, and then even the campesinos had light
in their houses. Señora Zapata subscribed to Spanish periodicals, but no
one read much. Mostly the family sat around talking about the usual
things that a hacendado family talked about in those days: henequen
prices, the weather, the recent hard times under Carrillo, the uncertain
future. For the grownups there were a good many serpents in the Eden
that the children would later remember with such fondness. More than
once they overheard their father lamenting that everything was going
bad, although usually he tried not to show that he was worried when
they were around. Their mother, too, seemed often worried and
preoccupied.

Before bedtime, Señora Zapata and her brood, accompanied by some
of the Maya workers, would retire to the little chapel to say the rosary.
At night everyone slept in hammocks except the parents, whose room
was furnished with the hacienda's only bed.

Weekends were apt to be less patterned and more lively than other
days. All the haciendas were at that time linked by narrow-gauge tramways like the ones still to be seen at Uayamón. Traveling in iron-
wheeled carriages drawn by mules, neighboring hacendados and their
families would come to visit and usually stay the night. The young Zapatas would have children of their own class to play with and more mis-
chief to get into. On Sunday afternoons, long platform wagons,
normally used to transport henequen, were loaded with youngsters and
drawn around the estate in the Yucatecan equivalent of a hay ride.

The most memorable day of all, however, was August 4, Santo Domingo's feast day. A priest would come, and the family, which normally
attended Sunday mass at the nearby village church, heard the service in
the hacienda chapel. This was followed by a great feast for the estate's
campesinos, visiting kin, and neighbors from miles around. In the afternoon there were bullfights. These were rather primitive affairs, corre-
sponding in almost every detail to those that Stephens had watched
almost a century earlier: the ring a wooden corral with a stand rigged up
to hold the Zapata family; the matadors from no further off than Mérida;
and the bulls rented. Only a couple of the animals would be killed; the
rest would be recycled. Although not exactly in a class with the spec-

tacles that Hemingway was witnessing at about this time in Spain, everyone enjoyed themselves. Except, of course, the bulls.

In the evening, bands played and everyone danced. "Until midnight there were firecrackers and rockets going off," one of the younger Zapata brothers, Eduardo, recalls. "There were all kinds of paper streamers hanging from the ceilings, even the trees. Everyone danced the native dances, around the big house, in the corridors, in the supervisor's house. All the young people danced together, us, the workers, everyone. Many people would get very drunk from the beer and tequila—but not the family, of course! . . . It was always a very wonderful fiesta. We all looked forward to it with great excitement."

Calle 62, south of the plaza, is about as busy and crowded as streets in Mérida ever get, which means it's about as busy and crowded as streets anywhere ever get. The narrow thoroughfare is jammed with trucks, cars, buses, roaring motorbikes, and swarms of pedestrians, the latter squeezing their way between honking vehicles and the walls of shops like cattle in a loading chute.

In the midst of all this stands a colonial town house that looks like a hundred others in Mérida, chipped, faded, run-down, with a unisex barbershop embedded in its corner. I check the little slip of paper in my pocket to make sure I have the right address. Then I ring the hard-to-find bell and wait for what seems a long moment, trying not to be swept away by the current of people squeezing past me. At last a short, elderly woman with an uncertain smile on her face opens the huge gateway door enough to let me introduce myself and slip through. There is one more tight fit. The carriageway is not quite large enough to comfortably accommodate the car that reposes there. But once I get past that, I am in a different, perfectly beautiful—and beautifully quiet!—world.

"Well," says Señora Rosa María Zapata, coming up behind me, "welcome to our home." At the same time, Señor Manuel Zapata approaches from the patio, and repeats the same words.

There are many things I like about this home I have been welcomed to, but underlying them all is the awareness that it comes by its beauty unaffectedly. No interior decorator has striven for effects here. During the century and a half of its existence, the house has grown, expanded, almost like some organic living thing. Everything that pleases the eye, which is almost everything, reflects a process of adaptation to this particular city, to its culture and climate, to five generations of a family that has civilized tastes. In modern Mérida, there are very few such residences left.

Half of the interior space is given over to a large patio surrounded by long, wide galleries. The marble tile of the floors is a soft blue-gray and white. Rounded columns with frilled Ionic capitals support the arches, which not only flank the patio but, garnished with rosettes, span the twenty-foot-high ceilings of the gallery. Cane chairs and dark mahogany chests and highboys line the inner wall. At the wide, arched doorway of one of the rooms stands a grand piano. And in the patio itself, palm trees and a riot of flowering shrubs shade gravel paths. If you picture a defrocked Romanesque cloister set down in the exuberant tropics, devoted to the contemplation of peaceful pleasures available in this world rather than the next, you will have the right idea.

I am invited to make myself comfortable at the dining room table. It, the chairs, sideboard, and china cabinet are all massively Italianate, with so many nymphs and cherubs frolicking on every available surface that their protrudent buns and boobies give the cedarwood a knotted, almost carbuncular texture. Señora Zapata tells me that she and her husband acquired the set more than half a century ago on their honeymoon in Mexico City. Huge as the pieces are, they do not fight for space in the large, high-ceilinged room. Neither do the artless portraits of Manuel's parents and grandparents on the walls.

Señora Zapata has large, smiling eyes and a wide, smiling mouth, both made up just now because she is off to meet a friend and do some shopping. But before she leaves she responds to my admiring reaction to the house with the conventional polite disclaimers. "Oh, but it is so difficult to keep it looking nice these days. We can't get servants anymore. It's just like your country. In the old days, we had a man from the plantation here, very good, very respectable. He died here. Now we must manage with this young fellow who comes, starts cleaning the house, then says he has to attend a class at school. When he comes back he works for perhaps an hour and then he says, 'Excuse me, I have to go to the movies now.'" She shrugs good-naturedly, not at all as exasperated as her words would suggest. "But they are all like that," she says, "so what can we do?"

When she leaves, Señor Zapata, who is obviously very proud of his wife, says, "She was a fine concert pianist, you know. She graduated—laureate—from the Academy of Music in Quebec. She comes from an old Mérida family, like mine. They went through the same sort of troubles, the same hardships. It hasn't always been easy for her. Everybody had to split up, to do different kinds of work. For a long time she had to give piano lessons to earn money. But"—he waves all that away with his hand—"we seem to have pulled through somehow."

All things considered, Señor Zapata has pulled through very well indeed. In his mid-seventies, he is still a very fit and distinguished-looking man, with a fine complexion, silky white hair, lively blue eyes. He takes a predictably jaundiced view of the federal government's socialist policies and their effect on the regional economy; but he is temperamentally more objective than some others of his age and class, and his recollections of the past are detailed and sharp-edged. He remembers that when Carrillo Puerto took power, his father was so concerned for his family's safety that he shipped Manuel, his sisters, and their pregnant mother to New Orleans by freighter. The ensuing year of exile was not a very happy time. His mother was often melancholy and he himself was very homesick. He shows me a sepia photo of Señora Zapata that was taken at this time. She is holding in her arms the infant Fernando, born in the States. She looks unsmilingly at the camera, her face careworn and prematurely aged.

Señor Zapata also recalls the dreadful day, perhaps a decade later, when this same Fernando decided to climb one of the watchtowers that overlooked the fields of henequen at San Domingo. The towers were small, bare platforms atop windmill frames, and when he reached the top, he slipped and fell off. "It was terrible. Poor Fernando landed on his back and we thought he was surely dead. For three days he lay in bed, as though he were numb, paralyzed. But then he started to be all right again."

This memory reminds Señor Zapata of the purpose of the watchtowers, and, in a more general way, of the unrest that occurred in the early 1920s. "We were always watchful for fires in the fields, both those that started naturally and those that were deliberately set. No; it wasn't the Indians working with us who set them. They were peaceful and friendly to us even later, when Cárdenas came in and took our land away." He tugs impatiently at the lace tablecloth. "You hear all these stories of how cruelly the Indians were treated in the old days. But the way I understand it, in the days of my grandfather, each hacienda was a little town. The foreman had to be the policeman; so naturally he had to punish people when someone kidnaped a girl or got drunk and beat his wife. It wasn't just meanness. The Indians themselves would say, 'Give him twenty strokes!' That's what I've heard. But by my father's time, the haciendas were less isolated, so there was no more need for that. The workers were treated well. In his day they were paid in American gold.

"Anyway," he continues, "it wasn't our people, it was the other ones, the agitators, that Carrillo Puerto set against us. People have told me that in his speeches Carrillo would tell the Indians that if they wanted money, they should take it; and if they had guns, they should use them. And they did. There were holdups of the payrolls on the way to the plantations. People were killed for no reason except to rob them. While Carrillo was in power and for a while afterward, we children were not allowed to go to San Domingo. The roads were not safe. Our clerk was held up. The fellow who drove the mule for him was killed. I remember the clerk saying how brave he was, how he got out his pistol and started to shoot. Ha! He wouldn't have been alive if he had done that. He just ran away and saved himself!"

One of Manuel Zapata's many enthusiasms was being a ham radio operator. In the 1930s, after Cárdenas confiscated the haciendas, and he found himself numbered among the poor-as-mice young men whose threadbare collars had shocked Doña Ana, he decided to put his hobby to work. "I got a permit, improved my equipment, and made a radio station," he says proudly. "That's how I made a living. Here in Yucatán they even called me one of the pioneers in radio."

During World War II, when Cárdenas's successor returned the haciendas and factories to private control, Manuel managed San Domingo and his father's twine factory. He also succeeded in pulling off a great financial coup. He went to Washington, and persuaded a supply agency in the Defense Department to give his company an exclusive contract for as much cordage as it could produce. "That was what really brought money back to the family," he says with a satisfied grin. "We invested it in real estate. That is what we have now."

I ask him what has become of San Domingo, now that henequen production is, more than ever, a government-controlled monopoly. He gives the tablecloth another tug. "What you would expect. The house is in ruins. There is no money to keep it up. One day they take a door. The next day they take another. You tell the police, but they don't do anything. . . . It used to be a pretty place when it was kept up. But they are like ants, eating a cake little by little."

His face brightens. "But come," he says, "I want to show you something." He leads me to a long table on one side of the gallery. It is covered with books, mimeographed papers, trays, and what looks like parts of a high school chemistry set. "See here," he says, lifting a jar of liquid. "I am doing chemistry on the henequen plant; on how to effectively extract a wax from the outer part of the leaf. It compares very favorably with the carnauba wax from Brazil, which is used to wax cars and floors. We could be very competitive, using henequen. Also, there is the vegetable hormone, Hexcogenina, which henequen produces. It is a contraceptive. Only now they get it from the juice. I want to demonstrate that it would be more practical to extract it from the wax." Señor Zapata waves a sample of the wax at me, the way Joann Andrews had brandished her little jars of Calakmul honey. "In spite of all the problems," he says defiantly, "I am not ready to give up on henequen yet."

When I am about to leave, I ask him if he feels that in the old days things were better, not just for him and his family, but for the majority of Yucatecans. He takes a long time thinking about his answer. Finally he says, "Better? Better than when? The 1930s? There is a little more freedom for everybody now. And tourism has helped, so economically the situation is a little better, or it would be if it were not for inflation, which is a terrible mess."

Another pause. He smooths out the tablecloth where his tugging has wrinkled it. Then, with a small sigh he murmurs, "Yes, I suppose I would have to say that for most people things are perhaps a little bit better now."

SIX

Valladolid

Officially the War of the Castes did not get under way until July 30, 1847, when the Maya overran a small settlement of whites and mestizos called Tepich. But it had its real beginning six months earlier, and twenty miles to the north, at Valladolid.

Valladolid lies midway between Mérida and Cancún. Of the peninsula's three great colonial cities—the others being Mérida and Campeche—it is the one that has been most savaged and yet least touched by time. Since the end of the era of Spanish rule, as well as for more than fifty years after the Maya rebellion, time stood still here. Even now it isn't exactly hurrying to catch up.

On the evening of my arrival at the Hotel Mesón de Marquez, the owner, Señor Escalante Ruiz, had told me that until fifteen or twenty years ago, a number of large old houses still stood abandoned on the outskirts of Valladolid. They have since been leveled to make way for pastureland or new construction. But in the central part of town, notwithstanding all the pillaging and burning that transpired here, a Spanish *hidalgo*, resurrected from his churchyard tomb long enough to take a little midnight stroll, would have no trouble finding his way around.

Even by the standards of colonial times, when having an old name and "pure" Spanish ancestry counted for as much or more than being rich or powerful—granted, they often went together—the hidalgos of Valladolid were notorious for their almost pathological snobbishness. These "Creoles" (the term, though elsewhere appropriated by peoples of mixed black and white derivation, still refers, in northern Yucatán, to persons of pure Spanish blood) regarded any commercial activity other than cattle ranching as being beneath the dignity of descendants of the conquistadors, and disdained their peers in Mérida for their mercantile instincts. They built grand houses that proudly displayed their ancient coats of arms, and generally conducted themselves in a way that makes one think of a bunch of Don Quixotes—only more arrogant, less appealing—tilting their lances at the windmills of nineteenth-century change. When Stephens arrived at the city after exploring the ruins of Chichén Itzá, he was struck by the number of "large buildings that stood roofless . . . with here and there, as if in mockery of human pride, a tottering front that has blazoned upon it the coat of arms of some proud Castilian . . . whose race is now entirely unknown." The observation suggests that Valladolid's proud and inbred Creole families were not successfully reproducing themselves; yet they preferred to see their neighbors' houses crumble into ruin rather than allow mestizos, much less Indians, to live in the streets near the plaza they had reserved for themselves.

Not that Valladolid was a ghost town by any means. It was on the eastern frontier of the civilized Hispanic world, linked to Mérida by road, but, by preference, culturally and economically isolated from the capital city. Nor did it have much commercial contact with the other frontier towns—Tizimín, Tihosuco, Peto, Tekax—which, like itself, were positioned along an arc, now roughly conforming with the boundary of Quintana Roo, which was then demarcated by the green walls of a hostile and all but impenetrable jungle. Still, this was the home of Yucatán's vicar-general, as well as the site of one of the first cotton manufacturing factories in Mexico; and it could boast a population of 15,000. One can only surmise that Stephens had it in for Valladolid, perhaps because only the Campechano owner of the factory, and its American manager, themselves outsiders, made him feel welcome. At any rate, he described the city's people as being, in general, good-for-nothings with a mania for cockfighting.

Whether that particular assessment was fair or not, the American explorer was a remarkably observant and astute fellow, and occasionally he sounds as though he had a crystal ball tucked away in his saddle bags. In another entry concerning Valladolid, he makes the following comment:

> The city . . . had some notoriety, as being the place at which the first blow was struck in the revolution now in progress against the dominion of Mexico, and also as being the residence of General Iman, under whom that blow was struck. The immediate consequence was the expulsion of the Mexican garrison; but there was another, more remote and of more enduring importance. There, for the first time, the Indians were brought

out in arms. Utterly ignorant of the political relations between Mexico and Yucatán, they came in from their ranchos and milpas under a promise by General Iman that their capitation tax should be remitted. After the success of the first outbreak the government endeavored to avoid the fulfillment of this promise, but was compelled to compromise by remitting the tax upon women, and the Indians still look forward to emancipation from the whole. What the consequences may be of finding themselves, after ages of servitude, once more in the possession of arms, and in increasing knowledge of their physical strength, is a question of momentous import to the people [of Yucatán], the solution of which no man can foretell.

The situation that Stephens refers to here was an ongoing conflict between Yucatán—or factions in Yucatán—and the Mexican government. Actually, the root cause of the fracas was the angry commercial rivalry that had been developing between Mérida and Campeche ever since 1821, when Mexico (including Yucatán) had declared its independence from Spain. Neither city had any ideological sympathy for the idea of centralized control emanating from Mexico City; but in trying to further its own interests, Campeche sided with the central government's effort to exercise its authority in the peninsula, which Mérida predictably opposed. For a time, Campeche—and the Mexican government—were the winners. However, Campeche quickly discovered that it had as little liking as did Mérida and the rest of Yucatán for the laws imposed by the central government under President Santa Ana, particularly when these called for the conscription of Yucatecan troops to help fight the revolt that broke out in Texas in the late 1830s.

This is where the General Santiago Iman whom Stephens mentioned comes in: He was a captain in the state militia who, at Tizimín, started his own revolt against the central government in 1840. When he defeated the Mexican garrison at Valladolid, all Yucatán joined in the rebellion and drove the government troops from the peninsula. But the crucial fact, overlooked in the heady days following Yucatán's declaration of its independence from Mexico, was that Iman would never have taken Valladolid if he had not had the radical idea of enlisting the frontier Maya into his improvised army, promising them they would be released from church taxes if they came to his aid, which they did by the thousands.

As Stephens notes, when the immediate crisis was over, the government in Mérida tried to forget about Iman's promises, although it did
create a surprisingly liberal constitution for the "sovereign nation" of
Yucatán. However, when Santa Ana made an effort to recapture the
peninsula in 1842, the government in Mérida once more enlisted the
Maya with promises of land grants and freedom from taxes; and again,
with their help, Mexican troops were driven out of the Yucatán.

After that, in the years 1844–46, relations between Yucatán and the
Mexican republic kept changing so quickly that hardly anyone could
keep track. First Yucatán's ruling class, which seemed to be holding all
the cards, made its peace with Santa Ana and rejoined the republic,
pretty much on its own terms. Then Santa Ana reneged on the terms.
Then Yucatán redeclared its independence. Then Santa Ana, needing
all the help he could get now that the Mexican-American War was under way, repromised to honor Yucatán's right to control its own affairs.
Then the government in Mérida agreed to re-rejoin the republic. Then
Campeche, realizing that its fortifications would be no defense against
the U.S. fleet's new explosive shells, rebelled against this latest pact and
led a popular uprising against the (for the moment) procentralist government in Mérida.

Well, if your head is spinning, think of the average Yucatecan citizen
at the time. In particular, think of the average Maya Indian. The government had not overtly reneged on all those promises concerning tax
reductions and land grants. But there had been so many thousands of
Maya volunteers whose demands must now be satisfied that it had decided the best thing to do was to do nothing. After all, it had its hands
full dealing with the various political factions that supported or opposed
ties with the national government. Indeed, the War of the Castes would
be well under way before Yucatán's whites and mestizos—the *ladinos*—
would fully realize that this was a race war, and not just one more power
struggle between the peninsula's pro- and anticentralist parties.

It *was* still that when what happened at Valladolid happened. In Jan-
uary 1847, only a few years after Stephens's visit, a local political chief
at Peto, Antonio Trujeque, raised an Indian battalion to take advantage
of Campeche's latest revolt against the government in Mérida. After
occupying Peto, they moved north and fell on Valladolid, thereby un-
leashing those "consequences" neither Stephens or anyone else could
have foretold.

But before the Indians get to Valladolid, it might be a good idea to
take a longer look at the Maya as a "modern" people, divorced from the
spectacular but long-extinct civilization that still eclipses their present
ethnic identity (so much so, indeed, that some newcomers to Yucatán
are surprised to learn that the Maya still survive in a sense that, say, the
Aztecs or the Toltecs do not).

It is an interesting thing, the way the Maya of the countryside and
the hamlets impress those who are not they. Almost everybody, myself
included, remarks on how likable they are. And almost always this observation is followed by a reference to their stoic patience, their good-
natured, if also somewhat passive, acceptance of whatever life dishes
out to them. At the hotel, Señor Escalante Ruiz had said, half-
enviously, "If a Maya's truck breaks down, he puts up his hammock in
the trees and goes to sleep. Providence will provide help in its own good
time." Even in-depth studies like those that made dreary little Chan
Kom—"the village that chose progress"—famous among anthropologists delineate the Maya's conservative attitude toward the human condition as something to be accepted and endured with as little fuss and
as much good grace as possible. In his travels through the hacienda
country, Stephens repeatedly noted what he perceived as the Maya's
submissive nature, their patient fatalism. He describes one of them kissing the hand of the foreman who has just given him a whipping for some
offense; he tells of another enduring, without any change in facial
expression, an operation without anesthetic, on the veins of his legs,
that sounded so excruciating that I groaned just reading of it; he men-
tions a third who buries his young wife in a shallow grave without any
trace of emotion, and on and on. Good American Yankee that he is, he
concludes that "veneration for masters is the first thing [the Indians]
learn, and these masters, descendants of the terrible conquerors . . .
have lost all the fierceness of their ancestors. Gentle, averse to labor
themselves, they impose no heavy burdens upon the Indians, but understand and humour their ways, and the two races move on harmoniously together, with nothing to apprehend from each other, forming a
simple, primitive, and almost patriarchal state of society."

In view of the horror that was about to envelop the Yucatán, it would
be easy to say that Stephens, in this passage at least, was being something less than prescient. But then, as we've seen, he seems to change
his tune later on, when he gets to Valladolid and starts wondering what

might happen now that the Indians have guns, and know how to use them.

The fact is that he is right in both of his observations. The War of the Castes was not a plantation revolt. On the contrary, the Maya of northwestern Yucatán—the ones he sees as venerating their masters—generally sided with the ladinos in the struggle that was to come.

No, Stephens changed his mind because, on the frontier lands outside Valladolid he ran into Maya of an altogether different breed. These were the Huits, the Indians of the eastern jungle. As Nelson Reed remarks in his excellent *The Caste War of Yucatán*, their numbers were estimated at anywhere from six to twenty thousand, "but to count them was like counting the birds in the forest." They wore loincloth-like shorts, their women went about barebreasted, they lived off the land as hunter-gatherers as well as maize growers, and they worshiped forest gods along with Christian saints. Until recently, they had never been more than tenuously under the control of the ladinos—or dzul, as the Maya called all whites and mestizos. But now the jungles were being increasingly invaded and cleared not only by settlers intent on growing corn and sugarcane, but, in the north, by cattle ranchers. Indeed, the Huits had a special grudge against the aristocratic families of Valladolid, who were high-handedly expropriating more and more of their communal lands for pasturage.

Stephens was a cool customer, but in his description of an encounter with the Huits we can sense something of his uneasiness, even though he was remembering the occasion from a long way off. "We met a large straggling party of Indians," he tells us, "returning from a hunting expedition in the forests along the seacoast. Naked, armed with long guns, and with deer and wild boars slung on their backs, their aspect was the most truculent of any people we had seen. They were some of the Indians who had risen at the call of General Iman, and they seemed ready at any moment for battle."

These were the Maya whom Trujeque would lead to Valladolid, and who, once inside the city, proceeded to settle scores in their own way. There is no glossing over the fact that the Maya, so likable in their peaceable moods, could be as revolting as anyone else when they revolted. For six days, drunk on aguardiente, they looted the city. The captured colonel of the state militia and a paralyzed curate were among those butchered by machetes; but Valladolid's aristocratic families were the Huits' particular targets, without regard for age or sex. Young girls were raped, then tied to the grillwork of the great houses and mutilated while their families were forced to look on. Almost a hundred civilians were murdered. Bodies were carried through the streets. Some were castrated, some were reportedly eaten.

It wasn't officially a Maya rebellion. The Huits had been led to Valladolid for the familiar purpose of helping to unseat one government party in order to replace it with another. But this time things had gotten out of hand. And what had happened in Valladolid would set the pattern for the war to come.

The drunken Maya who had sacked Valladolid went back to their forest homes expecting the ladinos to come after them and punish them. They didn't, which from the ladino point of view was a bad mistake. But Yucatán was in political turmoil—again. The governor of the centralist party in Mérida had been exiled to Cuba, but one of his aides, a fellow named Cetina, was on the loose in northeastern Yucatán, trying to do what Santiago Iman had done seven years earlier, namely, start a counterrevolt with the help of the Huit Maya. While he was sending envoys to the Maya chiefs, and the politicians of the newly installed neutralist party—the ones who didn't want to get Yucatán involved in the Mexican-American War—were nervously debating the international crisis on the one hand while trying to ignore the real implications of the Valladolid massacre on the other, the Maya were quietly mobilizing along the frontier. Evidently it wasn't an overnight conversion; more a matter of momentum gathering gradually but irreversibly. They knew their strength now. The shamans were predicting a great shedding of ladino blood; and the men who would lead the rebellion, notably Cecilio Chi and Jacinto Pat, were winning more and more adherents. When some of their messages were intercepted, the commandant at Valladolid ordered the arrest of Chi and Pat—by, ironically, that same Trujeque who had led the Huit Maya in what was supposed to have been the orderly overthrow of the Valladolid garrison.

By the time Trujeque was convinced that the two Maya leaders were up to something, they had escaped into the jungle. A couple of days later, Chi and his followers struck at the small settlement of Tepich, butchering all members of the twenty or thirty ladino families who lived there. Only one survivor managed to escape to the nearby, larger town of Tihosuco with the terrifying news that the War of the Castes had begun.

Panic swept through the ladino world. Incredibly, however, no one as yet fully understood the real implications of the uprising. Cetina, the agent provocateur for the deposed centralist government, was perceived as the guiding genius behind the Indian revolt; and for several weeks the politicians and state militia concentrated on hunting him down. Cetina himself was apparently led to believe by Pat and Chi and other Maya leaders that they were willing to act as his allies. In fact, however, the Maya leaders were by now committed to a policy—a final solution—of their own: they would annihilate all whites and mestizos in the peninsula.

They almost succeeded. It was a guerrilla war, with no holds barred on either side; but the Maya knew how to play this game better than the desperate ladinos, who were often cut off and surrounded before they knew what was happening. By now the Cocomes Maya were raiding south of Mérida, and the Chenes Maya were moving on Campeche. The tactical pattern was usually the same. First the isolated haciendas and small settlements in a region would be overwhelmed, then the larger towns besieged. The ladino militia would make forays into the jungle, only to be ambushed again and again. The towns would be sur-rounded, the Maya closing the circle more tightly every night with con-stricting barricades, built of the rocks with which the soil of Yucatán is so liberally strewn. The militia would charge out, suffer heavy losses, breach the stone barricade, and find that the enemy had disappeared into the jungle. The next morning the barricade, like the wood at Dun-sinane, would have moved closer to the town walls, seemingly of its own accord. From behind it, the Indians would lob the heads of captured ladinos at the defenders, or pop up briefly to dance about in blood-stained militia jackets or ladies' dresses.

Finally, the desperate garrison commander, ammunition low and morale even lower, would organize a retreat to the nearest untaken town on the road to Mérida or Valladolid. Terrified women, children, old people would gather in the square with whatever belongings they and their burros and horses could carry. The able-bodied townsmen and whatever state militia were available would form a front and rear guard, and the untidy exodus would get under way. Sometimes most of the refugees would make it to the next town—which would eventually also be besieged—and sometimes there would be a massacre, with the Maya rebels setting up stone roadblocks to halt the advance of the moving file, then leaping out of the surrounding bush to strike the strung-out line at various points along the narrow road, taking on the desperate troops in hand-to-hand combat or slaughtering undefended civilians with their machetes.

It was this latter scenario that occurred during the evacuation of Valladolid in March, 1848. The commandant, his supplies and troops depleted by offensives to the south that had turned into disastrous routs, had no option but to abandon the city. He and his advisors decided that a trail that led north to Espita before turning west toward Mérida would be the safest route. The way was opened by cannon volleys and the charge of a 500-man assault battalion. At dawn, when the road seemed clear, the ten thousand citizens that still remained in the city, of all ages and classes, began to move through the streets north of the plaza, escorted by another regiment of troops. But they had barely gotten under way when an overloaded carriage broke down, halting the column. Led by Cecilio Chi, the Maya rebels, who had already infiltrated the southern part of the city and set it ablaze, made the most of the delay. When cannon, positioned at the south side of the plaza, raked the streets with grapeshot, they fanned out, climbed across roofs and back walls, and fell on the rear of the long column of civilians.

From where I am standing at the northwestern corner of Valladolid's plaza, I can see them, the attacking Maya, howling their war cries, swarming across the square, leaping from walls, firing from the rooftops. The defending rear guard is quickly cut to pieces, while the surviving troops run through the streets trying to save their own necks.

The evacuation becomes a total rout, beset all along its line by sporadic Indian attacks. Some groups of militia fight bravely; others, completely demoralized, scatter and run. Abandoned carts and carriages, along with the uncounted bodies of hundreds of men, women, and children, litter the rutted trail. Still the tormented column moves onward, with gunshots, war whoops, the screams of the dying resounding again and again at one point or another along its miles-long length.

The fact that any of the exhausted fugitives finally reached Mérida after enduring days of incredible hardship was due to the inability of the Indian forces to function, over an extended period, as a modern army that could take tactical advantage of the victories it had won. Though expert in guerrilla warfare, the Maya were easily distracted by the booty at hand, particularly when it included, as it usually did, large quantities of aguardiente and other booze.

In the aftermath of the evacuation-turned-rout, the rebel leader, Cecilio Chi, hosted a great celebration for his men in a town not far from what was left of Valladolid. One of those who witnessed this weeks-long binge was the captive Vicar of Valladolid, Manuel Sierra O'Reilly. I mention him partly because I am staring at San Bernardino, the massive Franciscan church where he had officiated at mass during those last fateful days before the bloody exodus from Valladolid began; I can hear his voice calling out, with more than customary zeal, for God's protection, and I can see the frightened faces of his flock as they ardently echo his Amens.

But that aside, he also interests me because his personal history so vividly illustrates the precariousness of human existence, the thinness of the line that divides those who survive during a turbulent time from those who do not. Father Sierra had already stepped up to that line several times during the preceding month, when he had taken part in a series of meetings with Cecilio Chi, hoping to negotiate a settlement that would save Valladolid. He would have been very much aware that envoys on similar missions had sometimes ended up, minus their private parts, hanging from trees. The truce he helped arrange was quickly broken; but Sierra himself survived not only the negotiations but the fall of Valladolid. The Maya, for all their hatred of the dzul, retained their respect for the Catholic liturgy, and they needed qualified priests to pray to the Virgin and the Santos just as they needed shamans to pray to the gods of the bush. Sierra was hauled about among the Maya villages and encampments, performing the usual functions of a rural priest, but always aware that if he made a false move the blow of a machete would end his rather stressful ministry.

Which did not prevent him from undertaking a remarkable escape. Knowing that he would not be allowed to move in the direction of ladino forces, he undertook a long, tortuous journey to the northern coast. By pure luck he found an abandoned canoe somewhere near present-day El Cuyo. Starving and ravaged by fever, he traveled west-ward to the burned-out settlement of Río Lagartos, only to be recaptured there by a band of Maya. That same night, however, he escaped while his captors slept, and without any provisions he somehow managed to paddle along fifty miles of mangrove-choked coastline to Dzilam, which had recently been retaken by ladino troops. He appeared among them, as Reed remarks, like a Lazarus risen from the tomb.

During the months of Sierra's captivity, an extraordinary turn in the seemingly inevitable course of events had occurred. After the fall of Valladolid, there had seemed no way the Maya revolt could be crushed. By the end of May, virtually all of the Yucatán was in the hands of rebel forces except Campeche, cowering behind the walls that had originally been built to protect the city from pirates, and besieged Mérida, its population inflated by the thousands of refugees, many of them sick or dying, who crowded the convents and churches, the arcades of the plaza, the commandeered homes of residents who had fled. The governor prepared to announce the evacuation of the city. The citizens braced for a fighting retreat to the little port of Sisal, where there would almost certainly not be enough vessels available to carry them away.

And at that crucial moment, the insurgent Maya simply decided to go home, back to their villages, their families, and their milpas in the bush. The winged ants that were the harbingers of the rains had come. It was time to plant the maize that was and still is the Maya staff of life, as well as the focus of their religious beliefs. As Leandro Poot, the son of a rebel chief, would explain long after the event, "My father's people said to themselves and to their brothers, '¡Ehen! The time has come for us to make our planting, for if we do not we shall have no Grace of God to fill the bellies of our children' . . . and in spite of the supplication and threats of the chiefs, each man rolled up his blanket and put it in his food pouch, tightened the thongs of his sandals, and started for his home and his cornfield.

"Then the Batabob [chiefs], knowing how useless it was to attack the city with the few men that remained, went into council and resolved to go back home. Thus it can be clearly seen that Fate, and not white soldiers, kept my father's people from taking [Mérida] and working their will upon it" (*The Caste War of Yucatán*, p. 99).

Leandro Poot was certainly right about the white soldiers. Whether he was also right about the role of Fate depends, I suppose, on whether one looks at things from a Maya point of view or not.

At any rate, from then on, the tide turned against the Maya. The ladino militia, by now experienced in the Maya way of making war, and greatly heartened by the lifting of the siege of Mérida, followed the Maya to their villages and cornfields and attacked them there. The rebels remobilized, and for more than a year the fighting continued to rage, particularly in the south and east; but now it was the ladinos who were on the offensive. One by one, the wrecked towns, Ticul, Tekax, Peto, Valladolid, Ichmul, were retaken. Cecilio Chi, hiding out deep in the forest, was murdered by an aide who was sleeping with Chi's wife. In September 1849, Jacinto Pat, the only one of the Maya leaders who had some grasp of modern concepts of strategy, was killed by one of Chi's lieutenants. By the end of that year, almost all of the settled areas that the rebels had won were again in ladino hands. Yet the eastern Maya, the Huits, never accepted defeat. They retreated back into the forests and jungles of what is now Quintana Roo, formed an extraordinary cult centered on a Speaking Cross, and in spite of repeated attacks by government forces, continued to make most of the eastern third of the peninsula virtually off limits to whites until well into the present century.

Even in this age of world wars and mass exterminations, the carnage wreaked by the War of the Castes is hard for us to comprehend. Between 1847 and 1850, the Yucatán lost nearly half of its approximately 500,000 inhabitants. Thousands fled the peninsula, but it is estimated that close to a third of the prewar population perished in the revolt. In terms of percentages, if not total numbers, few conflicts anywhere have exacted such a dreadful toll.

Valladólid never did recover. For generations after the War of the Castes officially ended, it was still thought of as the city where the Maya first whet their appetite for white men's blood. People were afraid to settle that far to the east again. In a hit-and-miss sort of way, the unconquered Huit Indians were still apt to pick off lone travelers on the road, or vaqueros searching for cattle in the bush. But the deeper fear, of course, was that the Maya might again rise up *en masse* and once more overwhelm the town itself. Long after Mérida had regained its economic footing and had begun to prosper as never before with the advent of the henequen boom, Valladolid remained, not a ghost town, exactly, but a town with a lot of ghosts. Even now, walking the streets on a quiet evening, one can feel their presence.

In the second of the two patios around which the Mesón de Marquez is built, a pair of yearling whitetail deer stare at me with wide, glistening eyes from their wire mesh enclosure. Nearby, in a fairly roomy cage, a fat coatimundi paces back and forth, working off his dinner.

Noting my interest, Señor Mario Escalante Ruiz asks, "You like animals?"

"Very much," I tell him. "Wild animals especially."

"I like them too. We still have them around here; but nothing like it was. Just a few years ago, in the market you would see skins of jaguars and pumas that you could buy for nothing."

"Jaguars!"

"Oh, yes. There used to be a lot of them up in the northeast; there are still some in Quintana Roo. And deer! Venison was an entrée served at every restaurant. It's very good that the government has prohibited that. Of course the Maya still kill a lot. They sell it under the table, but it's maybe only 10 percent of what it was."

I tell him that not all of it is under the table: "When I first went to the mercado at Mérida years ago, I saw dozens of tiny, badly mounted fawns for sale. They must have still been in the womb when their mothers were shot. This time there weren't so many, but they were still being sold."

"Ah? Well, it is no longer legal, I am sure of that. Perhaps the inspector just looks the other way."

We both look at the caged deer. They could be considered lucky, I suppose. They must have been at least a few weeks old when their mothers were killed.

"I have a little piece of land I am preparing so these two can grow up in safety," says Señor Escalante Ruiz. He adds, "I have friends who hunt; they used to just drive the road at night, with lights. Bam, bam, bam! There is no sport in that. But that has been against the law for about ten years. Now they still go in the jungle and hunt; but it is more difficult for them."

We walk back together to the front patio. In the rear one there hadn't been much room for things to grow, what with the deer pen and the swimming pool; but here everything is shadowy green and cool. And quiet. There are only a couple of guests taking their evening meal in the hotel's little restaurant. This may or may not be because a couple of modern hotels have been built at Chichén Itzá, so that tourists who want to spend a couple of days at the ruins can overnight right there instead of traveling the twenty-five miles back to Valladolid. Señor Escalante Ruiz has done his best to keep pace with the changing times. The rooms in the rear wing of the Mesón have all the modern comforts; and there is a very good gift shop just inside the entryway. But despite the alterations and additions, the house, at least the front part of it, retains much of its traditional colonial look.

"My great-great-grandfather bought it in 1882. Even then, it was a very old house. Perhaps the Creole family that originally owned it were killed during the Caste War, or else they didn't want to live here afterward. Many people were afraid to try again. When the new Creole families came, everything was gone. And there were many small outbreaks, small guerrilla wars that the Maya would start every ten years or so. I remember my great-aunt telling me that back then there were hardly any roads, and nobody felt safe living in the haciendas. Here in town, at least, there were soldiers, guns, policemen. But it was only in about 1900, after the railroad got started here, that people began to feel safe. And even so, when I was a boy, Valladolid still had fewer people than it did when the Caste War began."

We are sitting at the end of the arcade, near the kitchen. The smell of roast pork hangs heavy in the air, making up my mind for me about what I will have for dinner. I take time out to order a margarita and the *cochinita píbil,* then focus my attention once again on Mario Escalante Ruiz. He reminds me a little of José Ramón Foraster, the pleasant Spanish businessman who shot the puma in Campeche; but I suspect there is more emotional depth to him, and a quiet, critical intelligence at work behind the easy smiles and easy manner. He is in his young middle age, putting on weight, but still a handsome man. There is nothing of the patrician about him, although he belongs to the fifth generation of one of those "new" Creole families that he has just been mentioning. These families, intermarrying with the few survivors of Valladolid's original aristocracy, quickly established themselves as the new elite of the eclipsed, half-empty town. Although they did not limit their commercial enterprises to raising cattle, they maintained the rigid divisions that separated race from race and class from class. They also retained Valladolid's traditional attitude toward Mérida. "My grandfather didn't know any people there," Mario explains. "Creoles in Mérida and here are not connected. We still live in different worlds, although I'm not sure why. Certainly I liked Mérida when I went to school there."

When I ask him to tell me a bit more about Valladolid's social structure, he says, a little impatiently, "Yes, yes, of course there was class consciousness. There still is." Then he grins, "But I bet you don't know that this was one of the first places in the Yucatán where the Revolution got started. That's right! They don't write much about it in the history books, because Valladolid is not important anymore! They only write about when Alvarado brought the Revolution to Mérida in 1915. But in 1910 there were already revolutionaries here. Rich and poor, everybody here wanted a change from the government of Porfirio Díaz. What? Well, yes, there was some killing. The revolutionaries killed some of the government people: eleven soldiers and officials. And they put about thirty others in jail. There are a lot of tales from that time. My grandmother told me about a nephew of hers. He was wealthy but he was also an alcoholic. Six months before the Revolution, the *jefe político,* who didn't like him, put him in jail. And while he was in jail his friends told him his mother was very sick. Well, he asked the jefe to give him just a few hours with his mother, but the jefe said no, even though he had only a few more days to be in jail. And his mother died without him seeing her. So, when he was free, he heard about the revolutionaries, and he joined them. He became one of the leaders. His picture is in the mural on the second floor of the City Hall. And on June 4, 1910, when the revolutionaries took the City Hall, he cut off the head of the jefe with a machete. He sent the head to the man's mother. She lived right over there"—Mario waves his hand in the appropriate direction— "in the second house on the south side of the square."

"Actually," he says, "the Revolution didn't much affect things here. We don't have anything like henequen, and since making money from henequen was all the Mexican government cared about, they left us alone. My grandfather had a hacienda, a cattle ranch; but he also planted cotton and he had a sugar mill. My father had a big business in wood. He set up three sawmills for mahogany and red cedar in the jungle. The biggest was at Colonía, which is between Tizimín and El Cuyo. Back then it was a boom town, maybe eight or ten thousand people. Now it's nothing, although there's still a mill there.

"I remember those forests, the way they were before. When I was twelve or thirteen, the government started to build a road from here to the Caribbean. My uncle was a contractor, so he invited me and my brother to come with him as far as Chemax. It was only ten kilometers away, but I remember how excited I was. It was another world. Tall, tall trees, and full of animals. Monkeys, wild pigs, big flocks of turkeys that crossed the trail. The jungle was beautiful. And then, by 1960, 1965, pfft! almost all gone! In about ten years, maybe 70 percent gone. . . . Well, my father cut a lot of that wood, I don't deny that. In a way I am almost sorry I saw it the way it was before."

Mario falls silent for a while, then resumes not quite where he had left off. "Maybe because I live here all the time, I don't see the changes, even though I suppose I am part of them, just as my father was part of the cutting of the forests. You ask about the castes. Well, here I think it was a little different from the way it was in Mérida. For example, our parents never said, 'Don't play with the Maya.' We played with them in our houses, their houses. We played ball in the streets. Maybe every three hours one car would pass us." He stares reflectively out at the garden where an elderly English woman is sitting by herself, reading a book and pulling absently at her nose. Then he says, "Still, when I think of that, I see how different it was for us: a different education, a different lifestyle. There are maybe thirty Creole families here. My wife is a Creole. We all went to a little private school when we were children. There were just three teachers, but then, we were not that many students. . . . Anyway, what I am trying to say is that maybe changes happen whether we try to make them happen or not. There are not many economic opportunities here in Valladolid. The young people leave. I came back, after three years of law in Mérida, to help my father. But most of the young people don't come back. My father had three children. Now my sister lives in Mexico City, my brother in Chicago. I am the only one who lives here. It is the same for all the other Creole families here—"

At that moment, he is interrupted by the forward rush of a beautiful little Maya boy, maybe 6 or 7, whose great, heavy-lidded eyes and incandescent smile seem to take up the whole of his small, round face. There is no hesitation, no shyness in the way he approaches the master of the Mesón de Marquez. Ignoring me, he puts his elbows across Mario's thigh, gives him the full force of that marvelous smile, and half demands, half pleads for, the money for some ice cream. Mario returns the smile, rumples the child's straight black hair, and fishes out some change from his pocket.

When the little boy has dashed off, Mario turns the brooding remains of his smile on me. "You see what I mean? Things are changing even here, for good or bad. Not because of revolutions or government edicts, but just because things have to change. The young Maya and mestizos go to work in Cancún and they are never the same after that. And we"—he shrugs—"we are dying out."

The next morning, an hour or two before I am to leave, Mario's nephew kindly shows me the way to one of the two large cenotes that explain why, in 1543, Valladolid was founded here and not somewhere else. The nephew lives in Chicago, and he and his wife have come down here on a three-week vacation to escape the winter cold. He is a plump, swarthy young man, thoroughly Americanized. He is an undertaker, and like so many people in his profession, he is an extrovert, friendly and very talkative.

He knows the proprietor of the little thatched-roof café that overlooks the cenote, and waves to him as we enter the walled enclosure. I am not sure if there is an admission fee, or whether visitors are expected to order something, but in any case we do neither. We stroll under the trees to the edge of the cenote and look down. Far below, the water, not yet brushed by the morning sun, is perfectly still and—unusual in cenotes—thinly coated with green algae. "I used to swim here when I was a kid," says the nephew. "It didn't have all that slime back then. Cousteau and his bunch came here, right? They tried like hell to reach the bottom, but they couldn't do it." He laughs. "Maybe there isn't one, just like the Indians say."

He is happy to have escaped, for three weeks, the Chicago cold. "Man, those winters up there are something! They really kill the old people. All they have to do is go outside and it just gets to them, gets in their lungs. We start getting a lot of them around Christmastime."

What he likes best about Valladolid, besides the fact that it never gets cold, is the peace and quiet. "There's started to be a little bit of crime here lately, mostly guys breaking into cars, right? But nothing violent. Nothing at all compared to Chicago! And there's not much drugs. Alcohol, yes, but not drugs. Marijuana grows wild around here, and some of the Maya grow it too; but it's a lot of risk. If they're caught, they stay in jail forever unless, of course, they got the money to buy their way out."

But peace and quiet, the absence of crime, the warm climate are not enough to entice Mario's nephew into thinking of returning to the ancestral home, even though he is not at all satisfied with his situation in Chicago. "It's pretty dull here," he says. "They still go by the old rules. You can have a mestizo girlfriend or something like that, but the mamas really watch their daughters close! That's why so many of the guys here are gay."

For the obvious reason, this observation reminds him of why he is no longer happy with his work. "This AIDS thing is serious. It's all over the place. Before long it'll be down here if it isn't already. They need to make a law that their bodies have to be cremated. I mean, when you embalm them you got to take out all the blood, right? You can talk all you want about taking precautions, but it's still dangerous. I may decide to do something else for a living."

On the way back to the Mesón de Marquez, he talks about his uncle. "Mario married his first cousin, you know. I guess there must be something wrong with one of them. Anyway, they can't have kids of their own. Those kids they adopted are the luckiest little Maya kids in the world. Everybody says so."

I stop in my tracks. "Adopted? Maya kids?" I remember the little boy's wonderful smile, and the way Mario had looked at him. If it hadn't been for the racial difference, if this were not Valladolid, I would have recognized the relationship instantly.

"Yeah. A boy and a girl. Mario dotes on them. I wouldn't be surprised if they adopt some more. It's really something, huh? Maya kids! A while back, nobody would've ever thought that something like that could happen. Maybe not even Mario. But I guess times change, even here. Anyway, those are some lucky kids!"

I am no longer listening to the nephew. I am listening again to Mario Escalante Ruiz. We are dying out, he had said. And he had also said that changes happen not because of revolutions and government edicts, but because things just have to change.

I feel curiously chastened. I had not understood how intensely he must feel it: the realization that "things have to change."

I also feel a little awed. I think now of what he didn't say, but could have: that, sometimes, at least, things change because love can accomplish what revolutions and government edicts cannot. It can transform Mario Escalante Ruiz, this scion of a proud old Creole family, into the Pied Piper that I, just for a moment back at Chunchumil, had merely wished to be.

North of Valladolid, the landscape is tamed and open looking. But once I turn east at Tizimín and get past Colonía Yucatán on the road to El Cuyo, the country changes. There are a number of little hard-scrabble milpas stuck out here in the bush, but a good bit of the second-growth forest still remains. Vegetation crowds up to the narrow road, and vines and tall grass spill onto the tarmac. In some of the trees hang green plastic boxes, meant to entice and trap swarms of the African killer bees that have invaded Yucatán, creating problems for the region's beekeepers and even killing livestock, including one of Joann Andrew's thoroughbred fillies.

No cars pass, and there are no campesinos walking along the road, although some must have passed recently: the flies have just begun to settle on a big rattlesnake, not quite five feet long, which lies stretched out on the pitted tarmac. A machete has lopped off its head, which lies nearby, and its rattles, which have been carried off as a memento.

This is a good road for birding. Yellowthroats, Yucatán jays, kiskadees, and warblers zip in and out of the undergrowth. There are quite a few raptors along here too: several roadside hawks living up to their name by perching at the roadside, a gray hawk soaring across a rough pasture, a pair of gray-headed kites gliding overhead.

Then, way off in the distance, I spot yet another hawk sitting in a lone dead tree. He politely holds still while I pull over to the side of the road and focus the binocs, but he has his back to me and I can't make out his markings. So I decide to have a closer look.

I struggle across a one-time clearing that is now overgrown with low, thorny underbrush that snags my trousers and unties my shoelaces every few steps. A sudden, scuttling rush just ahead of me makes me jump. But it is only an old friend, well met in a new setting. Armadillos are one of the more abundant wildlife species on the place I own in southern Mississippi, and I am very fond of them even though they Roto-root the garden without my permission. They are not terribly bright, but they have interesting little ways about them. When feeling amorous, for example, they copulate front-to-front, just as people usually do; and the female, who has the unusual ability to defer ovulation until she's good and ready to become a mother, always gives birth to quadruplets that are of one sex or the other, never both. The armadillo's main forte, however, is digging—for worms, grubs, beetles, centipedes, and other such delicacies. Which makes me wonder how it can make a living here in northern Yucatán, where the soil, what there is of it, is so underlain with limestone and covered with rocks that the Maya have to use pointed sticks to plant their kernels of maize. Yet the animals obviously thrive in this harsh environment. Or would, if the Maya didn't enjoy eating them so much.

The one I have startled, and been startled by, hurries off a few yards and then, forgetting all about me, resumes its hunt among the roots and stones for something to eat.

This seems to be my afternoon for encountering unalert wild creatures. The "hawk" is next. All this time, while I have been blundering through waist-high scrub, it has kept its perch in the dead tree, pivoting its head this way and that, obviously aware of me but reluctant to leave what it considers a very satisfactory observation post. Which it now proves itself to be. The bird spreads its wings, lifts off, and swoops down into the brush; the next minute it is back on the same branch, holding a small snake in its talons. Before it begins to attack its squirmy meal, it gives me a hard look, as though I might be thinking of inviting myself to dinner. By now I've had a close-up view of the bird and know what it is: a laughing falcon. To hear one live up to its name, I will have to wait until I meet the bird again in the jungles of Sian Ka'an. Right now, it has its mouth full.

Circling wide around the tree, I find a narrow footpath that is heading, as I am, away from the road. Before the coming night is over, I will regret that I hadn't noticed its beginning at the roadside, and followed it instead of wading through the scrub.

Ahead, the cleared land comes to halt at a dense wall of second growth about twenty feet high. The trail burrows into it, and so do I. Intrusive branches and vines have been recently cut back by a machete, and I expect at any moment to come on an opening containing a patch of beans and maize, a thatched choza, and a Maya family not at all amused to find a nosy gringo blundering onto their *parcelito*. I have my apologies all worked out in Spanish, but what if they only speak Maya?

But there is no opening. The trail just goes on and on, a narrow tunnel winding in and out among the offspring of all those trees that were fed to the voracious mill that Mario Escalante Ruiz's father had once owned. There are a good many big trees left, not necessarily ceibas, which were presumably spared because their wood was not marketable, and these give a scale to things. East of Tizimín, the rains are more generous than they are around Mérida, so the woodland here—described as "seasonal deciduous" in the language of silvaculturists—is greener than the scrub forests to the west. Yet despite the palms and palmettos and all the tropical broadleafs, everything seems dry and brittle, the ground not excepted. Again and again, the trail skirts places where the riddled limestone crust has collapsed, leaving shallow, broken cavities into which the roots of surrounding trees climb down, searching, not just for water, but for soil.

After walking maybe a mile and a half, I decide I'd better turn back; I still have some traveling to do before the day is done, and anyway, I'm feeling pretty tired. So I about-face, walk maybe a few dozen yards, then suddenly realize that something is keeping me company, moving parallel to the path just out of sight behind a screen of dappled vegetation. It isn't being noisy, but it isn't trying to be very quiet either. And to judge from the way the leaves stir at its passage, it has to be a pretty good size.

There is nothing for it but to have a look, although I am worried about moving off the trail. Not *afraid* worried. Just concerned that the racket I'm bound to make mucking through leaf litter and undergrowth will scare whatever-it-is away before I can get a decent look at it.

I needn't have worried. My fellow traveler is a *tamandua*—a collared anteater—and he is as foolishly unwary as the armadillo and the laughing falcon had been. As I approach, he hurries on ahead a little distance, but he doesn't make any effort to keep out of sight. Mostly I get a rear view of him, his back covered by rather long, golden brown fur encircled at the midriff by a wide sash of dark black hair. But at one point, deciding to have a look at me out of one beady little eye, he pauses and turns sideways, showing off to full effect his stunning profile.

I am enchanted. Surely, with the anteater, Nature's fanciful adaptation of form to function has gone as far as it can go. My tamandua's head isn't a proper head at all—just an arcing extension of the neck that, at a midway point where the small eyes and ears and perhaps a tiny brain are lodged, becomes a long tapering snout. Since its nostrils as well as its small mouth opening are at the very end of this extraordinary proboscis, I can only surmise that, for its size, an anteater must have the longest nasal passages as well as the longest tongue in the animal world. But it's the overall assembly, not just the tubular front end, that gives the animal its wondrous appearance. The prehensile tail is not festooned with long hair like that of the giant anteater (which reportedly once ranged as far north as the Yucatán but is gone from the area now); rather, it is the perfect counterpart for the neck and nose. Furry at the base but hairless at the tip, it has so much the same curve, and more or less the same length, that one half expects another set of small eyes and ears at that end too. Add to all this the fact that anteaters are terribly pigeon-toed, walking, as it were, on the sides of their feet, with their long digging claws turned up and inward, and you have a very, very weird-looking little animal. Actually, my anteater doesn't look all that little—about three feet long from stem to stern. But subtract the nose and tail and there wouldn't be much left.

Anteaters, of course, eat ants, along with termites and bees. Their long, sticky tongues are the equivalent of flypaper, and when they break open an anthill or hive and the disturbed inhabitants come pouring out they just lick them up like gravy off a spoon. Although they must have a very high pain threshold to cope with food that stings and bites as it goes down, they seem otherwise to be the most helpless and dim-witted creatures imaginable. Yet the campesinos say that they can give a good account of themselves if cornered by dogs, sitting up on their haunches and using their formidable-looking digging claws as weapons.

It is lucky for me that my anteater's route presently takes him across the trail I had been following. I had been so intent on keeping him in sight that if he had led me off in some other direction I might have had a hard time finding the path again.

As it is, I risk a turned ankle by running most of the way back to the van over the ragged, stony ground. During my unscheduled ramble, the sun has made its way to within an hour or so of setting; so now I have to make up for lost time. But it isn't just that. I feel exhilarated; I *want* to run.

El Cuyo is about as picturesque as a public restroom. A row of dreary cinder block dwellings climb the sandy street on the landward side of the dune, and that, plus a concrete quay and some fishing boats, is about it. Three young fishermen are lounging outside a little tienda. They are looking seaward, and so do I. The wind is really up now, and strong lines of waves are charging the shore. Far out, through the binoculars, I can see even larger ones lifting and breaking on the reefs. El Norte is coming in, say the fishermen. El Norte is the cold wind that occasionally swoops down on Yucatán from the northern Gulf during winter and early spring. The fishermen are resigned to the fact that there will be no fishing tomorrow, maybe not for several days.

When I ask them about the road along the barrier dune that reportedly links El Cuyo with Río Lagartos, they hold a conference. "That road is not so good," one of them says.

"Well," says another, "it is only this end that is not so good. After that you can go all the way. No problem."

They circle the van, examine the tires. One shakes his head, another shrugs noncommittally, a third smiles. I look worried.

"There are a couple of places where the sand is soft, but you can make it," says the smiling one. "After that it is easy."

"You won't get to Río Lagartos until after dark," warns the doubtful-looking man. "Maybe to Las Coloradas, but there is no place to stay there."

"I don't care about that as long as the van can make it," I tell him.

"You can make it," says the smiling man.

Finally the noncommittal one casts his vote. "I think you can make it," he says.

I am willing to be convinced. I don't want to go all the way back to Tizimín. And the idea of seeing this rarely visited part of the coast appeals to me.

The smiling young fisherman waves at me as I turn the van down the sand track behind the tienda. "¡Una gran aventura!" he yells encouragingly.

Adventure indeed. Later I would admit to myself that if I had had any sense, I would have turned back as soon as I hit the first stretch of soft sand. Instead, having just barely managed to get across it, I convinced myself that the bad stuff was behind me now. And after plowing through a second spot as chancy as the first, I was positively certain there couldn't be more than two places like that on the road. Besides, other cars had gotten through; I could see the tracks—

Now, when I am almost through the fourth stretch of deep sand, the van says, "To hell with it"—and digs in.

By this time, it is almost dark and El Norte is coming on strong and cold. I can hear the surf nearby and see that the beach is narrow. I wonder nervously about the tide; but there is a narrow stretch of dune vegetation between the beach and the road, so I figure that at least that is one worry I can scratch, even if the surf is getting all whipped up. And this time, unlike that night on the road to Uayamón, I am adequately provisioned: cigarettes, toilet paper, the makings of an iceless martini, Off!, a couple of boiled eggs. It may get cold, even with the windows up, but I had known beforehand about these sudden cold spells and have a sweater in my bag. Better a little shivering, if it comes to that, than swarms of mosquitoes.

So I am feeling resigned, psychologically relaxed, even a little pleased for taking this predicament in stride. The morning will bring help, even if I have to hike all the way back to El Cuyo to get it. Meantime, like a Maya, I will figuratively hang up my hammock and go to sleep.

And then it begins.

Actually, it had been going on for some while; but I had been so tensed up, so preoccupied with the nervous-making drive along the sandy track that I had hardly noticed I was scratching myself. Now I notice. I really notice. I am itching like mad.

I pull up my shirt, pull down my pants, shine the flashlight. All I can see is the redness of the skin where I've been scratching. What the hell have I got, I wonder, a Yucatecan case of the crabs? red bugs? jungle rot? Whatever it is, it is having a field day with my private and semiprivate parts. I try Off!, which burns the raw skin, and an unguent for cuts, which doesn't do much one way or the other. I consider getting into the surf to ease the burning itch, but decide not to try it. During a hike along the beach track between Sisal and Chuburna I had learned through painful experience that the dune vegetation of northern Yucatán comes equipped with every conceivable type of thorn and armored seed—hooked, barbed, stiletto sharp—that old Mother Nature had been able to dream up on one of Her bad days. Tennis shoes and socks hadn't guaranteed protection then, even in broad daylight, so venturing out now in the pitch-black night, with only a feeble flashlight beam to pick the way, doesn't seem like a good idea. I'm in enough pain already.

Finally, after a couple of hours of misery, I remember the chunk of *Aloe vera* that the Cobbs had given me when I left Ticul. And wonder of wonders, it really seems to help a little, although the inside of my skin still feels as though it is lined with steel wool. Finally, around midnight, cold, with El Norte vibrating the roof of the van, I fall miserably asleep.

I am awake before dawn and as soon as there is light enough to see by, I make my way to the beach, naked from the ankles up. As it turns out, I needn't have worried about being raked by thorns and thistles. Here, the grasses, sedges, and strange red vines all hug the sand and are generally less hostile than those at Sisal. The surf is, if anything, rougher than on the previous evening, but not as cold as the wind. Gratefully, I let it roll me about like some old log, only now and then holding myself still long enough to soap up and watch the dawn erupting through the salty spray like molten lava. After about an hour of this rough-and-tumble immersion—oh, frabjous joy!—the worst of the horrible itchiness has eased itself out of my tortured skin.

I let the wind dry me off, conclude that some sort of loathsome tropical chigger has assailed me, give myself a working over with *Aloe vera*, and bethink myself of the hike back to El Cuyo that lies ahead.

I needn't have worried. Not about that, at least. El Cuyo, or at least a sizable share of its male population, is awaiting me at the van.

There are five of them, and they have just arrived on the scene. They are posed in various stages of getting out of a very old and rusty sedan, frozen in attitudes of surprise, staring at me.

I still cringe, thinking of the fine anecdote they must have made of me when they and their buddies gathered for a round of beers at Las Coloradas that night: "And so we were on our way to Las Coloradas in

Manuel's car, to wait out El Norte; and a few miles out of El Cuyo, here is this van stuck in the sand ahead of us, right? And just as we come up, who comes up from the beach in the cold wind, bare-assed as Adam, but this tall gringo! No, no, not one of the French or Italian ones that take off their bikinis every chance they get. This one is a crazy American. Oh, no, he says, he wasn't swimming. It's just that he has this little rash. A little rash, Mother of God! He had let a swarm of *garrapatas* get all over him and didn't even notice until they were dug in!"

Garrapatas, my rescuers cheerfully inform me, are tiny ticks that congregate in great numbers in some wooded or scrubby areas. Actually, I had heard of them before. Stephens had graphically reported his own run-ins with the little horrors, and Joann and a couple of other people had warned me of them too. I just hadn't paid attention. They have a nasty way of sprinkling themselves like seeds on the unwary passerby, and if one doesn't notice them and get out of one's clothes fast enough, they burrow into the skin, causing that horrible itching irritation that I have so feelingly described.

Having amiably marveled at my ignorance, Manuel, the car's driver, who looks like Anthony Quinn in *La Strada*, helpfully suggests that I apply gasoline to the affected areas. Gasoline—unlit, of course—is, after all, a powerful insecticide. However, confronted with my obvious reluctance, and the fact that most of the ticks have either been scratched off, drowned, or suffocated in *Aloe vera*, he and his friends grinningly allow that gasoline might prove a little painful on my much abraded skin, and that getting into a change of clothes—which by now I have hastily done—ought to be remedy enough.

That settled, the little problem of the stuck van is quickly dealt with. My three advisors of the previous evening, none of whom are among this group, had neglected to mention the most essential equipment one needed when traveling this treacherous road, to wit, some extra manpower. Now, with five husky fishermen putting their backs to the job, the van is out of the sand trap on the first try. When it is the sedan's turn, it digs itself in at about the same spot. It is a heavy old wreck, so it takes a little more lifting and shoving, but in no time we have it on solid ground too. When Manuel sees me reaching for my wallet he waves his finger at me. "We help you, you help us. No problem!"

I invite them to lead the way, and Manuel squeezes the sedan past me on the narrow track. Then, with everyone laughing and hanging out the windows, offering final warnings about garrapatas and assurances that the road ahead is okay, the ancient car bumps and lurches its way out of sight.

After that harrowing beginning, the rest of the drive is pure pleasure, though the washboard track makes for slow going and a long haul. El Norte has not brought rain, not yet at least, and the windswept day is bright as brass. The barrier ridge is an uncannily beautiful world in its beach-desert way. Where it begins to broaden out a little, widening the distance between the ocean and the Río Lagartos estuary, it becomes a dry, abstract setting for some sci-fi movie in which stark, savage-looking agaves neatly alternate with stunted chit palms in a spartan equilibrium. The dune is so low that from the elevation of the van seat I can see the narrow beach—part of the sea turtles' nesting grounds that Joann and ProNatura are helping the government to protect. At one point, a gray fox dashes across the road. I wonder where, in this dry, sandy world, it can find fresh water to drink.

The roadbed is firm and better graded now, the going easier. In the lagoon, salt pans extend for miles, anywhere from four to forty acres in size, gleaming in the sun, their rectangular surfaces only mildly ruffled by the wind. Depending on the degree of their salinity, they display a range of colors that run the spectrum from pale aquamarine to vermilion. Also depending on the salinity, the low paddylike levees that separate them are or are not bedecked with hundreds of gulls, cormorants, shorebirds.

Presently, far out in the lagoon beyond the salt pans, the water turns a lobster pink. I drive out along one of the tracks atop the levees to get a closer look. There are thousands of flamingos out there, far more than at Celestún, like a mist catching the first light of rosy-fingered dawn. When I turn off the engine, I can hear their distant gooselike voices. At Río Lagartos, I have been told, there will be a guide and boat for hire, so tomorrow I will have a closer look.

On the landward side of the estuary, a couple of sudden pointed hills, covered with scrub, loom above the mangrove forest. Only they aren't hills. The Maya were here, mining the high-grade salt deposits thousands of years before the white man came.

Salt is what Las Coloradas is all about. When I pass through the little company town, with its few rows of cement block and wood-and-thatch houses, the place seems almost deserted. No sign of Manuel and his friends, or the rusty gray car.

Then, after a few more miles of tall yucca and short palms and wind-whipped sea, the road turns sharply south and crosses a bridge to the mainland at a bottleneck narrowing of the lagoon. From here on there is a stunning series of landscape transitions, a hop-skip-and-a-jump from one ecological zone to another. First come the mangroves, then dense tropical woodland interspersed with lovely little lagoons and marshy savannahs, hammocks, and strands of palms. I stop the van now and then and scout the water edges with the binocs. Egrets and great blue herons stalk their own reflections, and coots bob among the reeds. But if any of the crocodiles for which the estuary is named are in the neighborhood, they have the good sense to keep out of sight.

As the road and I head west again, the lush, watery greenery abruptly gives way to fierce, jungly scrub. Sea grape, palms, acacias, mesquite, and assorted cacti—some very tall—struggle for footing in the dry, stony soil. Boat-billed flycatchers flash back and forth like golden ar-rows. Hawks and buzzards throw their shadows across the dusty lane.

I am told that, thanks to a timely evacuation, no lives were lost when Hurricane Gilberto ripped across this northern coast not long after I was there. And since then, Río Lagartos has put itself back together. I just hope that the ubiquitous cement block construction of modern Mexico has not replaced the wood plank walls that made so many of the brightly painted little houses here unique in Yucatán.

I am also told that the Hotel Nefertiti survived the storm, which gladdens me because I liked Don Bernardo, the proprietor, if not the hotel itself. Despite its beguiling name, it was, and presumably still is, a mega-eyesore. At five stories (two unfinished) it must be the tallest building on the coast between Progreso and Cancún, looming over the little fishing village like an upended concrete bunker.

In fairness, the thatch-roofed cabana adjoining it, the center for what little social life there is in Río Lagartos, almost excuses the exis-tence of the hotel itself. The cabana overlooks the lovely, curving bay, with its moored fishing boats and squadrons of cormorants and pelicans. You can sit on its somewhat ramshackle deck in the evenings, drinking beer, eating tiny fresh-caught shrimp, and watch the sun behind you casting out one last great net of smoldering light across the eastern sky—catching, perhaps, a flight of flamingos heading home to Las Coloradas.

So here I am on this first evening, glad to have come to roost even though I am not exactly comfortable. El Norte, humming across the deck, is a little more cold than my sweater is warm. From behind me comes a clear penetrating female voice that rises sharply above the conversational hum in the cabana's kitchen, dominating it absolutely. The voice is enunciating Spanish in the sharp-edged, self-delighting way that only someone who has triumphantly mastered all the intricacies and little nuances of a second language would be likely to employ. That, and a certain midwestern flatness in the accent, tell me I am in the near-presence of a fellow American.

I am still listening to that voice when Don Bernardo enters the cabana. He is a somber-faced man in late middle age, whose features, like those of many of the inhabitants of Río Lagartos, are decidedly more Caucasian than Indian. He takes a long look at me, sitting in windswept solitude on the deck, and comes over, frowning worriedly.

"You aren't cold?"

"Yes, but I like it out here. The sunset is very pretty."

"Ah. If pretty sunsets were money, everybody here would be rich."

We introduce ourselves, and I ask him to join me.

Don Bernardo is Río Lagartos's leading citizen, and he conducts himself accordingly. He is courteous, dignified, and very, very serious about everything. Gravely, he asks me if my room is comfortable, and complacently believes me when I stretch the truth and tell him yes. When he asks about the shrimp, I can honestly say that they are very tasty; but he is less confident of his cooks than of the Nefertiti's concrete modern decor. "Not too overcooked?" he asks doubtfully. "Americans do not like seafood overcooked. I tell them"—he waves toward the kitchen—"but they don't always listen."

As though summoned by the gesture, a woman emerges from the kitchen and swoops confidently down on us. She is well built, in her early thirties, nice-looking in a no-nonsense sort of way. Even before she takes a seat at the table and introduces herself as Susan Kepecs of Madison, Wisconsin, I knew that the voice I had heard earlier, commanding Spanish so flawlessly, must belong to her.

She jumps right in, asking where I'm from and so forth. When I de-

scribe the adventure of driving along the road from El Cuyo and getting
stuck, she is amused. Don Bernardo, however, shakes his head. "Americans should not take that road," he says flatly, as though its perils
threatened only them. And when I make a joke of my encounter with
the garrapatas, describing myself as being "*muy estúpido*" for allowing
them to colonize my body before I was even aware of them, Don Bernardo frowns. "No, no," he says, as though speaking to a child. "You
should *never* describe yourself as stupid." He gives me a grave look
through his glasses. "I do not want to offend, but it is not manly to say
such things about oneself."

I consider the various ways I might respond to this, settling finally on
no response at all.

Susan decides to change the subject. Flamingos—which she rightly
assumes I wish to see—are a topic ready at hand, so she talks about their
value as a tourist attraction. Don Bernardo seems pleased to let her take
on the role of hostess; and she, I notice, rather plays to his attention as
audience even when she addresses me: "During the winter we get some
tour groups of bird-watchers coming here; but it really isn't enough.
What we need is something else. Development is going to come. The
only question is what kind. I've been working with the government
agencies for a year to get the necessary permits—you can't imagine what
a mess that is!—so we can start a small institute for ecological
studies—"

"The students and professors would stay at my hotel," says Don Bernardo approvingly. But he has heard all this before. "You go on talking
to Susan. She knows everything. I have some small matters I must tend
to." He gets up and shakes my hand. "In the morning I will have my
guide and boat here to take you to see the flamingos." Then, as he is
about to turn away, he gives me a final sobering look. "And remember,"
he says, "a man must never describe himself as stupid. People will take
it the wrong way!"

Susan watches him depart. "He's such a wonderful man," she says.
"A real old-fashioned *patrón*. There aren't supposed to be any more of
them, but there are. I suppose it's all a bit feudal, but it works; at least
here. Everyone looks up to him and everyone depends on him. Here at
the hotel he has way more people than he needs—look at all the women
in that little kitchen, and you're the only customer! But he feels it's his
duty to support them all. And their children and great-aunts and second

cousins." According to Susan, this obligation extends to a wide range of local people, including fishermen in need of loans, the workers and hangers-on at the inland ranch he owns, the drivers and guides who work for him, the part-time girlfriends in nearby towns whose children he supports.

In an emotional way, Susan is more than a little dependent on Don Bernardo herself. Although she has a perfectly good pair of educated, liberal-minded parents of her own back in Wisconsin, she makes no bones about Don Bernardo's appeal as a father figure; she even takes his name when she lives here. She has been coming back to Río Lagartos for ten years now, ostensibly doing archaeological research for a graduate thesis on the salt-mining activities of the ancient Maya. But it is clear that her real enthusiasm and concern are invested in the present and future of Río Lagartos itself. "If you sit around that kitchen long enough, listening to the women gossiping about the same things day after day, your mind starts turning to mush," she complains smilingly. But she is proud that the talk includes her, that she is so accepted here. Around the hotel, she has become Don Bernardo's trusted second-in-command, his advisor on the future of this little out-of-the-way village.

"What I'm really afraid of is that the same thing will happen here that's happened at Cancún. There's a beautiful beach out there on the barrier island, just asking to be developed. Of course I'm worried about the flamingos and the environmental destruction; but it's the people that concern me most. Everyone here is so—I don't know—so unspoiled. They mostly just do things the way they always have. They don't know what crime is. In Cancún . . . well, you don't hear much about it, but American girls have been raped there. And to add insult to injury, you have to pay the police to fill out a crime report. Here, I can sit on the dock at three in the morning and feel perfectly safe."

When I ask Susan how the Río Lagartos nature reserve is faring, she says, "The salt operation at Las Coloradas is creating lots of ecological problems, but if I can get a research center going here, with transfer credit for American students, it would help preserve things. And it would create some jobs, bring in some money. Without changing things too much." Her eyes flash angrily. "I'd just *hate* to see the same thing happen here that's happened at Cancún!"

Susan is not yet aware that, before long, SEDUE, with the help of

ProNatura, will establish a small research station at the reserve, staffed with Mexican biologists. If she could know about that, I wonder how she would react. She is so possessive about Río Lagartos, so involved and so close to the scene. She sometimes seems to feel that the fate of the little community must depend entirely on her.

I have become fascinated by the different ways Americans adapt to life in this still not-quite-assimilated butt end of the Mexican republic. I don't mean the turistas, including itinerant flying Dutchmen like myself, but those who, for one reason or another, end up spending months, years, a whole lifetime down here.

I think, for example, of the Cobbs, living out their retired lives in Ticul. They have made a tiny corner of this land, never an English possession, temporarily, if not forever, England. They are the most benign of all possible colonialists, interested in the local culture, never condescending, always willing to smooth the rough edges where their own lives and the very different lives of their neighbors intersect; but never, even for an instant, conducting their lives in other than a very English sort of way. I think of those comradely lovers, Barbara and John, self-immured at Celestún. They are children of the Age of Liberations, so excruciatingly enlightened that they regard any prejudice as a capital sin; yet after a couple of six-month stints in the country, they are so fed up with the region's bureaucratic and social customs that they shut themselves away in their work and their shared life, knowing more about the ducks in the estuary than the fishing village where they have lived a year of their lives. I also think of the American manager of a tourist agency I met in Mérida who has lived in Yucatán for a decade and surrounds himself with expatriates like himself; and the elderly husband of a wealthy Yucatecan woman who has never learned to speak Spanish. And of course I think of Joann Andrews—without, I must admit, knowing exactly what to think. What I suspect is that she is one of those rare people who create their own worlds according to the needs of their particular personality, wherever they happen to be. She enjoys ruling the roost, no doubt, but essentially she is independent of tribal customs, whether those of equestrian Virginia or equatorial Africa or provincial Yucatán. Yucatán is simply the place where she has happened to end up; and she has made the most of it. Whatever else, she is no exile in a foreign land. No more, at least, than truly individual people are wherever they happen to live.

And now I think of Susan Kepecs. In contrast to Barbara and John at Celestún, she is ardently engaged in the life of this little fishing village. And unlike the Cobbs, when she lives here, she leaves as much of her nationality behind her as she can. Indeed, she has very little good to say about her own country, the fountainhead of crass commercialism and materialistic values, of social hypocrisy and injustice. She enjoys going native, and she particularly likes being accepted as a member in good standing of Don Bernardo's extended family.

She is, in fact, a mass of contradictions. In one respect she is a sort of cross between a missionary and a Peace Corps worker, preaching a gospel of enlightened change. Yet at the same time she wants desperately to keep foreign influences of any kind out of Río Lagartos. She loves its people just the way they are even as she laments the narrowness and mind-killing banality of their uneventful lives. She tolerates and even seems to need in Don Bernardo a deeply Hispanic masculine dominance that she would not put up with for a minute in her own father or any other American male. And she wants to save Río Lagartos not just from Us, but from Itself.

After we have talked for some time about her life here, I remark that it's too bad people aren't flamingos. We could put them in reserves. She laughs, but she isn't really amused. It's no joke, after all. Sooner or later she must decide either to confront or just plain ignore the schizophrenic dilemma that troubles the sleep of all well-intentioned people who share the modern-day version of the White Man's Burden: how to go about destroying less complicated Third World cultures in order to save them.

I am tempted to suggest that she might want to shift her priorities: If she concentrated on saving the flamingos and the estuary for their own sakes, these simple fisherfolk might inadvertently end up saving themselves without any other help from her. But I have a feeling she doesn't want to hear this.

"I don't know," she sighs. "I sometimes think I understand the people here better than they understand themselves. *I* understand *them;* but they don't understand *me.* There are just some barriers that you can't ever break through. "

SEVEN

Cancún

You either like the big, splashy resort scenes or you don't. Personally, I don't; but I have nothing against Cancún. It's easy to make jokes about this encapsulated Xanadu on the shores of the tropical sea. But from my own specialized point of view, Cancún is a tradeoff. Inevitably, it and its resort satellites have loused up miles of lovely Caribbean coastline; but they have also deferred, quite inadvertently, a lot of environmental mayhem in the rest of Quintana Roo. The natural resources of this long-isolated region of the peninsula were due to be exploited by government planners whether a Miami-Beach-in-exile had materialized here or not. Some ill-conceived projects were already under way even as Cancún was a-building. Consider the program that encouraged local ejidos to switch from milpa agriculture to cattle ranching. Only after hundreds of thousands of acres of forests and jungles had been duly burned and cleared did everyone discover to their great amazement that most of Quintana Roo's stony and porous soils were incapable of becoming productive grazing land. Other quick-fix schemes were in the works—still are—but by the late 1970s, the sudden excrescence of Cancún was attracting thousands of surplus young Maya, not to mention surplus young Mexicans from other regions, to its bright lights, like the proverbial moths to the beckoning flame.

This internal migration has helped slow the destruction of Quintana Roo's natural environment. What it does to and for all those surplus young Maya is another question—one for which Barbara Montes, a Cancún resident since almost before the place existed, has a blunt and ready answer: "The minute they move here, they're lost."

"Here" is Cancún City, not Cancún. Hardly anyone actually *lives* in Cancún, the glitzy hotel zone strung out along the slender strand of beach that separates Laguna Nichupte from the Caribbean. The people whose livelihoods depend on the resort do their living in the service city a mile or two inland. Only it isn't just for service people anymore.

Thanks to an invasion of budget-conscious and/or adventure-seeking tourists, Cancún City has become a resort town in its own right, offering a less packaged sort of nightlife than they would get in the plush enclaves on the beach. Despite the computerized programing that went into its planning, the place has outgrown itself several times over. Ironically, a new service population has been spawned to service the service city. Waiters and busboys have as rough a time finding affordable lodging here as they do in Aspen, buses are packed, drugs circulate, and the broad expanses of the Avenida Tulum are choked with bumper-to-bumper traffic.

There aren't many places where you can escape the hustle and the noise, but Barbara Montes's home, hidden by high walls in a comfortable cul-de-sac on the eastern edge of town, is one of them. The only sound, other than our own voices and the rattle of coffee cups, comes from the cool fall of water in a stone fountain. The fountain is enclosed in a miniature glass-walled atrium at the edge of the raised living room.

Barbara Montes is telling me what it was like to live here during the early 1970s, when Cancún was rising, almost overnight, from the mangrove swamps. "If anyone saw the change as it happened, I did. When we first came here in the early 1970s, there was no land link with Chetumal; the road ended at Tulum. Isla Mujeres was the only tourist spot on the coast back then, and my husband had a boating business there. Even though he came from a wealthy family, he worked when it suited him; and he loved boats. In 1976, when tourists started coming to Cancún, he moved the business here. In those days it was what the Gold Coast in California must have been like: the dirt was flying, everything was expensive, there was a scarcity of goods; the hotels were going up three or four at a time and the 'dozers were filling in the mangrove swamps for the golf course. . . . After that, things settled down for a few years; everything was planted, it was sort of peaceful, we knew everyone. But then it all started booming again. I can't say I like what's happened. There's supposed to be a moratorium on new construction in 1992, but the 'controlled growth' has already gotten out of hand. It's a benefit, of course, that people have jobs and all that. They still keep flocking in from all over Mexico, not just Yucatán. They want the economic opportunity, the healthier environment. But how many places can handle a growth rate of 25 percent a year? There used to be no crime, but now there's a lot of drugs coming in from Belize. Just a few months ago this house was broken into. It's really sort of sad. I don't even know the place anymore."

Barbara Montes presents this account of Cancún before-and-after in a flat, disengaged voice, as though she were reading from a newspaper. She isn't disengaged—anything but—yet this is the way she wants to come across: all business, even when the business at hand is, with her, a passionate avocation.

In some ways she is the counterpart in Quintana Roo of her good friend, Joann Andrews, in Mérida. Her efforts, however, are more concentrated. She and the citizens conservation group she has helped to found, Amigos de Sian Ka'an, are concerned exclusively with a single, crucially important project: the preservation of Sian Ka'an, an enormous biosphere reserve further south along the coast, which I will soon be visiting.

Even if she were not important to my own interests, I would have heard of Barbara Montes here and there along the line. Like Joann, when she took a husband, she also married Mexico. A New Yorker, she moved to hectic California in the 1960s, and became a buyer for a chain of specialty shops. Then, in 1969, she went to Puerto Vallarta on a vacation. And there, in the sort of encounter that normally occurs only in a Hollywood script, she met a dashing Hispanic man with a cultured voice who promptly fell in love with her. They married, and for several years led a drifting sort of life: a year in a fishing village south of Puerto Vallarta, a couple of years in Mexico City, another year in Sonora on the Sea of Cortés, and then a move to Yucatán where Barbara's husband had his roots. He was, as it happened, the scion of the Monteses, that fabled Yucatecan dynasty that, along with the Molinas (into whose family his grandfather had married), once enjoyed an all but absolute control over the henequen market in the years before the Revolution came to the peninsula. Montes, according to some reports, had problems being the sole heir to a distinguished family name. He was something of a rebel; and although he sometimes chose to live in out-of-the-way places, he also apparently liked to travel in the fast lane, literally and figuratively. Not long before he died in an auto accident, he and Barbara had separated. There were no children, so the Montes name died with him.

Barbara still maintains close ties with her in-laws. "My mother-in-law and a few of her friends were the last of the old high society, the real casta divina. I remember her reading the newspaper and exclaiming, 'Oh, another mixed marriage!' They all knew the old stories, all the details of who pulled off a great financial coup when, and who got what in the wills. They didn't go in for the 'high life' though. They weren't trying to impress anybody. It was all very Catholic, ultraconservative, family-related. To tell the truth, I found it pretty suffocating. So did my husband. He was elegant and well mannered, very much of that world; but he was a nonconformist, a critic of his own background. A lot of those families still live off the old money, or their names and social position. But he didn't care about any of that. . . . It's true, though, that whether he did or not, he *was* a Montes and was accepted everywhere. You could get away with a lot if you belonged to the old society."

Barbara Montes looks around her very modern home—her "sanctuary" as she calls it. "Some of my cousins-in-law are like sisters to me. The whole family has been wonderful. One or another of them is always calling me out of the blue. So I don't get lonely. . . . But I could never go back to that way of life."

She has her own life now. At the time of this first meeting, she is a successful real estate agent, selling time-shares, although she will later give that up. She does not strike me as a particularly "happy" woman; but it is obvious that she is proud of her independence, her self-reliance.

She is saying: "Like a lot of people who watched what has happened here—who participated in what has happened—I felt a strong personal need to 'save' some part of this wonderful coastal area."

"Ah," I remark innocently, "so Sian Ka'an is sort of a way of making amends?"

"What? Amends?" She repeats the word as though it had distasteful connotations. "Amends? Certainly not. The only way I would make 'amends' for something would be to stop doing it. The fact is, the development was going to happen anyway, whatever I did or didn't do."

I had already been very much aware that she was an exceedingly handsome woman. Now, when her feathers are a little ruffled, she is out-and-out beautiful. She fixes me with a cool, put-down stare. In a firm, quiet voice she says, "I've never been sorry for anything I've done."

I feel chastised. And impressed. Also fascinated. I wish that, like Barbara Montes, I could never be sorry for things I've done. And that, like her, I could learn how to start over, start living a satisfyingly independent, not-too-lonely life. I would like to talk to her about such things. But she isn't having any of that. The fascination, alas, is not mutual. After an hour of trying to make myself seem interesting, my only claim to her attention is my potential usefulness as an ally in the effort to save Sian Ka'an.

She has picked up where she left off: "Even before I came here, I was always interested in nature, in anything that moved, really; but it wasn't a developed taste. When my husband and I lived south of Puerto Vallarta, there wasn't much to do besides go boating. No electricity or telephone or anything. I got to be friendly with a giant iguana on the terrace. I'd watch a tarantula for hours. And there was a snake that liked to stretch itself out on the windowsill. Afraid? No, not at all. I'm the sort who, if I see a boa sunning itself, I want to see if I can touch it. . . . But it wasn't until we lived in Sonora that I got seriously interested in wildlife, particularly birds. I had Blake's bird book with me, and I guess that started me off. I became very intense about it. I began taking photographs. It's a serious hobby now. I'm working on a guidebook of Yucatán birds."

Of Amigos de Sian Ka'an, she says, "It's not like in the States, you know. The reason we were able to come into existence was because international conservation groups prefer to give funds to nongovernmental organizations in developing nations. But in Mexico the only way a nongovernmental organization can work is if the government more or less supports it. So it isn't always easy. The advantage that Amigos has is that everyone, from the fishermen on the reserve to the businessmen in Cancún, has a practical interest in making Sian Ka'an work. But it's a constant effort. Really, it takes a lot to burn me out, but there are times . . ." Her voice trails off, then comes on strong again: "The important thing is that we're surviving. We've started several management programs with the ejidos in and around the reserve. All sorts of projects: drip agriculture, which doesn't use as much land as milpa, the cultivation of wild fruits, handicrafts, like making baskets out of vines. There are about 800 people living within the reserve's boundaries, and the trick is to keep them living in harmony with it. You have to work within the culture, of course; good intentions aren't enough. It took a year and a half to get our ejido projects going. The people had to identify their own needs and ask for the help. If you're from the government, they don't want to hear what you have to say. In Mexico, when the government changes, it changes from top to bottom, so programs have no continuity. But we have our own paid Maya agricultural technicians working with the people now, and other ejidos are expressing interest. The Indians aren't dumb, you know; if they see the advantage, they'll accept it. If we can just get things going at Sian Ka'an, we can export what we're doing to the rest of Quintana Roo. And if we do that, we'll have done what we set out to do."

She smiles a businesslike smile, a little pinched around the edges, and glances at her watch. She has an appointment with someone who may be interested in buying a time-share in a condominium. "It isn't just the problem of dealing with the people on the reserve," she says, seeing me out. "If it were, it wouldn't be so bad. . . . But I'd better not get started on that. Let's just say you need time and a lot of patience. I just hope we have enough of both." Another quick, brisk smile, friendly but dismissive. "For now, anyway—you'll see for yourself—Sian Ka'an is in pretty good shape."

Barbara Montes had left the "problem that isn't just—" hanging in the air. She is too discreet to talk politics with someone like me. But I have a pretty good idea what she alludes to, as would anyone, resident or not, who is even briefly exposed to how the system works in Mexico. As far as I know, it is unique to that country—and, since I keep referring to it in a piecemeal sort of way, I might as well say my piece about it here.

If you can imagine the liberal and far-left wings of the Democratic party controlling all three branches of government in the United States, at both the federal and state level, *for seventy years*, you might have some conception of how things operate south of the border. What you end up with is a government of, for, and by bureaucracy. Huge government agencies, all dependent on a single more-or-less socialist political party, all underfunded and overstaffed, almost all corrupt to varying degrees, control every aspect of the country's political and economic life. Unlike more totalitarian regimes, however, this bureaucratic system is not overtly oppressive. Democratic forms are carefully maintained, "equality" is celebrated, and opposing candidates within the PRI, the dominant governing party, often have genuinely different platforms. Private enterprise is tolerated for the good and sufficient reason that it is the only viable sector of the nation's economy. And even within the bureaucracy itself, individual administrators sometimes beat the odds, gallantly initiating sensible programs, accomplishing some good things. Yet, in principle and in practice, it is against the interests of the central government—that is, the PRI—to encourage its own agencies, or the unions, or the ejidos, or businesses whether private or government-controlled, or even private nonprofit organizations like Amigos de Sian Ka'an, to run their own shows and do too good a job of it. That sort of initiative fosters independence of action—a desire to break away from government control altogether; and that is the last thing that the PRI and its huge party-controlled agencies want to see happen. Therefore, new initiatives are deliberately discouraged if they in any way challenge federal authority. Better that the ejidos should remain in debt peonage to the national banks, that the whole economy should operate on a colossal workfare-welfare system, that the nation, which is as rich in resources as the United States, should remain chronically poor, than that this unwieldy one-party bureaucratic system should be modified, much less dismantled.

The instructive thing is that the system does work, in the sense that it successfully perpetuates itself. Most of Mexico's citizens are in some way dependent on it. There is no need for death squads or a KGB or anything like that. A certain amount of carefully rationed protest is allowed. And if any dissatisfied wheel in the collective machinery squeaks loud enough—for example, a big labor union demanding a pay raise— it gets a bit of what oil there is to go around. For the rest, intimidation works wonders. If the enterprising campesinos on an ejido try to sell their produce without going through the government middleman, their debt to the national bank comes suddenly due. If a businessman supports an opposition party, his income tax is ruthlessly audited by the same tax collector he's been paying off for years—which means that he faces potential bankruptcy, since Mexican income tax levels are deliberately maintained at levels too high for anyone to actually pay. And of course, if a worker in a government agency should make any waves at all, he wakes up one morning without a job. There are no directives

from on high, no official policy, concerning all this. Powerful bureaucrats and politicians at the grassroots level take care of their own
troublemakers.

Very well, then; but in practice, how does all this affect a private
group like Amigos de Sian Ka'an? Barbara Montes would not say. But
the next day I will meet a man named Arturo Ornat who is a little more
forthcoming. He has handed in his resignation as director of Amigos,
and is about to return to his native Spain. He is an austerely beautiful
man in his early thirties who—give him a tonsure and a cassock—could
have stepped out of an El Greco painting of a saint. He is a zoologist
who knows a lot about tropical ecosystems, but perhaps not enough
about human nervous systems and the egos that control them. "I am
told I am introverted," he says in his deep, quiet voice. "Am I? I don't
know. I like sports, after all. . . . But perhaps it is true that I don't understand people."

No one had asked him to resign. Ostensibly, he is going home to finish up his doctorate. But in fact he feels that he had become a liability
to Amigos. He had made himself unpopular with people in the state and
federal agencies that control Sian Ka'an by criticizing their policies, or
lack of policy, in public.

"I hope new times are ahead," Arturo sighs. "The country's current
president, Salinas, is more open to private groups, not a hard-liner. He
is something of an ecologist, an intellectual. Still, he cannot change
the PRI. . . .

"What can they do to us? Well, they can keep us from doing our
work. We have begun these projects; but they say that it is the government agencies that should do that, that we do not have the authority.
Never mind that they do not have money, and that they can offer no
continuity to the research. It is *their* reserve. They want to put us in a
box, to be a cocktail group that raises money and gives it to them. So
we protest."

We are sitting on the screened porch of the Ornats' home in Puerto
Morelos, a pleasant pink-roofed beach house in the northern part of
town. In the big, comfortably ramshackle living room, Arturo's pretty
wife is carrying on a running conversation with their two young children, keeping them out of our way. "Mexicans are very good at not making decisions," says Arturo, sounding like an American. "There should

be decisions made about how to divide the work at Sian Ka'an: what should be the role of SEDUE, the state government, the private groups, the ejidos. . . . That's what is really missing, the coordination, the setting of long-term goals. That's what I said in the newspapers."

He smiles a melancholy smile that would have made El Greco's heart go flip-flop. "My successor, the new director of Amigos, is very committed and he has no enemies. He has worked for SEDUE so he understands the politics. You see, so far we have been working as a group of friends, concentrating on the biology, the ecology of Sian Ka'an. But we are not expert at administration. Probably it is time for Amigos to be more stabilized, more politically astute. The new director is better at that than I am."

I have the sad feeling that this gentle-minded man has the sad feeling that he has failed. I wish I could cheer him up, but I don't know what to say.

A month later, in Chetumal, I will have a long conversation with Alberto Rodriguez Hernandez, who is in charge of SEDUE's Department of Ecology in Quintana Roo. His doctorate is in hydrological engineering, and he doesn't know a thing in the world about ecology; but he is wonderfully candid and up-front for a bureaucrat, and, amazingly, he doesn't care whether I quote him or not. Almost cheerfully, he confirms one after another of the criticisms that outsiders make about Mexico's government agencies. He says he does his best against the odds, and I believe him. He has actually succeeded in adding a couple of biologists and a botanist to his staff of thirty-five "including secretaries." However, most of the personnel, he admits, are hopeless. "They are just transferred from the Department of Public Works. They belong to the union, so of course they won't work after three in the afternoon, or on weekends. I'm ashamed to say that two or three people carry most of the work around here, but there's nothing I can do about that."

In the same outspoken way, he holds forth about the disappearance of funds, the inadequacies of fiscal budgets ("My six game wardens are hired by the year"), the lack of communication between government departments, the low salaries ("I am paid the most and I only earn $300 a month!"), and the tangles of red tape that must be dealt with.

In a way, this is a familiar litany. In the States and everywhere else, bureaucrats complain, almost always off the record, about some of the same problems. But it's a matter of degree. In Quintana Roo as in all of Mexico, such problems are about as serious as they can get. The sense of inertia is crippling. Arturo Ornat was right about that: there is no direction, no setting of realistic long-term goals.

Señor Rodriguez Hernandez is willing, even eager, to acknowledge these shortcomings. Yet the most interesting thing that this bright and rather likable man reveals is an attitude of which he himself is perhaps not aware: unworkable as it is, he does not really want the system to change. Why not? Because he intuitively understands that any real change in the status quo would involve a challenge to his authority. And of that, he is very, very jealous.

When I mention Amigos de Sian Ka'an and Arturo Ornat, his brows knit in a small frown. Suddenly he seems a different sort of person.

"Los Amigos? Well, let us say it is an organization that has good intentions. What is wrong is that they want to rule the reserve. And that is not possible! Sian Ka'an has to be ruled by SEDUE. That is the federal law. What happened was that the SEDUE manager of the reserve—the ex-manager—got into a very friendly relationship with Amigos. He gave them a lot of influence in the reserve. Somehow he started to make his own decisions about such things." He pauses, stares out the window of his large, bleak office. "And he was a subordinate of mine. I don't believe that was correct, do you?"

In a way, I can see his point. At first glance, the situation seems analogous to, say, letting the Sierra Club take over research projects or make policy decisions at a U.S. national wildlife refuge. Actually, that might not be a bad idea, considering how the Department of Interior runs those refuges. But the comparison doesn't really hold up. In the United States, the government may do a poor job of managing the refuges, but they are managed. In Mexico they aren't. Moreover, in the United States, private conservation organizations can harass or cooperate with public agencies as they please. In Mexico, they either cooperate, or they are the ones harassed. Ironically, Sian Ka'an is perhaps the only large natural reserve in Mexico (though it may soon be joined by Calakmul) where a major effort is being made to work up an ecological inventory and to educate the indigenous human population to apply principles of sustainable yield. But SEDUE can't possibly do this job on its own. Which is why Sian Ka'an can use all the amigos it can get.

The issue that is surfacing here, however, has much more to do with territorial imperatives than with ecological goals. Señor Rodriguez Hernandez is saying, "Not long ago, Arturo Ornat came by to 'shake hands,' so to speak. He said he wanted to start a new stage of cooperation between SEDUE and Amigos. I told him I was pleased with his attitude. But the problem, as I see it, is that there are *political* intentions on the part of Amigos. I don't know what sort. I'm confused myself. But with all these articles, these criticisms of SEDUE and myself . . . it cannot be as simple as it seems to be."

I want to tell him that it really is that simple: that there are some people out there who just want to save Sian Ka'an; that all they want to do is make the reserve work. But I can see that Señor Rodriguez Hernandez's mind isn't operating on that level. He honestly wouldn't understand.

I'm feeling a bit confused myself about the ins and outs of the situation by the time I head back to my hotel. But one thing seems clear. If the new director matches up to Arturo Ornat's description of a man who can work with government agencies (and time will prove, happily, that he can), then Amigos de Sian Ka'an needs him badly.

Cancún City isn't as expensive as the Hotel Zone on the beach, but it's still one of the pricier watering holes for tourists in Mexico. However, on this visit there are still several reasonably priced little restaurants north of the bus station on Avenida Tulum. Their days, however, are numbered. They will soon be cleared away, along with the block that housed them, to make way for a huge McDonald's (or is it Burger King?) geared to make money from—guess who? Not tourists so much as the city's service people who come here on their nights off.

That belongs to the immediate future, however. Tonight, after eating at the budget restaurants three evenings in a row, I decide that I'll behave like a proper tourist and take dinner at one of the classier establishments south of the glorieta. It is pretty late, and there are only a few other diners at the restaurant I select, so I have my waiter almost to myself. We strike up a conservation. His name is Cristino. He has a nice friendly way about him that is more than a matter of angling for a tip. He tells me he comes from a small village east of Valladolid, where his father is a campesino. He is 20. He has five brothers and sisters, all younger than he and still at home. He has been working in Cancún City for almost a year. "I want to get a good job at a hotel, you know, but it's not easy. My friend, Ernesto, works at the front desk, and he is trying to help me. But I need to learn more English."

He seems pleased by my interest in him; and when I have finished eating and paid the check, he asks if I have any plans for the rest of the evening. I tell him I am as free as a bird. "Well, then," he says, "I am off duty now, and my friends have already started celebrating. Maybe you would like to join us?" He adds quickly, "You don't pay. The drinks are free."

"A celebration?" I ask, not much wanting to butt in on a wedding party or something like that.

"Yes, yes," he says, "Antonio is going to your country."

He points to the rear of the restaurant. The place is otherwise almost empty, but back there, a couple of tables have been put together to accommodate seven or eight men, some still in their white waiter's shirts. I had half heard the sudden spurts of laughter, the chattering voices coming from that direction, but until now I'd been too busy paying attention to Cristino and a plate of pompano and prawns to look in that direction. Now, when Cristino assures me I really would be welcome, I decide, Why not? and let him lead the way.

Antonio is beaming, and a little bit foxed. He wants to know right away where I am from, and when I tell him, he says in English, "For me is Peetsburgh in Pennsla—Pennseelvania. Do you know this place? This Peetsburgh?"

I tell him I only visited it once a long time ago, but that it seemed like an interesting city.

"Seelvia says it is very nice place that I will like."

I take a seat and am handed a glass, a half a lime, and the bottle of tequila that is being passed around. Cristino introduces me to everyone at the table. Three or four of the young men, including the guest of honor, Antonio, are waiters or busboys at the restaurant. But there is also Cristino's friend Ernesto, who works at a nearby hotel, and a couple of off-duty waiters from other restaurants. Now and then the rather harried-looking manager of this establishment, Felipe, sits with us, but never for long.

"Now I go to Peetsburgh, I wish I speak better English," Antonio says to me. He is a handsome fellow, more mestizo-looking than Mayan, with a bland, dazed smile. "Better!" says one of his buddies in Spanish. "You don't speak English at all!" Everyone laughs, including Antonio. "Your girlfriend isn't bringing you to the United States for your good conversation," says Felipe, who is making one of his brief appearances at the table. Another round of laughter. "Green card, green card," one of the other waiters intones in a hunching, panting voice.

For my benefit, Ernesto, the hotel clerk, explains that Sylvia is a turista who fell in love with Antonio while she was down here on a vacation. She has sent him a plane ticket and money to get him to Pittsburgh, and will sponsor him when he applies for a green card—a work permit. "Cristino and I met her when she and Antonio were at the disco Caramba one night. Nice looking. Good dancer. She's rich. Has her own car, apartment, everything." He rolls his eyes toward the ceiling. "Why doesn't God give me a girl like that who will pay my way to the United States? Only Miami, not Pittsburgh."

"Does it happen often?" I ask.

"Like that? No. They don't take us back with them. But here! While they're here, they pay our way. With my help, even Cristino gets girls, right, Cristino? And he's just a dumb Maya, not good-looking like me!"

Cristino grins sheepishly.

"That's what the American girls come here for," says Felipe. "I see it all the time. They go after the waiters—"

"Hotel clerks too!" Ernesto interjects.

"—like they were going shopping. In my opinion, it makes them feel more powerful. It's like they are buying a person."

"So what?" Ernesto exclaims. "They can buy me anytime. But it's not really that. They just want to go crazy, to have a good time."

Casually, I remark that I have heard that the American girls occasionally get in trouble. Felipe frowns. "It is as I said. They think, some of them, they are buying a toy, and they can play with it or not. Sometimes the toy doesn't like that."

"Nobody gets in trouble that I know about," says Ernesto. He throws an arm around my shoulder. "We love Americans."

One of the other waiters chimes in: "Americans are all right. They spend money. It's the Italians and French I don't like. They nag all the time and don't tip."

Someone says, "Antonio loves Americans for sure!" and Antonio, looking glazed, waves his glass of tequila at everyone.

Felipe makes a wry face. "Actually, it is the truth. We 'love' Americans. This place was made for the Americans. The kind of food, the way people dress, everything. We want to be like you. Nobody cares what happens as long as you Americans go home happy. You know, even the wealthy Mexicans don't come to Cancún anymore. They feel out of place. In their own country! If a Mexican family comes in here, you watch; my waiters treat them differently. If some blonde nice-looking Americans come in and ask for shrimp brochette, those shrimp brochette come out of the kitchen flaming. But for the Mexican family, no."

While finishing this last sentence, Felipe gets to his feet and heads toward the front of the restaurant, as though his commentary has reminded him of his duties. Two couples, evidently Americans, are still being served by a lone waiter. He hovers over one table, then the other, making himself agreeable.

I divide my attention between Ernesto, who is frankly drunk, and Cristino, who is beginning to mellow out. After a third hit of tequila on top of the beers I'd had with dinner, I am somewhere in between.

Ernesto comes from Izamal, a large, picturesque colonial town, all faded yellows, between Mérida and Tizimín. He is older, better educated, and more sophisticated than Cristino, and speaks English quite well. His family, though poor, is blue-collar urban. "When I finished primary school, my father said, 'All right, if you must study more, you can; but I can't help you.' So I said okay, I would do it on my own. So I went to Mérida and studied very hard for five years. The government gave me a *beca*—a grant—but I needed to pay for books, food, room, everything, so I got a job as a cashier at a bank. It was very hard for me, working from nine until two, and then going to school from three to eight. And at night, I studied. After five years, my father said, 'That is enough education. Now is a good time to help me.' He is a truck driver, and makes 3,000 pesos a day, which is not enough for a family to live on, not now with all this inflation. So I told him I would go to Cancún, and either make the money to help him, or else, if I was a failure, I would come home."

"It's hard to save money here in Cancún," says Cristino. "It's too expensive."

Ernesto vigorously concurs. "I am earning 10,000 pesos a day, 300,000 a month; but a tiny apartment costs 200,000."

"My room costs 120,000," says Cristino. "But there is no water, no toilet. Only one for the whole floor."

"Everything is different here. At home it doesn't cost as much. And it is more quiet, traditional, you know? But if you want to sleep with a girl, a nice girl, you have to know her two years and then you have to marry her. And I can't afford to marry anyway. Here, I find an American girl and we go dancing and I sleep with her the first night. And she pays! But still, there are clothes, haircuts, other things. . . . What I need is to work for a bigger hotel and make more money. But it's always the Mexicans who get the best jobs. For instance, if you are working for a hotel and you want to be an assistant manager, do you think the boss will promote you if you are a Yucatecan? No way! He tells his company to send someone from Mexico. Even the government does that. . . . Do you know the main thing I have been able to do for my family so far? I have bought them a refrigerator. And I help pay for my brothers' education. Before they were on the lowest step, but now, because of me, they are moving one step higher, you understand? You know what my father told me? He said, 'You are very smart because you are making money. I have worked all my life but I couldn't buy a refrigerator; and you have bought one after working only a little while in Cancún.' I didn't say anything. I didn't want to hurt my father. I didn't want to tell him that the reason he could never buy a refrigerator was because he had no education!"

Cristino listens quietly while Ernesto talks. He tends to defer to his friend; and I suspect it is not just because Ernesto is the more experienced hand, and may help to get him a job at a hotel. Ernesto is Hispanic-looking. Cristino, if he is not pure Maya, might as well be. We talk frankly about this, now that, as another bottle of tequila makes the rounds, Cristino is catching up with me and I am catching up with Ernesto.

Does Cristino think there is prejudice against the Maya? "No-o-o," he says, then reconsiders. "Well, yes. There is some. The higher class are the mestizos, and they can order the Maya to do anything."

"I don't order you to do anything," Ernesto growls.

"Yes, you do," Cristino smiles. "But not in a bad way. Some people do it in a bad way. And sometimes they act like you are not even there."

For a fleeting second, I see Anita and her family staring through the ejido women at Uayamón. As though they weren't there.

"The Mexicans call all of us mestizos," says Ernesto. "It's our accent. But in a way they're right; we're all mixed. There's more Indian blood in Yucatecans than in people anywhere else in the country, but the real difference is that if you grow up in the country speaking Mayan, then you're Maya; and if you grow up in town speaking Spanish, you're mestizo—'Spanish.'"

"Well, I am not mixed blood," says Cristino. "I am real Maya. My father and mother both were Maya. The first five years of my life, until I went to school, Maya was all I spoke. That is why the Maya are the poorest people. They don't know how to change. It is a tradition with them, especially on the ejidos. Some of them don't even like to go to town because they don't have preparation. The government is trying to teach them; but it is very hard for them because they know they can't speak Spanish well. My family is like that. They are not so ambitious because they don't have the education. My brother works in Valladolid, but he doesn't make any money because he is only an ignorant Maya. And my father is the same. He didn't want me to go to Cancún. He said, 'Who is going to help me with the milpa?' Now he doesn't say that anymore because I send him money to buy the corn and other things. But he is still poor and ignorant. He doesn't understand that I want to improve myself." Cristino shakes his head. "It's hard. First I had to learn to speak good Spanish, and now I must learn to speak good English."

"Ha!" snorts Ernesto. "Do you know what they are doing now in Mérida? They are teaching the Maya language in the schools! Talk about dumb!"

Cristino nods but he is not really listening. He seems far away. Impulsively, I ask him the question I seem to want to ask everybody.

"Lonely?" He thinks about that for a second. "Yes-s-s. Yes. Sometimes I am lonely here. But I go home every two weeks. I am glad to see my mother and little sisters. And my father. Only, when the time is up, I am ready to come back to Cancún."

"Here I find him girls," Ernesto says in a voice that is becoming very blurred indeed. "Even though he's a dumb Maya and can't dance; or speak good English."

Cristino unfurls his good-natured smile. "I get girls right here, at the restaurant. Ask Felipe."

Felipe has returned to the table, but he doesn't sit down. "All right, you drunks," he says. "I've got to close this place soon, so you better drink up. Has anyone wished Antonio good luck? This is supposed to be his goodbye party, you know." He lifts the half-empty glass he had left at the table and says, "To Antonio!" We all loudly echo him.

Antonio is in a state of beatific, drunken bliss. He lifts his own glass "To Seelvia!" and everybody shouts, "To Sylvia!"

Ernesto, who can hardly hold up his head, nevertheless hoists his glass on high. "To Pittsburgh," he mutters.

The rest of us bellow, "To Pittsburgh! To Pittsburgh!" The friends on either side of Antonio pound him on the back.

I find myself thinking soap opera thoughts: What is she like, this Princess Charming, this Sylvia de Peetsburgh? Does she really mean to rescue Antonio or simply buy him? Will they live happily, if not forever after, at least long enough for Antonio to take root in the United States?

While the near-empty bottle is making its last round, I suddenly remember Palenque and the beautiful Elizabeta. I wonder what has happened to her. What will happen to her. Or Armando, for that matter. Or Barbara and John. But then I remind myself that much of the pleasure of meeting people on a journey lies in the fact that you can't stay tuned in to the ongoing story. You never have to know how the tale ends. I have had enough of that, of knowing how things end.

EIGHT

Sian Ka'an

People who have been where I am coming from will know how it is: The everyday background grief is one thing. The totally unanticipated shocks of anguish—as though the dying and the death had happened yesterday—are something else. They spring at you without warning from the nowhere of some random association. Tonight, for some reason, I impulsively removed the long-expired packet of air freshener that had been dangling from the rearview mirror ever since I bought the van three years ago. I had hung it there in a futile effort to defend the nice new upholstery from the aroma of our much cherished old mutt, Teddy, who smelled to high heaven no matter how often he was bathed. He had died at a ripe old age just a month or so before I left on this journey. Occasionally the faint trace of his doggy smell still hovers in the van when there is no air stirring. It wasn't the thought of Teddy, however, but the absentminded act of removing the useless packet of deodorizer that suddenly summoned the dead voice—not talking to me, but to the dog: "Don't listen to him, Teddy," it said soothingly. "He doesn't mean it. Of course you don't 'stink.' You just smell a little bit strong."

Just that, the smiling voice coming as from a living presence sitting in the seat beside me. That, and the memory of the long, beautiful hands ruffling Teddy's ears.

But I am learning. There is no way to brace myself against the first sudden rip of pain, like adhesive being yanked from a half-healed wound. But I can take deep breaths and remind myself that these moments come less frequently now, that I am doing better. Deliberately I herd my thoughts away like schoolchildren from the scene of a terrible accident.

I concentrate on the fireflies. There are hundreds of them turning themselves on and off around the van. Soon after dark a brief but heavy rain had fallen, and now that it is over the fireflies have decided to put on this light show for my benefit.

The van is perched where you wouldn't expect to find one, not even in a television commercial. Namely, a jungle hammock in the middle of a vast mangrove swamp on the southern edge of Sian Ka'an. The little sortie that has ended up here will be the last of my attempts—they can only be attempts—to explore the great reserve and its surroundings.

I count my blessings. It has been a wonderful day—the last and maybe the best of a whole run of wonderful days that had begun with the chicleros' trail, and the almost-meeting with the phantom jaguar. I just have to keep reminding myself that things are getting better. That I am getting better . . .

In Maya, Sian Ka'an means "birth of the sky," though nobody now knows just how this area of southern Quintana Roo came by the name. At any rate, even if the significance is lost, the reserve is large enough to handle a name like that—1.3 million acres, or roughly a tenth of the surface of Quintana Roo (although that includes a lot of reef and open water). Calakmul may rival it someday if proclamations can be translated into policy, but right now Sian Ka'an is the premiere biosphere reserve in Mexico and one of the last great wild places remaining in Central America. Despite the lack of adequate funding, and the aforementioned conflicts between state, federal, and private agencies, it does exist in fact. There are surveyed boundaries. There are wardens. There is a research station where a few on-again, off-again research studies are conducted. And as Barbara Montes says, some headway is being made in efforts to get the people, mostly fishermen, who live in the reserve, and the several thousand others who live on the surrounding ejidos, to coexist with their environment instead of destroying it. Best of all, despite a lot of logging and overhunting in some areas, the place is still basically a wilderness.

From a plane you can see what the brochures are talking about when they describe the reserve's ecology as "hydrologically complex": Along the coast there are two huge, island-dotted bays, Ascensión and Espíritu Santo, lots of lagoons, and long strands of barrier beach. Behind them, vast alternating expanses of mangrove forest and salt-, brackish-, and freshwater marsh are dotted by tear-shaped *petenes*—that is, hammocky islands of forest surrounding large cenotes and maybe—no one seems sure about this—freshwater springs like the ojos de agua near Celestún.

Gradually, as the eye travels still further inland, the marshes merge with the jungle canopy: tens of thousands of acres of "semi-deciduous" and "semi-evergreen" woodlands of varying heights, some subject to inundation, some not, all containing a variety of plant and tree species unimaginable in a temperate-zone forest.

That's what you see from the air. It should look a lot like the Everglades, and in fact it rather does near the coast. There is no "river of grass" but there are marshes and mangroves, bays and hammocks, even the same type of flat, porous limestone shelf underlying all the rest. At ground level, however, it doesn't look like any other place I've ever seen anywhere.

But then, at ground level, I am like all the six blind men in the fable combined, trying to describe an elephant by feeling up a few little parts of his enormous anatomy.

I get my first "feel" in the vicinity of Laguna de Muyil, on the northwestern edge of the reserve. The highway passes an archaeological site here that boasts some rather more impressive ruins than those at nearby Tulum, including a causeway leading to a Maya observatory; but they haven't been worked on much, and they lack Tulum's spectacular view of the coast. There is, however, another sort of view available nearby that is, to me, more interesting, if not as pretty-pretty as Tulum's rocky headlands and blindingly blue sea. Here, moreover, there intervenes between the ruins and the view the bonus of a lovely green and gray jungle, full of sinuous, melted-looking tree trunks embellished with the usual flaring roots and ropy vines. In its flatland way, it is as impressive as that other jungle on the slopes at Palenque where my peninsula journey had begun; and this one is not just a tiny fragment of its former self.

The caretaker at the ruins tells me of an unmarked spur trail that leads out into the savannah. After a bit of stumbling around, during which I pass empty deer enclosures, empty crocodile pens, and an empty blue mesh "aviary" meant to house butterflies—all breeding projects begun and then abandoned because of political pique or insufficient funding—I finally discover the path's barely visible beginning, and follow it through head-high marsh grass to an observation tower. I say "tower" for courtesy's sake, but in truth it abuses the language to apply such a sturdy word to this rickety construction of half-rotted poles. When I attempt to climb it, the first rung on the wooden ladder breaks warningly under my weight; but eventually, with only one more rung giving out on me, I reach the platform on the top, which consists of half a dozen sagging boards.

But I am high up and have my view; and a very impressive one it is: a miles-wide cyclorama encompassing jungle edge, a broad crescent of tawny marsh, and the whole of Laguna de Muyil merging at a distance with a much larger, bluer expanse of water, the Laguna de Chunyaxche, which in its turn merges with the cloudless blue of the Caribbean sky.

As I have earlier remarked, views are all very well. But it's wildlife that I want to see. It is still fairly early in the morning. I pick the soundest-looking of the platform boards to settle on, and sit and wait. And wait. A place like this—all these edges, these "transitional zones"—has got to be positively crawling with wild things.

Only it isn't. A couple of great kiskadees flashing yellow and cinnamon brown against the forest wall; a white dot so far off that even with the binocs I can't positively identify it as an egret. And that's it. When I finally descend from my perch, I reflect somewhat grumpily that even in the ravaged Everglades I would have had a lot more to show for three hours of watchful waiting.

When I express my disappointment to the caretaker, he concedes that there aren't many birds or animals hereabouts. He gets to his explanation for the scarcity of wildlife in a somewhat roundabout way, first invoking God and the saints to punish politicians for their corruption, economic planners for the runaway inflation, state authorities for their indifference to the plight of poor people like himself, and the jefes of neighboring ejidos for their incompetence and nepotism. Only when he has got all that off his chest does he remark almost off-handedly that store-bought meat is impossibly expensive; so if a man wants meat for his table, he goes out and kills it himself. Oh, no, he says; local people don't sell what they shoot; it's strictly a matter of domestic consumption. But oh, yes, he admits, all mammals larger than a wood rat, as well as many different species of birds, are candidates for the cooking pot.

After thanking the well-meaning fellow for taking time with me, I head back to the van. But as I climb in, he comes running up. "Wait, wait," he says. "You want to see the wild animals? I can tell you how; but you will have to walk."

A little too cavalierly, I assure him I don't mind that.

"Then what you need to do is follow the chicleros' trail! If you go far enough into the deep woods [*la selva pura*], you will have better luck seeing the wild animals."

In the generous Yucatecan manner, he sees me on my way. We walk along the highway for perhaps a quarter of a mile, then turn into a large milpa where dead, scorched trees poke above low underbrush, and a campesino's choza shows its thatched roof in the distance. The trail turns toward the little house; but directly ahead is a small opening in a dense wall of jungle growth. "There it begins," says my guide. He accepts my handshake and one of the two soft drinks I have brought with me, then watches as I duck my head and enter another world.

The forest here is not quite like anything I have seen so far in my travels. What amazes me is that it can exist at all. Even by the standards of the stony Yucatán, this is stony ground. Indeed, by the time I have gotten a mile beyond the milpa, it is nothing but stone, jagged and broken, as though it had been bashed repeatedly by some gigantic mallet. It is the sort of terrain one expects to find on a barren, scree-covered mountain slope, not the floor of a sea-level jungle. And, whatever its technical classification, this is a jungle, albeit composed mostly of second-growth trees. Its potential height at maturity can be measured by the chicle-producing *zapotes* along the way, easy to spot because of the V-shaped wounds that invariably scar their trunks. These trees produced the world's supply of chewing gum before synthetic substitutes arrived, and for that reason they were spared when loggers or milperos worked this forest over. Now they outreach, but not by all that much, the trees that rise in dense ranks around them, struggling for a saving share of light, moisture, and what little soil there is. And they *do* struggle! One sees it in their contorted shapes and the searching way their roots take hold of the rocks, breaking them, in the slowest of slow motions, into smaller and smaller fragments. Some trees, unable to maintain a footing, have tipped over, but still their exposed roots clutch upended slabs of stone in a desperate grip.

The trail that the chicle gatherers have kept open with their machetes is, in the most literal sense, a tunnel, burrowing its way stubbornly through this green gridlock of crowding, shoving trees. It seems often to follow a low ridge, so straight, and so totally composed of jumbled rock that I wonder, at first, if it might be the remains of some ancient Maya causeway; but then decide not, since the uncleared ground on either side, though half hidden by broad-leaved undergrowth and pockets of duff, is just as stony.

Here, as everywhere in the Yucatán, the always irregular surface of the ground is abundantly pocked with large cavities—which the people hereabouts call *rejolladas*. Some are so small and regular in their circumference that they look man-made, deliberately drilled through solid rock. They haven't been; but there are occasional signs of the human presence: piles of stone, boundary markers with dates on them, and in one spot, the name of an ejido that I can't make out. These are of fairly recent vintage, however. The earliest of the markers dates from the early 1970s. Not so very long before that, if local reports can be believed, Mexican officials, missionaries, and gringo explorers sometimes had a way of going into this country and not coming back out.

The infrequent markers aside, there are only the slashes on the zapotes to remind me that this trail exists for more practical reasons than to facilitate my rambling through Quintana Roo's outback. Actually, the ramble turns into a hike in earnest after the first mile or so, and after another mile or two it is an endurance contest all the way. The cranking rocks have split one of my already overstressed tennis shoes along the sole; and I wonder whether they, or my ankles, which are repeatedly turned on the uneven footing, will give out first. At one point, I mutter to myself, "Jesus, it's like walking on broken coral." To which I mutteringly reply, "You idiot, you *are* walking on broken coral." For that is what the Yucatán peninsula essentially is: a dead reef exposed by the ebbing of ancient seas.

Actually, the most annoying problem is that I have to keep glancing at the ground, taking care where I put my feet; a fall, a seriously sprained ankle, would definitely be out of order here. But on that account I can't do a very good job of surveying the surrounding bush; which is very frustrating. I am out to see what I can see, specifically, some of the wildlife the caretaker had half-promised me; and I have the powerful intuition that it is certainly here. At moments there are shadows of movement just at the corner of vision, the rippling stir of small and not-so-small creatures moving quietly away. I glimpse a bird now and then. Most are just flickering shadows in the dappled light, but I spot a violaceous trogan for sure, as well as some sort of wood creeper, and a couple of white-eyed vireos. The vireos bemuse scientists because when they are breeding in the United States they frequent thickets and edges; yet here on their wintering grounds they live only in dense forest habitat like this. Such habitat is rapidly disappearing in Central America, which probably explains why populations of white-eyed vireos are declining.

Mostly what I see are butterflies, hundreds of yellow and blue ones, but now and then an exquisite little art deco charmer that sports a dash of heliotrope at the tips of its narrow wings and a yellow stripe near the base. I tell myself that the butterflies alone are worth the bother of this hard walking; but I don't believe it. I am greedy; I want something more. It would help if I could just see the tracks of Something; but among these roots and rocks there is no hope of that.

Whether deliberately or by chance, the trail skirts several craterlike depressions that contain sizable grottos under their shelving rims. They are not cenotes, but they hold pools of black, stagnant-looking rainwater. One of them is quite large. I have no difficulty picturing a jaguar crouching on the limestone rim, waiting for some thirsty whitetail or brocket deer to take its chances. I remind myself consolingly that this part of Quintana Roo, along with neighboring Campeche, is el tigre's last stronghold in peninsular Mexico. At Puerto Morales I had been told of a big male that had frequented the vicinity of a small village not far north of here. It had spooked the human inhabitants in the course of helping itself to some of the resident dogs and calves; and after months of trying, local hunters had finally killed it just a few weeks before my passing through. Everyone in the village was said to have eaten jaguar meat that day.

I, of course, do not expect to see a jaguar; although it does strike me as a trifle unfair that a bunch of unappreciative campesinos should have had a privilege that I cannot even hope to someday hope for. Actually, as far as this expiring day is concerned, I would gladly settle for a glimpse of a toucan or a small iguana; but I am beginning to conclude that I must be content with my solitary trogan, the pretty butterflies, and the delicate satisfaction that comes of haunting jaguar-haunted woods.

This resigned and accepting frame of mind, as I have discovered time and again, is just the mood that woodland creatures wait for before allowing themselves to be seen. I sit myself down, as I have already done several times along the way, at the edge of a small *rejollada*—partly to check myself for garrapatas, partly to rest my tired, rock-clutching feet, but mostly to give anything that wishes to oblige a chance to come to me. A last chance, as I tell myself. I have about five miles to cover, or re-cover, before getting back to the highway and my van; and if there was ever a trail I wouldn't want to travel in the dark, this is it.

So there I am, sitting with my bottom between a rock and a hard place when, suddenly, along comes an agouti, delicately picking its way through the trees not a dozen yards away. Agoutis and their near cousin, the paca, are considered delicious eating by the indigenous peoples of Central and South America, so they are relentlessly hunted throughout their range; but even where they still exist in fair numbers, they are shy and secretive. A couple of times, on nocturnal forays along back roads, I have caught paca in the van's headlights; but this is the first wild agouti I have ever seen.

It is a beguiling, dainty little creature. Only its head and paws attest to the fact that it is a rodent; its trim brown body and delicate legs ought by rights to belong to a pygmy deer. At one end, its nose twitches nervously; at the other, there is no tail to speak of. It is unaware of me; but it has somewhere it wants to get to. It moves purposefully across the jumbled rocks, not pausing to nibble leaves or ferns; and in less than a minute it is out of sight.

When, after a decent interval, I get up and head back toward the road, I am feeling like someone who has just gotten an unexpected check in the mail. I make no attempt now to be quiet as I move along as quickly as the terrain will allow. Returning from a hike by the same route, one never expects to see as much as one did on the outbound journey. Besides, I have had my thrill for the day. Or so I suppose.

But as I've already remarked, the whole point of the unexpected happening is that it happens when you don't expect it to. I have got about two-thirds of the way back to the highway. The sunlight, copper red, inserts itself through small openings in the canopy at a low, sharp angle. The sole of my left sneaker is waggling as loose as a gossip's tongue. My ankles, though not properly sprained, have been turned so often that they hurt like hell. The forest, but for my passage, is as still as an underwater cave.

And then it isn't. Nothing very loud: an odd scuffing sound, a light, stony patter, a low grunt, and—maybe I imagine it—a brief, distant sound like a frightened squeal.

Suddenly there are shapes, gray and low, moving fast among the crowded trees, three, four, a half a dozen of them—running *toward* me! I stand there transfixed, knowing what they are even before they dash across the trail, but hardly able to believe it. The closest of them passes not more than twenty feet in front of me. Then a seventh animal, a bit separated from the others, rattles a stone as it crosses the trail right behind me. It is already almost out of sight when I about-face. When I look frontward again, the last of the others is vanishing in the undergrowth.

These here-and-gone-again animals are javelina, or peccary, as my reader will have probably guessed. They are the only wild swine native to the New World; although if you want to be technical about it, they are taxonomically not proper pigs at all, what with their more complicated digestive track and odoriferous musk glands and three-toed hind feet. But they look like wild pigs and act like wild pigs and really are wild pigs, whether the Old World's boars and warthogs want to claim them as kin or not.

Of course I'm not thinking about any of that at the moment. At first I am not thinking at all, just repeating "Oh, wow! Oh, wow!" over and over in a breathless whisper. But when I do start considering the almost literally overwhelming thing that has happened, what I keep hitting on is not just the wonderful fact that I've been allowed a brief but extraordinarily close look at these bristly fellows, but that I've been given that look because they were badly frightened. Only, not of me.

I'd seen the same sort of thing happen often before. Always, however, there was a human cause: deer, foxes, coyotes practically running over me in their eagerness to escape the hunter or pack of hounds or noisy hiker who had scared them. Whereas this time, I am certain that whatever caused those javelinas to panic was not human at all. No gunshots, no voices, no thwack and slash of a machete cutting through vines and brush. No sound of any kind coming from that all-but-impenetrable jungle to my right.

I fairly shiver with excitement. "I know you're there," I say silently, "maybe just behind that wall of trees."

I stand there listening for a considerable while. But the forest is holding its breath every bit as much as I am. In part, perhaps, because the javelinas have left a musky reek behind them, similar to that of our old dog, Teddy.

I finally move on, hobbling like a little old man by the time I get back to the ruins. It is something after six, but the caretaker is still there, talking with a couple of friends. He gives me a big grin and a wave, and asks if I have had any luck. I tell him I've seen some javelinas, without mentioning the how or why of it.

"Ah! Good to eat," he says approvingly, as though I had shot one and stowed it away somewhere. "But you got to cut out the bad-smelling sac right away." Grinning, he holds his nose. His friends laugh and nod.

I shake his hand and earnestly thank him for showing me the chicleros' trail. But there is no way in the world that I can explain to him how really grateful I feel. I can just barely explain that to myself: How this tenuous contact with a beast that prowls the tangled landscape of my imagination as surely as he does the nearby forests has made me conscious of a regenerative process that has perhaps been going on, imperceptibly, incrementally, ever since the day I left Anita's house.

I suppose everyone has some one aptitude that they most prize in themselves. In my case it had been a certain simple-minded awareness, even an expectation, that there were all sorts of adventures—modest marvels, believable mysteries—crouched in excited ambush along whatever path I happened to be following at the moment. And because I wanted them to leap out at me, they often did. It had made life interesting.

Then that different sort of ambush had occurred; and along with every other appetite that gave me pleasure, I had lost that one faculty that had always kept me wanting to go on. I was sure it was gone for good. I almost *wanted* it to be gone for good.

Yet now, here I am, at this nowhere place called Laguna de Muyil, shaking hands with this smiling caretaker, suddenly realizing that that lost part of myself, like the broken-off tail of an anole or a glass lizard, has been slowly, secretly, growing itself back again.

"*Gracias, gracias,*" I keep saying as I get into the van.

The caretaker waves. "*Vaya con Dios,*" he says.

When I settled in at the Sian Ka'an research station, I knew the obvious sorts of things about tropical forests that just about everybody knows by now: that they contain the lion's share of the world's fauna and flora;

that they are still being destroyed at a lunatic rate; that their shallow soils are almost invariably ill suited for the agricultural development that is imposed on them; and that the upshot of it all is likely to be a major screw-up in the planet's weather patterns.

But when I left the reserve a few days later, I knew a good bit more than that. I learned, just for example, that tropical forests and jungles do not go about regenerating themselves in the same way that temperate forests do. In the temperate forests, where trees have developed strategies for surviving a cold season, their seeds, which contain the potential for a whole new forest, have a period of dormancy; they wait until conditions are right before they start shooting up. But here in the warm tropics, seeds are not programed in that way. As soon as one drops, the new tree starts growing. The seed has to move fast; if it doesn't, it will be quickly devoured, more often by ants and other insects that live on the forest floor than by birds and beasts. So the seed begins to shoot up—and *then*, when it is a small sapling, its period of latency begins. It waits in the wings, like an actress's understudy, until the demise of some overshadowing tree allows for an opening in which it can start growing like mad. What this arrangement means, in terms of the whole tropical forest community, is that the genetic information necessary to its many tree species is stored in their "latent" sapling offspring rather than their vulnerable, perishable seeds. This setup greatly narrows the species' chances of survival if the forest in which it lives is burned or bulldozed away. In a temperate zone, if a woodland is clear-cut and the area is then left alone, sown with its dormant acorns, cones, nuts, whatever, the same sort of forest will eventually grow back in its place even though it may take a hundred years or more. Whereas when a large tract of tropical forest is cleared—too large for the birds, bats, and monkeys in surrounding woodlands to re-sow with the "fresh" seeds they've consumed—that forest is gone for good.

Or so the scientists think. They aren't really sure, because the whole field of tropical biology is still very new, and because there are so very many species of trees to learn about, and, most of all, because the subject is almost unbearably complex. In fact, that is the main thing I learned at Sian Ka'an about tropical forests and jungles: that nobody was going to get to the bottom of things where they were concerned, not in a thousand years, even assuming there were more than a few revenant bits and pieces of those forests and jungles left by then. Which, the way things are going, doesn't seem too likely.

Ingrid Olmsted, the plant ecologist at Sian Ka'an, would be the first to admit she hasn't got to the bottom of things, but she knows more than anybody else about the forests of Sian Ka'an. She breaks open a leaf she has picked up and sniffs it. "Sometimes," she says, "different species are so alike that you have to cut the bark and look at the color of the sap, or check the scent of a leaf."

We are walking on an old logging road that cuts deep into a shadowy forest, somewhat taller, less stony-looking, but just as dense as the one at Laguna de Muyil. "Look," she says, "there's a young mahogany. All the big ones have been logged." She gives the unprepossessing sapling, no taller than she is, a sober, rather moody stare. "Think of it. Two hundred and fifty-three species of trees have been identified in this forest. That is a *lot* of species of trees. Yet only the mahogany, cedar, and a few others are used commercially. There are a great many other trees that could have commercial value if only the lumber companies were required to market them along with the more popular types of wood. If they would do that, the forests could be better managed on a sustained-yield basis. Which is so important, you know, because the forests are Quintana Roo's most important resource. Using them wisely would be the best way to keep the region in a somewhat healthy state."

When I ask her if there has been any progress made in that direction, she gives me the same glum look she had given the young mahogany. "There have been attempts. I hope it will happen. But the bureaucracy, the bureaucratic problems." She shrugs. "To understand *that,* to explain *that,* you would have to write a book."

Despite the fact that all the sizable mahogany and cedar have been extracted from it like molars from a mouthful of teeth, the forest we are exploring is mature. Ingrid pauses often and tilts her head back, methodically scrutinizing the canopy to see what wild fruits are coming into season. But now and then she takes time out to answer my questions, or identify something interesting: the ridged-back legume, *Casalpinia violacea,* climbing along the boughs of certain trees like a column of green horseshoe crabs; the huge clusters of pineapple-like oncidiums that seem to have a marked preference for the zapotes; the long, wavy-leaved *Tillandsia bulbosa,* in which a species of stinging ant makes its home. She even allows herself a mild excitement when she comes on a delicate lavender flower glowing in the tangling vines at the base of a dead tree. "Ah!" she exclaims. "*Ipomoea heterodoxa.* I've never seen it in bloom before. It's a species of morning glory, on the threatened list. But no one knows its actual distribution."

There are many palm species in Sian Ka'an. On this walk we do not see the rarest of them, the kuku, which regenerates only once in half a century, and survives in only three isolated groves—one of them on the shores of Ascensión Bay. But there are others, including the chit, the miniature palm of the dunes, which here in the jungles grows quite tall; and the look-alike nakash, which only grows on the Yucatán peninsula. Of them all, the chit is the most useful to the Maya. They still use its leaves to make thatch roofs and brooms, and its trunk to construct the walls of their chozas. And because it is resistant to salt water, it is essential for the construction of lobster traps—a vital consideration in an area where lobster fishing is the chief source of income. Ingrid says that, for good measure, they use it for medicinal purposes too, like so many other forest plants. She breaks off the leaf of a broad-leaved plant that looks like a dozen other broad-leaved plants she's been pointing out. "*Pilocarpus pacemosa.* It's supposed to cure kidney disease. And headaches. The Maya grind it into a paste and put it around their heads. I'm not sure in this case, but there are so many things like this that medical science hasn't taken up yet. The Maya have names for all of them."

I cite a study Arturo Ornat had mentioned, in which it had been found that the Indians used 185 different trees and plants for three hundred different purposes. Ingrid, who considers Arturo every bit as saintly as he looks, brightens at the mention of his name. "*Ja,*" she says, "he is right. Here at Sian Ka'an, the Maya are the ones who have really managed the whole forest in a sustainable way. Of course, some of them are too superstitious. They tell you stories about things in nature that you know aren't true—that certain harmless animals or lizards or snakes are dangerous. But on the whole they are good conservationists. They have had to be. When they were not being fishermen, they were being hunters and gatherers. That is still true to some extent. Most of the Maya down here do not work in Cancún or Puerto Morelos. Of course that will change. But if we can make things work here at Sian Ka'an, we can perhaps adapt the old way to the new."

Ingrid grew up in Germany—her accent is still pretty thick—and then lived and studied in the United States. When she came to Sian Ka'an, she first worked for CIQRO—Research Center for Quintana Roo—but she is now employed by Amigos de Sian Ka'an to find out whatever she can about the ecology of the reserve's vegetation zones. She is blonde, angular, and rather reserved.

"I feel free here," she says when, during a break in the morning's walk, she consents to talk a little about herself. "I can live in a more responsible way, without obeying rules and regulations. Of course I am not talking about bureaucratic rules, the politics, the corruption. I mean on a more personal level. Because this is a Third World country, the society is less structured. At this point I prefer the Mexican life-style—*en toto*—to the American or European way of doing things. I see more people here who are spontaneous and happy than I do in the United States or Europe, where television makes people dull. Also, the Maya don't have the same ideas we do about accumulating things. They are used to having just a one-room hut, a little land to grow maize and beans, a few animals, and that's it. You can't say, 'Look, there is a rich Maya, there is a poor one.' In that sense, they are all pretty much the same."

Like Susan Kepecs at Río Lagartos, Ingrid is ambivalent and tends to hedge when confronted with the other side of the Mexican coin. "I don't feel discriminated against as a woman. . . . But it's true; although a Maya woman may have standing in her home, she never messes in other things, never. In the mestizo social structure, it is somewhat different. But I also feel that when one comes here from the United States or Europe, one has a totally different preconception of what things should be like—for example, the woman's place in society. Mexico is really a very different country with its own attitudes about that. It's the same with the corruption. I don't see a solution to that because it is institutionalized. The amazing thing is that people deal with it and survive. And so does the country." She starts moving along the trail again. "I don't know," she says uncomfortably, "maybe it is because I am a biologist; I am used to being outside a lot; I'm not in need of the amenities as much as some people. Whatever the reason, I feel more alive here."

With that, Ingrid seems to decide that she has confided more than enough of her personal feelings to a stranger. Now and then she politely identifies a tree or plant and points out its idiosyncrasies; but mostly she maintains long silences, which I am not encouraged to interrupt, during which she studiously searches the tangled canopy for trees bearing fruit.

Then, after we have gone on for some while in this way, the silence of the forest is suddenly broken wide open by an astonishing succession of sounds that stops us both dead in our tracks.

It is the laughing falcon. By this time, I have seen the bird several times, usually perched, like that first one near El Cuyo, in an overgrown milpa. But only now, when it is invisible, does it decide to vocalize.

Everyone who hears a laughing falcon has his own way of describing its outrageous cry. Mine, I'm afraid, is a touch prurient: what comes across is a hysterically funny combination of depraved laughter and orgiastic exclamation. "Oh, stop," the falcon screams, "I can't stand it! Haw, haw, I can't stand it. Give me more, haw haw, oh more!"

It's been many a moon since I last belly-laughed; but now I make up for lost time, bending over, grabbing hold of a tree, joining the falcon in a helpless paroxysm of haw-hawing.

Ingrid looks open-mouthed at me. Then she looks in the direction from which the falcon's crazy laughter is coming. Then she looks back at me.

And then she joins our duet. I am so astonished to see her laughing that it almost sobers me. But the falcon, which had paused to catch its breath, starts up again, and so do I.

Afterward, when the falcon has called it quits and Ingrid and I have regained our composure, we go on as we had before. But a little while later, remembering that madly lascivious cry, I start chuckling. Ingrid gives me a nice, spontaneous smile that quite brightens her plain face. "I've heard it before, of course," she says, "but it never seemed *that* amusing."

"Maybe we both needed a good laugh?"

"*Ja,*" she concedes, "maybe so."

The research station at Sian Ka'an proved to be as starkly new-looking and underused as the one at Celestún. But at Celestún there had been a relaxed mood, a cohesiveness that was missing here, at least during my brief stay. The two American graduate students in residence were agreeable, bright young people, working hard at collecting data on the many migratory bird species for whom the reserve is a vital wintering ground. But both were concerned about relationships back home that might or might not withstand the stress of long separations; and they were worried about the prospects of getting jobs in their overcrowded field. On top of all that, they were discouraged by the hassles that attended their work at Sian Ka'an. When I met them they had just returned from Chetumal, the state capital. They had made the long drive in response to the unexplained summons of the director of the Quintana Roo research center; but when they got there, he was nowhere to be found, and his own secretary had no idea when he'd show up. They had waited around for a couple of days for a meeting that never took place. It was the sort of experience that is par for the course in Mexico, but that hadn't made it any easier to deal with.

What with the graduate students preoccupied with their private problems, Ingrid absorbed in her research, and the otherwise unoccupied warden-guard nursing an unrequited passion for the pretty young female student, there seemed to be a lot of noncommunication going on at the Sian Ka'an research station.

Not wanting to feel left in, I contributed my own sense of separateness to the rather forlorn atmosphere of the place. Now that I was tentatively rediscovering my own enthusiasms and abstract passions, I was less interested in vicariously absorbing those that emanated from other people. Even with the graduate students, I didn't broach the subject of loneliness. All I wanted—that I could have, at any rate—was to experience as much of Sian Ka'an as the place itself and the limited ration of time would allow.

Given the fact that Sian Ka'an is no Yellowstone Park where herds of elk pose helpfully for tourists in every other mountain valley, I did pretty well—or more exactly, I was done well by. For starters, a reception committee of seven or eight ocellated turkeys turned out to welcome me when I arrived at the research station. They promenaded along the edge of the clearing, pompously ignoring the warden, who lounged nearby; which either spoke well for the security they found here or, less favorably, indicated the low level of the birds' intelligence. Ocellated turkeys are more gorgeously plumed than the wild turkeys I am familiar with back home; but even where they are relentlessly hunted, which is almost everywhere except maybe Sian Ka'an, they seem less wary than their northern cousins. I don't know; maybe among turkeys the inverse relationship between looks and IQ actually applies.

My luck held. At daybreak next morning, I had a good look at several pacas without having to walk further than the distance from my bunk to the nearby window. Pacas are not ordinarily very sociable animals, but the oranges fallen to the ground in the little grove behind the station had brought a bunch of them together. They were obviously paranoid about their spotted, rather chunky little bodies being improperly camouflaged in the short grass; they hunkered down as best they could, and spent much of their time peering over their rounded shoulders, obviously expecting, as rodents so often do, the worst to happen. They seemed especially inclined to scrutinize my window, as though they could feel my eyes on them; and after a few nervous minutes they crept off, one after another, into the underbrush.

It was later that same morning that I accompanied Ingrid on her rounds and had the pleasure of sharing with her the laughter of the laughing falcon. Not long after that good moment, we came on a lovely little lagoon all but hidden by the tall forest surrounding it. It was difficult to approach, but when we did get through to its reedy bank, we were vouchsafed a rare and extraordinary sight. Or more exactly, two of them.

At about the height of the tree canopy, a very large white bird with black markings was gliding by, wings extended and unmoving, above the pond's still surface. I grabbed Ingrid's elbow. "What the hell is it?" I whispered. "It can't be a wood ibis; it's got—"

"Look!" Ingrid breathed. She wasn't looking at my bird. She was staring straight up above our heads.

When I followed her example, I almost levitated with excitement. Talk about a bird's-eye view! We were looking right up the skirts of a king vulture, perched on the limb of a dead tree, airing out its outspread wings in the hot morning sun.

I have little patience with the squeamishness some people indulge in at the expense of vultures. The birds are always beautiful to look at when they ride the thermals on outstretched wings; and while I will admit that some of the African species, and our own turkey buzzard, are a bit scruffy-looking when seen close up, others, like the black vulture, are quite handsome in their bald, beaky way at any distance. As for their taste for carrion, they are just a bit more specialized than a long list of other creatures, including dogs, that don't mind eating overripe meat when they get hungry.

But there was no doubt that these king vultures were in a class by themselves. My bird guide describes them as buffy white; but this pair looked white as new-washed sheets to me, with tails and broad wings edged in jet black for contrast. The most astonishing thing about them, though, was their heads—conventionally regarded as the vulture tribe's most ugly feature. In these birds, the naked, featherless flesh of neck, eye rings, and wattles, as well as the tip of the huge hooked beak, positively glowed with a brilliant mandarin orange, set off by delicate brush strokes of lavender and black, a veritable eye-feast of loud yet somehow harmonious coloration.

I gawked, gaped, and got a crick in my neck, while the bird above us obliviously continued to sun its beautiful (if also, perhaps, odoriferous) wings, and its mate, after settling in a tree on the other side of the laguna, seemed to lean from its perch and peer down at his reflection in the dark water.

"They're quite uncommon," said Ingrid, turning to make her way back to the trail and her survey of canopy fruits. "As a matter of fact, this is a first for me."

Following after her, I promised myself I would come back the next day on my own for another look. But when I did, and took what I thought was the same trail again, the laguna and its king vultures were not to be found.

During the rest of that day and the next two, and some of the night hours as well, I spent a lot of time cruising the two rough narrow roads that converge deep within the reserve and then proceed as one to the Glorieta Rojo Gómez, a boat landing on the Bahía de la Ascensión. As well as the trail that should have led to the king vultures but didn't, I sometimes followed others for a mile or two into the bush. This was the dry season of a very droughty year, so that in the more inland marshes and the seasonally inundated forests, only the larger *aguadas* and lagunas contained any water. At the terminus of one side trail, I risked my neck climbing to a platform that made even the one at Laguna de Muyil seem sturdy by comparison—both must be either gone or rebuilt by now—and from there I was able to take in a stretch of thirsty-looking savannah broken by stretches of stunted woodlands and a long pan of cracked, parched mud patrolled by a lone jacana, a rail-like bird with what must be the largest feet, relative to its size, in the whole bird kingdom. But the interior of the reserve is not the place for those who hunger for views. There are numerous stretches where the marshes open things up; but the only real elevations hereabouts are a few rubble heaps that were once Maya temples, and they are too overgrown and for the most part too inaccessible to serve as lookouts. Much of the time, the only view is straight ahead. The road barrels on, me with it, mile after mile, through dense forest, some of it, especially near the coast, quite tall, but most of it not. Every once in a while, as though letting me in on a nice little secret, it divulges one of its inhabitants. Tarantulas crawl, *chachalacas*, quail, and gray-necked wood rails run, and parakeets, trogans, and ant tanagers fly across the road in front of me.

And once, something slithers. It is easily the largest snake I've ever seen in the wild—a good nine, maybe ten, feet long. Certainly its body is longer than the narrow road is wide. A boa? I don't know. Frantically I brake, almost forgetting to put the shift into idle as I jump out of the van. I can see the ground cover shivering with the reptile's passage, and actually hear its long body scraping over leaves as it slides into the forest; but for all my desperate scrambling I can't catch up with it, and in a minute it is gone, taking its identity with it.

I try with some success not to react in a sour grapes sort of way. Better to have seen and not know than never to have seen at all, I tell myself. Little do I know that, the following night, that stoical philosophy will be put to a very severe test indeed.

During my night drives, the headlights pick up one pair after another of small, round eyes gleaming like rubies. By this time I am experienced enough not to imagine they might be what they are not. What they are is *pauraques*, hugging the unpaved road like their whippoorwill cousins back home, though in far greater numbers. They are easily confused by the approach of the van, poor things; and once routed, some of them will fly ahead of it for half a mile before finally ducking into the bush.

On the night in question, views of pauraque eyeballs and rear ends are all I have to show for an hour's drive. By the time I turn around and head back to the station, I have stopped expecting to see anything else.

Which is, of course, when the Something Else appears. Exerting themselves, the beams of the headlights just barely reflect and hold at the extremity of their reach a pair of eyes that definitely do not belong to a pauraque. Please wait, I whisper, giving the van some gas. At this point I will settle for a wood rat.

If you've never tried it, it's hard to describe the suspense of a game like this. I know what it is, what I want it to be, this animal hesitating in the middle of the road, startled, staring back at the staring, blinding lights. I can almost make it out now: smallish, the fur throwing back a little light, the coloration patterned—

Then the lights of the eyes blink out. The animal has turned its head, is beginning to move—and now it is gone with a run and a leap.

I stop, pointlessly, at the spot where it has vanished, and hop out of the van. The dirt road is too packed down to show any tracks, but I nevertheless crouch in front of the humming van, brushing away the bugs attracted by the headlights. "I know it was an ocelot," I tell myself. It had to be. I had glimpsed the markings, I am sure of it. And the size, the way it moved—other than the very rare and secretive margay, which would normally be climbing trees, not crossing roads, at this hour of the night, there is nothing else it could have been! But I hadn't really seen it, not clearly, not clearly enough. If it had only hesitated two seconds, literally two seconds longer! Even so, I am sure I have seen an ocelot. Almost seen. I am almost sure.

It's odd. In Campeche, when a certified ocelot had run across the track in front of the first jeep in our hunters' safari, I hadn't minded too much not seeing it. It was enough to know that the *tigrillo* had got away with its skin, and that I was in a place where an animal like that could still be expected to dash across a trail.

And now here I am in another such place, sure that what I have just seen was an ocelot. Almost seen. Almost sure. So I should be excited, thrilled. And I am, I really am. But at the same time I feel so frustrated I almost want to bawl like a disappointed child.

The next and last morning of my stay at the station, I take a final drive down to the Glorieta Rojo Gómez. Beyond an imposing stretch of *selva alta*—tall jungle—the road eases itself onto a narrow causeway. The mangroves take over. A few minutes later I am at the end of the line, surrounded by blue sky, blue bay.

And birds. Hundreds of birds. Great blue, little blue, green-backed, tricolored, yellow-crowned, and tiger herons; snowy, great, and reddish egrets; roseate spoonbills, white ibis, pelicans, cormorants, frigate birds; and scores of gulls, terns, shorebirds. In short, all the birds that were supposed to be at Laguna de Muyil when I was there and weren't, because they were all here.

El Ramonal is a small farm located a few miles inland from the glorieta landing. If one notices it at all, it is only because there are so few other signs of human habitation along this road. Yet there is a much better reason for taking note of El Ramonal than that. It is a "demonstration project" that actually works.

The Third World is strewn with thousands of pilot programs funded by governmental or nonprofit organizations, all meant to raise the standard of living of indigenous peoples. They are the latest and probably the most benign, though not necessarily the most successful, expression of the Western world's economic colonialization of the planet. Having decided what is best for the natives, agricultural consultants, engineers, government officials, or bright-eyed Peace Corps volunteers induce their charges to dig septic tanks or build dams or cover sewers or plant alien crops—or clear thousands of acres for cattle pasture. Then, like God on the seventh day, they see that their work is good (and that the funding has run out), and move on to programs new. More often than not, when the experts have departed, it turns out that the natives are not able or willing to repair the new generator or tractor when it breaks down, or afford fertilizer for the new supercorn, or feel comfortable using the new chemical toilets, or find a profitable market for whatever new crop they are growing, or cope with the local bureaucrats and planners who insist on getting into the act. Or, most likely of all, change their old way of doing things.

And yet, this ongoing effort does produce success stories now and then, and El Ramonal seems to be one of them. Here, a very simple but important concept is being put into practice: The concept, which Joann Andrews and Barbara Montes and a lot of other environmentalists have been pushing for some time now, is that it is possible for indigenous peoples to continue to use the natural resources they have always depended on in a way that (1) improves their standard of living, (2) takes account of a modern market economy, (3) does not altogether undermine their traditional lifestyle, and, most important of all (4) allows them to exploit natural ecosystems without destroying them.

In practice, this concept translates into something called drip irrigation. Because it relies on this unexciting-sounding methodology, El Ramonal is a farm utterly unlike the usual milpa operations in this region. It is a rather unprepossessing place to look at. The buildings are modest, and the whole spread is very small, just a few acres. The crops and citrus trees, neatly laid out in weeded rows, grow in spaces more aptly described as plots than fields.

Drip irrigation, as the name suggests, involves the direct application of small driblets of water to the root systems of crops. The method is by no means new. But its application in the Yucatán peninsula as an alternative to the milpa practice of slash-and-burn agriculture is nothing less than revolutionary. Its leading proponent in Quintana Roo is a burly, black-bearded, outspoken agronomist named Felipe Sánchez, whose research, funded by The Nature Conservancy, is being applied both at his own model farm project near Puerto Morelos and at El Ramonal.

Most of the Yucatán peninsula is a dry, stony region with very thin soils. Even in Quintana Roo, where rain is most abundant, the porous limestone crust absorbs moisture like a sieve. Ordinary trench irrigation would be impractical, since the water would have to be pumped in great quantities and at considerable cost from wells, and much of it would go to waste. Drip irrigation, in contrast, dispenses water parsimoniously, where and when it is needed, so the cost of operating gas pumps to bring water to the surface is not prohibitive.

The system is not suited to most large farm operations where land is tillable, since pipes or perforated hoses must be kept in service. "But of course, that's just the point," Sánchez declares in his usual emphatic way. "If you want to do some big-time farming, you should be someplace else, not here. Even if we had outside markets, which we don't, most of the peninsula is as totally unfit for large-scale agriculture as it is for cattle ranching. What we need here is a self-sustaining agriculture to meet the needs of local markets, including Cancún. And for that, with drip irrigation, you need very, very little land."

The peninsula may not be suited to agribusiness (henequen excepted), but to judge from the results, it can be astonishingly productive in terms of small family-operated plots of three or four acres. A traditional milpa will produce, on average, a single crop of one ton of corn per year on four hectares (approximately nine acres) of land. Whereas Sánchez, using drip irrigation and small amounts of fertilizer, has produced three crops per year totaling eighteen tons of corn on just *one* hectare. "We have done that for three years on the same plot, and we have reason to think it could go on indefinitely." He frowns and shrugs. "There are problems, of course. Insect pests become endemic; and you need to invest about $1,500 per hectare, although that is not so much considering the results. We did an extension service demonstration for the Indians in the 'Maya Zone' south of here, and they really got excited about the idea of three crops a year."

He lets out a short, barking laugh. "I asked them what they would do about their annual *pibilnal* ceremony—you know, where the shaman prays to the gods for a good crop—if they have three crops; and they said, 'Well, we will just have three pibilnals every year instead of one.' They don't really care about all that anymore, anyway. There's no religious feeling. The priest prays because he's being paid to do it, and everybody else has a good time, the women making tortillas, the men getting drunk."

Again that abrupt laugh; but almost immediately it is followed by an exasperated sigh. "We had a good program going with the Maya. It worked well in terms of production. But their ejido, their cooperative, wasn't allowed to sell the produce. The government took it, and the Indians never got the money. Naturally, they saw themselves as paid laborers, and like paid laborers everywhere, they weren't going to work hard at this program if the government was going to make all the profits. I expected that to happen, of course. What I hoped was that individuals would somehow try it on their own; but that was very difficult because you need some capital, you know, and most Maya are poor; and the national bank is not going to finance free enterprise. Maybe for a big landowner, yes; but the government wants to keep the campesinos in the cooperatives, where they don't have title to the land, and where they can be controlled." The clouded, impatient expression on his face relaxes into a sudden grin. "In 1986 all the finances for the program were closed off; so I thought, well, that was the end of it. And yet—I don't know how it happened—but at least fifty people, probably many more, are now growing vegetables on their own and selling them in Chetumal and Cancún! I saw some of the guys I had taught in the markets, selling their own produce. So some of them did find the capital. Some of them even have trucks!"

Again his mood changes. He is reflective now: "What I am hoping is that it will spread—a sort of agrarian revolution that the government will eventually have to support. . . . But even if that happens, sooner or later there will be problems. What I would like to do someday is start my own private extension service. The farmers have to be kept informed. Vegetables are not native to the peninsula, you know; it's difficult raising them here. Nematodes, diseases, pests—they all build up. People need to know about new varieties, the least harmful pesticides. I would have a couple of guys going around all the time in a pickup truck, seeing that the growers do things right. That's the sort of thing I would really like to do."

El Ramonal came into being as the result of a tradeoff. In 1982, when the movement to create the reserve was just getting under way, the Maya in the fishing cooperative at Punta Allen, which was to be incorporated within the proposed boundaries of Sian Ka'an, became alarmed that they might lose their rights to use the land resources of the area. So sixty-four of them petitioned the government to grant them a 60,000-acre ejido right in the middle of the reserve-to-be, where they could work their milpas and raise cattle. In other words, they threw a pretty big monkey wrench into the works at a crucial stage. The Sian Ka'an planning council, which was composed of representatives of the ejidos, Amigos de Sian Ka'an, and various federal and state agencies including SEDUE and CIQRO, called first one meeting, then another, and then another, to discuss the proposal. By the time the dust settled, twenty meetings had been held over a period of three years.

During these sessions, everyone got a chance to say their piece (several times over) and hash things out. In the end, the fishermen were given concessions on 12-acre lots, rather than the eighty acres requested by each of them. All the lots were to be located in a buffer zone along the existing roads in the reserve. In addition, the applicants would be obliged to respect the guidelines set up for the management of the reserve. What this meant in practice was that they would have to farm the land with intensive agricultural techniques rather than the milpa method of slash and burn (which wouldn't work on such small parcels anyway).

The amazing thing is that everyone, including the fishermen, eventually agreed to this arrangement. It took a long time to convince the fishermen-*cum*-farmers that the new way of farming would be more productive than the old. When they finally did come around, it was largely because Amigos de Sian Ka'an had by then come up with a pragmatic incentive: the idea of creating a model farm that would help them get started with the methodology of intensive agriculture. In due course Amigos got the needed funds for the project from The Nature Conservancy and the World Wildlife Fund. And that is how El Ramonal came to be.

As it turns out, only thirty of the small plots granted the petitioners, a total of about 400 acres, are being used—more than enough to supply groceries for the fishermen's families. This, at a savings, in terms of lands that would otherwise have been subjected to the slash-and-burn syndrome, of about 59,600 forest acres! Meanwhile, more and more people in ejidos abutting the reserve are expressing interest in the new agriculture, even though it remains to be seen whether government agencies will allow them to keep their profits or not.

Every situation is different, but the various morals of this little tale are generally applicable to any situation involving the establishment of a biosphere reserve in a Third World country—or anywhere else: A lot of patience is needed, as Barbara Montes had remarked with a heartfelt sigh. People have got to sit down together and hear each other out, no matter how long it takes. The proposed solutions must seem reasonably advantageous to a majority of the local people involved. And, when the time is right, the conservationist faction has to be ready to put some money where its mouth is.

Projects at Sian Ka'an don't always turn out so well, as Arturo Ornat and others who have been connected with the reserve can testify. Even operations at El Ramonal have been scaled down since I was there because of funding problems. But the reserve is still intact, the resident wildlife is in pretty good shape, and research does continue, however haltingly. For all the endless hassles involving funding and both personal and departmental conflicts, there is a chance that someday the whole of Sian Ka'an will become a "demonstration project" that the rest of the world might take for a model. What it will demonstrate, if that happens, is that even in this environmentally suicidal age, indigenous peoples can still live harmoniously—and profitably—with the natural world.

I am not green-thumbed, which may explain why I have never been able to get very intense about tame vegetables and fruit trees. I mention this because, for all my enthusiastic rambling on about El Ramonal, I spent only a few minutes admiring the little orchard and flourishing rows of beans, squash, peppers, and corn that Mardoqueo and Ezequeras Herrara, the Maya agricultural technicians who run the place, had so carefully laid out.

In fact, my most vivid memory of El Ramonal has nothing to do with farming at all. While prowling the edge of the cultivated area, I had noticed how closely the forest crowded up to it. I had also noticed that one of the farm workers was standing nearby watching me curiously. I suppose he was wondering why I wasn't asking him questions about the place. So I asked him a question: Were there any jaguars in the vicinity of El Ramonal? I knew there was a viable population on the reserve, but I was curious to know how close they might come to human habitations.

The young man's face broke into a large giggling grin. "*Viene*," he said. I followed him along the forest edge to a spot not far from the road. He bent over and pointed at a small patch of peaty soil cradled among rocks.

And there it was, a single large pug mark imprinted in the peaty soil.

"It looks fresh."

"Oh, it is fresh! Maybe two hours ago. He was here when I came to work."

"You *saw* him!"

The young man could hardly miss the raw envy in my eyes and voice. With a sort of bemused, uncomprehending sympathy, he shrugged, "Maybe he was waiting for you. But you came too late."

I spent one night on the beach north of Xcalac. Which was enough. The place itself is paradise in its littered, mosquito-ridden way, but my appreciation of its charms was somewhat dampened when I was routed out of my cot at three o'clock in the morning by a squad of soldiers brandishing flashlights and guns in my face. In fairness, they handled the situation pretty well, considering that my first response was to look outraged and scared while at the same time trying to roll up the van's windows. They didn't tell me to put my hands up or anything like that. And after they had checked my papers, asked me a few questions, and given the van the once-over, they were friendly enough, even apologetic about waking me up. We parted on the best of terms, enriched by the advice and cigarettes that they and I had respectively handed out.

I had no one to blame for the incident but myself, which naturally made it that much more upsetting. At Puerto Morelos and Tulum, posthippie wayfarers on the Gringo Trail that meanders south from Isla Mujeres to Guatemala had warned me that this isolated coastline of southern Quintana Roo was a favored landfall for smugglers shipping dope from Belize, and that it was therefore heavily patrolled. But I had never been in a duty-free drug zone before (unless you want to count California and south Florida), so the warnings had no resonance. Even the military roadblock on the only road leading to Puerto Bravo hadn't seemed anything special; they can be encountered anywhere in Mexico. But now these soldiers, in the nicest possible way, had assured me that I was lucky that they, not a party of drug smugglers wanting to use my isolated campsite as a beachhead, had disturbed my rest.

Actually, by the time the reassuring sun came up next morning, I was feeling sort of pleased that I had inadvertently chosen such an adventurous place to spend the night. At the same time, I told myself that, really, there had been no danger. The soldiers, not liking the idea of gringo tourists scattering themselves around down here, had just wanted to scare me off.

Later that morning, however, when I gave a lift to a cosmically cynical local resident named Roberto, he did not wholeheartedly endorse my assessment. "Oh, it is usually safe enough," he said, "except maybe if they don't know who you are. A couple of people have disappeared, not many. Really, there have been only three big busts down here the last year or two. The last one was maybe fourteen tons. Of course, it was just marijuana. Now, the really hard stuff, well! Who knows who gets paid off and looks the other way, eh? Even if I knew the answer to that, I wouldn't tell you."

But at the moment, that was literally neither here nor there, since I had left my last night's campsite behind and had not yet reached Puerto Bravo, where Roberto would get aboard. The high point of the drive was seeing a jet-black jaguarundi, my second good look at one, making a dash for the mangroves on the west side of the road. Evidently it had been stalking a bare-throated tiger heron when I disturbed it. At any rate, the bird was only a few yards from where the cat had been, obliviously perched on a dune bush at the edge of the beach.

But even without the jaguarundi bonus, this was a lovely drive as long as you didn't look too closely: a postcard-perfect tropical dreamland furnished with turquoise skies, a sea as blue as ink, mile after mile of beaches and bays, a spectacular reef just offshore, headlands crowned with rustling groves of coconut palms—everything you could ask for. But also, alas, a few things you could do without. Immediately behind this gorgeous belt of scenery lies a thirty-mile-wide swath of mangrove swamp and marsh, a marvelous and mysterious wilderness still full of wildlife, as I would shortly discover for myself, but it is also the home of trillions of thirsty mosquitoes that have no qualms about coming out on the beach to make a meal of hapless campers. The beaches themselves are often narrow to nonexistent; and in the shallows, underwater meadows of turtle grass discourage swimming. But these are minor blemishes on the countenance of this smiling coast. Even the occasional shacks, seasonally occupied by coco gatherers, aren't really eyesores. Most are just inoffensive sheds with no walls to speak of. The one I stopped at to eat my chocolate peanut butter breakfast had as a tenant a huge iguana that rattled noisily around under the tin eaves.

The real scenery-killer is the flotsam and jetsam sown on these shores by our own omnipresent species. And it is the prettiest places, the large coconut groves on the headlands, that are most befouled. Liquor bottles, cans, plastic containers, and tire rims lie everywhere, as well as more degradable stuff like smashed coconut and conch shells. Local people do their share to foul their nest, but most of the crud is delivered by the tide, courtesy of cruise ships and freighters miles out at sea. I tell myself I ought to be hardened to this sort of thing by now, but I'm not, I never will be.

Because I stop so often to take walks along less littered stretches of the beach, or wade far out through the turtle grass to swim in the quiet sea, it is high noon before I reach Puerto Bravo, a collection of a dozen huts and small houses that lies at the junction of the coastal road and the one leading back to the Cancún-Chetumal highway. The only watering hole is a cantina where you can get fresh fish, beer, and soft drinks. It is a pleasant, easy place: a thatched-roof palapa with beach sand for flooring and a thatch wainscoting for walls. Turkeys wander in and out. Under the tree outside, a sad-eyed spider monkey swings back and forth on his leash. Schools of small fish circulate in the shadows of moored boats, and frigate birds and gulls swoop down on them. While eating a brunch of beans and fish, I chat with the proprietor about spider monkeys. He says there is still a fair supply of them way back in the *manglares*, the mangrove swamps. A few years ago, he says, I might have seen them along the roads, but not anymore.

After leaving the cantina and getting through the military checkpoint at the road junction, I turn right, meaning to drive only a few miles on the northern half of the coast road before turning back and heading inland. I have scheduled myself to reach Chetumal before nightfall.

But then I see this man at the side of the road, signaling that he wants a lift. "Ooopf!" he exclaims as he climbs in, "you are my savior, Señor. I never would have made it with my sore feet. If I had to walk the whole way, I would have been crawling on my hands and knees!"

This is Roberto, a thick-set mestizo of about forty, with a dapper little mustache, angry eyes, and the smile of a cartoon shark. Right off, I misdoubt that his feet are all that sore. Also right off, I decide that I like him. He is good company for the duration of a sunny afternoon drive, though not, perhaps, for much longer than that. His wife, he tells me, divorced him years ago, and I can understand why. He has opinions about everything and everyone. Except when they concern himself, they are invariably uncharitable, but in the course of delivering them, he is entertaining and sometimes informative. Life is the villain he loves to hate; but he rails against its inequities with such gusto that one could almost envy him his discontent. By comparison, my own misanthropy seems anemic and insincere.

He was born on this coast, but he has been around, enduring one horrible job after another: as an underpaid seaman, visiting many ports, none of which he liked; as an underpaid worker for a timber company in Tabasco ("It was terrible. Sometimes I would be working up to my waist in mud!"); and most recently as an underpaid handyman for a Texas businessman who owns some of the beachfront up ahead of us. Of this man, Roberto says, "He was always getting angry at the men he hired. They didn't show up on time or they didn't work hard enough to suit him. So one day when they were clearing a landing strip he lost patience and started doing the work himself. I told him it was all right to work hard, but he shouldn't work *too* hard, not down here; but he wouldn't listen. So he got heat stroke or something! He could hardly breathe." Roberto chuckles delightedly, savoring the memory. "They had to fly him back to the States. He almost died!"

Although not fanatically devoted to the work ethic himself, Roberto deplores the lack of it in others. When a battered truck full of cheerful-looking Maya passes us, heading the other way, he says, "You see those fishermen? All drunk. They are on their way to get more beer, or anything they can get their hands on. It's disgusting. They work four hours a day for eight months, only it's more like four months because the weather isn't always right. They catch maybe sixty lobsters a day if they're lucky. The lobsters and the conch are how they earn their money. And as soon as they have enough, they buy liquor and get drunk! They smoke the grass, too. It's a normal thing with the Maya. The chicleros do it, they do it, the father, the son, they all do it. What? No, they don't grow it. They get it in Chetumal. Four months of the year they go there to live. What do they do? Nothing! They live off the government. The government lends them money for new nets, power motors, and then they never pay it back. Why should they? It's the way things are down here."

He goes on to give the government a few licks for controlling people's lives the way it does. But when I ask him if he would like to see the ejido system dismantled, he looks skeptical. "If that happened," he says, "the Maya would need another type of boss, a patrón, to take the government's place. They won't work hard on their own." He pauses and then, in a rare moment of self-deprecation, admits, "Even *I* don't work as much as I should if someone doesn't make me."

I tell him that that is the way it is everywhere. Nevertheless, it occurs to me that, cynical as he is, Roberto may be on to something. Privately, if not publicly, every invader or immigrant from temperate zones always has and always will complain about the sort of indolence that Roberto speaks of. Of course it is a truism that everybody everywhere who thinks he is possessed by a work ethic tends to lament its absence in everybody everywhere else. But even taking that into account, it is also a truism that what we Westerners, and some Eastern peoples too, describe as a work ethic has never existed even as a concept among the great masses of people in most tropical Third World countries. Undoubtedly, environmental considerations are a partial explanation for its absence. In the tropics there is no winter to survive; and the natives have better sense than to get out in the noonday sun like mad dogs, Englishmen, and workaholics from Texas. The Maya, for example, rarely store surplus corn from a good year in anticipation of a bad one; they don't even pick it from the stalks until they are ready to use it.

But I suspect that there is a more important explanation for the work ethic's failure to take root in equatorial lands. It has to do with the fact that, throughout the millennia, the people of these regions have never known anything but a collective—tribal—existence, combined with servitude. They can and do work hard when they have to, the women especially; but most of them can think only in terms of getting by, not of getting ahead. I see the same pattern all the time in the South among the descendants of black slaves and white sharecroppers.

That habit of mind may help to explain why Mexico's "permanent revolution" has been so successful in its weird, bumbling way. The "revolutionary" rulers, the politicians and bureaucrats, may be corrupt, incompetent, exploitive; but they adequately fulfill the quasi-paternalistic functions of the old patrón, and before him the Spanish priests and landowners, and before them the god-kings and priests of the Mesoamerican golden age, and before and after them all the jefes, the local chiefs. Indeed, the more I think about it, the more I suspect that the revolutionary upheavals that occur with such regularity in other Third World countries come about not because the dictatorial or oligarchical governments in power are oppressive, per se, but because they fail to honor the ancient contract that has always cemented the relationship between master and slave, patrón and peon, chieftain and tribal serf: the tradeoff between work (but not too much work) on the one hand, and a subsistence living (but not much more than that) on the other.

If my theory is right, the work ethic will always be confined to countries where the winters are long and hard, and where the inhabitants do not depend overmuch for their livelihoods on the patronage of those who run things. It isn't a very democratic thing to say out loud, but perhaps outsiders—including conservationists—who want to get things done in a place like southern Mexico ought to think more about the function of the patrón.

In any system of contractual bondage, griping is a necessary safety valve, and in Roberto this national habit is developed to an advanced degree. He is now inveighing against the robber patrons who have always managed to make it rich in this socialist country. For example, the governor back in the 1940s who logged off all the mahogany and cedar in the southern part of Qintana Roo and secretly sold it to the English in neighboring British Honduras (now Belize). And the three or four "Mafia" families who control the island of Cozumel, deciding who can and cannot open a shop or build a hotel there. And the powerful personage who has a monopoly on the supply of gasoline in Quintana Roo—which explains why motorists must wait in long lines for gas at one of the only three service stations in the booming city of Chetumal. "Why should he go to the expense of building more?" asks Roberto with angry relish. "He makes the same profit whether you wait in line or not."

On this stretch of the coast north of Puerto Bravo, the road is keeping a little more distance between itself and the beach. I can't make up my mind which is worse, the part that is hard-topped and pitted with deep holes, or the part that is washboard sand. The land- and seascape is not so various as it was further south, but it is still very pretty. The seaward side of the road is shaded by a continuous grove of coconut palms. Now and then there are solid-looking houses of cement block and stucco, which Roberto tells me are the vacation homes of Americans. He also gives me the depressing news that some American will start constructing a resort—the first on this part of the coast—in the next few months. Aloud, I wonder whether the area will seem so attractive to developers when the deadly "yellow" palm disease (caused by an insect-transmitted mycoplasm), which is presently devastating coconut palm plantations not far to the north, infests this part of the coast. But on this subject, which does not allow for much optimism, Roberto is unexpectedly optimistic. "You don't see the palms dying here, do you? The scientists don't know anything; they always predict the worst thing that can happen. Anyway, they have stations on the highway to stop coconuts from up there coming down here. What will happen is that our coconuts will be worth more."

I am getting a little worried about the time, and about having enough gas to get back to the highway. I forewarn Roberto that, sore feet or not, I will have to drop him off pretty soon. He assures me that his destination, a vacation house whose caretaker he is visiting, is only a couple of miles further on. Then, not wanting me to keep too close an eye on the mileage gauge, he expresses a sudden interest in what has brought me to this remote and hard-to-reach corner of Quintana Roo. I tell him of my visit to Sian Ka'an (its southern boundary, I know, cannot be too far to the north of us) and my general interest in wildlife.

"Ah, the wildlife!" says Roberto. "When I was a boy, the wild animals were everywhere around here. There were crocodiles in every place with a little water, big ones! But not now. Now if you see a deer or a jaguar or a turkey cross the road, it is something to talk about. The fishermen are the ones responsible. They shoot everything, any chance they get. The only thing they don't shoot is monkeys because they don't eat them. In Tabasco, now, those ignorant people will eat anything: monkeys, snakes, lizards, turtles. . . . Of course," he admits, "we eat turtles too." Encouraged by my interest, he goes on: "There are still some wild animals left. Before they made the reserve a few years back, and closed the road, we used to hunt at this quarry back in the swamp. Whenever there was a long drought, it was one of the few places that always held water, so the animals had to come there. It was nothing to kill twenty javelina at a time."

I ignore the "we." Instead, I exclaim, "A road? That goes *into* the reserve?" The mere thought that such a back-door entrance might exist excites me.

"Oh yes," Roberto says. "An old logging road. When it is dry enough, you can get in."

"It's dry now."

He shakes his head doubtfully. "But there is a guard there now. And a gate. They don't let you in anymore."

"Still, I'd like to give it a try. If only I weren't so low on gas!"

"Gas?" Roberto exclaims. "Is that all you are worried about? You can get gas at El Uvero; it's only a few miles past where I get off."

That does it. I had wanted in the worst way to explore this remote southern end of Sian Ka'an, but not even the most detailed of my maps suggested such a road; and none of the people at the research station had mentioned it. I will presently find out why.

About five miles further on, I exchanged handshakes with Roberto in front of a small vacation home in an area called Punta El Placer, and then moved on. The road zigged inland to pass through abandoned coconut groves succumbing to second-growth forest, then zagged back to the coast long enough to touch base with the tiny fishing cooperative of El Uvero. The local service station consisted of an open drum of gasoline, a rubber tube, and a plastic gallon jug. A woman with an understandably sour face got the gas "pumping" by sucking on the tube. Spitting out a mouthful, she gave me a look that blamed me for its bad taste. She told me she could spare me only two gallons. To my pleasant surprise, she didn't gouge me on the price even when I finally persuaded her to sell me three.

I still had about twenty slow, rattling miles to go, so it was pretty late in the day when I saw on my right a little shed where a uniformed guard was on duty. Sure enough, right across the road was a gate blocking the entrance to a narrow trail.

When the guard, commendably firm and unsmiling, refused me admittance, I held my breath and handed him an envelope I had pulled out of the glove compartment. In it was a letter-to-whom-it-may-concern written by the Mexican consul in New Orleans, stating that I was on an assignment in the Yucatán, etc., etc. This was the first time I had thought to test its power to open doors. Or rickety gates. Given the magical transformation in the guard's demeanor, I was sorry I hadn't flashed it around on a few earlier occasions when it might have proved useful. The guard nodded, smiled, made apologetic sounds, and trotted across the road to unfasten the gate. As I drove through, he gave the light-looking van a doubtful look. "It would be a good idea, Señor," he called after me, "not to drive in further than you can easily walk out."

At one time or another I had canoed and motorboated and even waded into the depths of mangrove swamps; but driving into one was a first for me. It was dry, of course, the faint track weaving in and out among the spidery roots of the stranded-looking mangrove trees. But it wasn't quite dry; there were low places where the baked gray mud had not fully baked, and the van's tires skidded and struggled for purchase in the deep grooves left by some enterprising vehicle that had come and gone this way before me. Of course I thought of the sand traps at El Cuyo, but I wasn't going to quit now, not when I was so close to, well, whatever it was I was looking for.

Presently, the track climbed a small slope and broke clear of the mangroves. An osprey, lifting off just ahead of me, announced the presence of water; and a minute later I was driving onto a narrow, ragged causeway that bisected a sizable excavation. The quarry that Roberto had spoken of! Whatever might betide, I had at least got that far!

Far enough, as it turned out, to have my first look at a gray and black crocodile, sliding unhurriedly into the water not twenty feet from the van. I was on familiar terms with alligators, but the only crocs I had ever seen in their natural habitat were a long way off in East Africa. Mexico can claim two crocodile species, the Morelet's and the Acutus. (The 'gator-like caiman, resident further north in Mexico, has its own separate classification.) Both species are endangered in almost all their remaining range, but the former is the more adaptable and widely distributed of the two; and here at Sian Ka'an, though not nearly as abundant as in olden days, it is still fairly numerous. Like the American alligator, the Morelet's can make itself at home in swamps, lakes, and fresh and brackish marshes. The Acutus, in contrast, is more particular, and pays the price for its discriminating tastes: it is now restricted to a few isolated salt marshes and lagoons along Mexico's Pacific coast, some isolated corners of the Caribbean, and the southernmost tip of Florida. Since it prefers to nest on the same sandy beaches and cays where tourists disport themselves, it has a hard time surviving even in those few places where it can still be found. In Sian Ka'an, however, the hardpressed creature has a fairly safe refuge; and in coastal areas like the one in which I found myself, the Acutus and the Morelet's coexist.

So which of the two was I gaping at? I hadn't the foggiest. I had read that the snout of *Crocodylus acutus* is narrower than that of *C. moreletii*, but without a basis for comparison I was no wiser for knowing that. I assumed that, since the latter were the more numerous species, and this was a freshwater pond, my crocodile was probably a Morelet's. But I would never know for sure.

Did I care? In this case, not much. I was looking at my first wild New World crocodile and that was enough.

The trouble with that sort of "enough" is that you can never get enough of it. I felt I was on a roll. Without even thinking about it, I pressed on.

Pressing on is the right phrase. I was presently being swallowed up by one of Sian Ka'an's petenes—the islanded hammocks that dot the reserve's wetlands. The dense vegetation that flourished here had all but overwhelmed the trail. Before long, I was instinctively ducking webs of branches and viny tendrils that slapped against the windshield. My poor van had no choice but to butt its way through, picking up a whole new set of scratches and scrapes along the way.

Deep grass covered the track. I suddenly noticed that the recently made tire tracks that had been so considerately leading the way were no longer there to follow. While I debated whether to turn around and go back, assuming I could find a place to turn around, I felt the van dipping into a depression that the grass had hidden. "I've done it again," I muttered, as the front wheels started digging into mud.

It was a sinking-stomach sort of moment. Of course, I wasn't lost and about to perish in the wilderness or anything like that. But this time I couldn't expect a carload of friendly locals like the ones at El Cuyo to come to my rescue, not on this going-nowhere trail, especially now that the reserve was off limits to poachers. I hadn't kept track of distances, but I was sure I hadn't covered more than three or four miles and could probably get back to the gate before dark. Tomorrow, no doubt, someone would be available to unstick my dispirited van . . .

All the same, I felt really down. I just didn't want my promising little adventure to end this way.

The vegetation crowded up so close on either side that I could barely get the door open wide enough to squeeze through. When I got down on my stomach and examined the situation, I found that only the right front wheel was seriously stuck. I had, after all, learned a little from hard experience, braking as soon as I started losing traction instead of trying to bully my way through. I also discovered that in spite of the encumbering grass roots, the mud was as soft as, well, mud. So, to make an hour's story short, I dug out a ramp behind the wheel with my hands—I could hardly have used a shovel if I'd had one—and stuffed it with branches and twigs. Then I got back behind the wheel, held my breath—and backed out. As nerve-wrackingly simple as that!

The upshot of this all's-well-that-ends-well little episode was that, now that the van was unstuck and I could leave the reserve, I decided that I wouldn't. I would spend the night here.

I had about an hour left before dark so I took a walk. I was hardly out of sight of the van, however, when the forest on either side of the trail erupted in a pandemonium of noise and fluttering movement. Booming hoots and frantic whistles showered down on me. Branches and vines stretching midway between the canopy and the forest floor sagged under the weight of large dark shapes.

Curassows! I had stumbled on a family gathering of the huge birds, all behaving in a way that struck me as very peculiar. On the two previous occasions when I glimpsed them, they had been just as high-strung, but, knowing that every predator, human and otherwise, would have liked nothing better than to eat them, they had quickly made themselves scarce. These curassows, however, behaved as though I were a jaguar or a puma: as long as they were physically out of reach, they obviously felt they could hang around and hiss and boo to their hearts' content.

Curassows are the size of turkeys but they look even larger, perhaps because of their more solid coloration. The males, otherwise outfitted in basic black from stem to stern (except for some negligible white touches underneath), display a spectacular yellow nob, like a huge gold nugget, at the base of their beaks; the females wear deep, orangy browns, nicely set off by salt-and-pepper feathering around the neck and face. In contrast to turkeys, the heads of both sexes seem outsized, owing to the pretty crests they wear, which curve forward as though they had been permed.

For what seemed a considerable time, maybe a minute, maybe two, I happily stood there suffering the curassows' abuse. Then the three birds on the right side of the track flapped heavily across to join those on the left, and, satisfied that they'd given me what-for, the lot of them finally moved off into the forest.

I had my compass with me for a change, so I didn't always stick to the trail as I wandered on. Behind the crowded shrubs and trees fighting for precedence in the narrow belt of sunlight the lane had opened up, the forest was taller than any I had seen at Sian Ka'an, and in places fairly open at ground level. One toucan, a coatimundi, and a host of elusive little songbirds later, I passed through a perimeter of high-and-dry mangroves and came to the edge of a small marsh, which looked like it might be the elbow of a larger one nudging into the hammock at an angle. It appeared to be dried up, but out toward the center egrets rose and settled in the shallows of water I couldn't see.

What I could see were the same strange, heavy tracks in the dry mud that I had last encountered in Campeche, when Ramón had pointed to them and murmured, "*Muy raro.*"

The sky overhead was losing light fast, the rose pink that had suffused it a moment earlier darkening into mauve. I knew I couldn't wait at the marsh's edge for long.

But as it turned out, I didn't have to wait at all. She—I don't know why I felt she was a she—was already there. Only the dark, rounded back, the twitching ears, the crown of the strange head were visible above the grass. But this wasn't like the ocelot—a case of being almost but not quite sure. Even before she lifted her curved snout into view for a wind-sniffing second, I knew I was looking at a tapir.

She had been moving through the marsh, about twenty yards away, on a course parallel to the one I was following, only heading the other way. But now she changed direction and meandered off at a 45-degree angle, still totally unaware that she was being watched. Before long there was only an occasional glimpse of her rump, and then even that was gone. The upper third of her body was all I ever saw of her; but that was one-third more than I had dared to hope to see, even after the encounter with the crocodile had made me greedy and ambitious.

I've already tried once or twice; but I can't really explain why, for someone like me, a moment like that is literally magical; something to be remembered for the rest of my life. During the firefly night that lay ahead, when the agony of another kind of remembering would make me almost forget I had ever thought of becoming whole again, I would hold on to that obscured but prolonged glimpse of a rare and ancient beast as though it were a charm that could protect and heal.

NINE

Belize

American and European visitors to Belize usually arrive by air, and immediately head for the balmy offshore cays. So the border customs station a few miles south of Chetumal doesn't have to make a good impression on anyone, and it doesn't try. The place is shabby, dusty, badly run. The guard who checks my papers makes me cool my heels while he stares at my passport as though it were a rap sheet. By the time he is done, my teeth hurt from the grinding I've given them.

It is not a nice introduction to a country that, in an incremental sort of way, I will come to love.

A couple of hours later, and I have ended up at a place where I hadn't planned to be with someone I have met by chance. Which is one of the interesting, if not always welcome, consequences of conducting a geographic journey the way most of us conduct our lives, namely, as a series of unpremeditated detours on roads that usually dead-end.

A dead end is where Roland and I are at. A couple of miles behind us lie the village of Crooked Tree and the wildlife sanctuary of the same name. The former is a relaxed-looking, funky little community of frame houses shaded by huge mango and cashew trees. The latter is a series of inland lagoons where one can see a great wealth of wading birds, hawks and snail kites, as well as Belize's last stand of mature logwood trees. The dead end belongs to the same ecosystem as the refuge, but, just as Roland had promised, it is "different." Around us lies a strange, uncertain-looking country composed of all sorts of landscape odds and ends. When the rains come, as they will in another month or so, the seasonal flooding will no doubt tie everything together. But right now the scene comes across as the outdoor equivalent of a low-rent apartment furnished with garage-sale accessories. The effect is by no means displeasing, just incoherent: there are groves of stunted oaks and stands of scrawny tropical pines; patches of dry, wintery-looking scrub; raw, muddy pastures that cattle have grazed to the nub; and small mangrove islands that seem out of place this far inland. Only the more distant view, of a wide, tawny savannah, makes thematic sense. Roland points to the low, dark wall of trees on its far side. "See that ridge?" he says. "That goes all the way up to Orange Walk. There are still some deer and peccary out there."

Roland is a poacher, one of several I have met and talked with in the course of my travels. Indeed, only two days earlier, in Chetumal, I had had an encounter with another one of that numerous fraternity. The fellow owned a little white hole-in-the-wall that sold only hamburgers; and to judge from the round, soft look of him, he was his own best customer. He had taken a special interest in me because he had once visited New Orleans and been very impressed, though not by its treasure trove of fine architecture or its lively nightlife; no, it was the fast food chains that had stirred his soul. "Ever since," he told me, with the misty, far-off look of an astronaut taking one more step for mankind, "I have dreamed of bringing a real McDonald's to Chetumal." He apologized for his small unplasticated establishment with a disparaging glance. "Maybe someday," he had sighed.

I don't know how we got on to his favorite avocation, but before long he was telling me, with an enthusiasm that was boastful and at the same time unpleasantly coy, of the depredations that he and his friends inflicted on the wildlife of southern Quintana Roo. He even illustrated his commentary with pictures from an album he kept handy: dozens of photos of blood-spattered bucks and does—mostly does—as well as javelinas, ocelots, turkeys, and curassows. He owned a jeep, and when I produced a map and asked him to show me where he went hunting, he shocked me by pointing to every little dotted trail between Tulum and the Guatemala border. Like wildlife butchers the world over—including those that trespass on my Mississippi property—he was simultaneously self-excusing, smug, and inconsistent while describing his exploits. The game laws were ridiculous, he insisted with an outraged roll of his big brown eyes. They forbade hunting at night with vehicles and jacklights—which was the only possible way to hunt in the jungle. At the same time, he admitted that there would still be plenty of game, even on the ejidos, if people would honor the bag limits and open seasons, which of course they didn't. While he talked, I tried to maintain

an air of casual interest, but he must have sensed my disapproval. At
any rate, he assured me, with another little eye-roll or two, that he had
become more conservation-minded of late. He only shot bucks these
days; and only for home consumption, of course! A minute later, however, he was bragging that he had shot twenty deer just this year—all
bucks, of course!—even though the last photos in his album were of
slaughtered does. When I left, he looked hurt that I hadn't finished the
hamburguesa I had ordered.

And now here I was, a couple of days later, touring the Belizean outback with another poacher for company. In principle, I ought to have
disliked this one as much as I had his counterpart back in Chetumal. I
wanted to, but I couldn't.

I had given Roland a lift at the junction of the Crooked Tree road
and the Northern Highway. When we reached the lagoon, I stopped on
the narrow causeway, which the van had to itself, and glassed the birds
assembled there. I got excited when I saw what I was pretty sure was a
rather rare rufous-necked rail, then really flipped at the sight of my first
black-collared hawk, one of the most beautiful raptors I'd ever seen.

"Ah," said Roland, "you like hawks?"

"I like hawks, snakes, monkeys—anything, as long as it isn't human," I told him, making a joke of what was not quite a joke.

When we had reached Crooked Tree, I asked him where he lived.
But instead of telling me, he had directed me through the village and
across a network of risky, muddy tracks to the place where we were now.
"You like nature," he had said. "So do I. On the back side of the lagoon
it is different, more wild. There are sometimes more hawks. Maybe also
some *jabirú*. I will take you there." It wasn't so much an offer as a
command.

Regrettably, the rare and spectacular jabirú stork, which I had seen
only once when both it and I were migrants in Tabasco, had declined
to show itself, although this area of Belize boasts several nesting pairs.
On my account, Roland was more disappointed than I was myself. But
he was able to show me a couple of black hawks, a gray-necked wood
rail, which he called a "clucking hen," and, very close up, a nonven-
omous snake about six feet long. He said it was a "brown-headed" or
"brown-tailed" snake—I forget which—but it looked solid gray to me.

When we had seen what there was to see, I asked him if he was ready to go back to Crooked Tree. He shook his head, so we sat against a tree and talked for a while in English—that being the official language of this former British colony. After months of making do with my not very fluent Spanish, I was ready for the change.

Roland could have been either "Spanish," as mestizos are known in Belize, or a "white Creole"—a person having both black and white blood in his veins, with the latter predominating. He had black, wavy hair, olive skin, a blandly open face.

As soon as we were settled, he asked me, rather shyly, if I were a Christian. I gave him a sideways answer, gesturing at our surroundings and saying that my church was out here. He frowned at that, frankly registering my quasi-scientific pantheism as some sort of heathen mumbo-jumbo. But he recovered quickly and redeemed me with a forgiving smile. "That's all right," he said, "I like you, mon. I will pray for you." He went on to talk about his own recent conversion. His parents were Baptists, he told me, but in spite of their objections, he had become a Pentecostal. "I have already felt the Holy Spirit descend on me," he said. "I don't smoke or drink or take dope or whore. I got a nice clean girl, you know? Her name is Helena. She's saved too. I don't want to get her into no trouble." He grinned sheepishly and looked away.

That he and his parents had abandoned their traditional Catholicism was no surprise; throughout all of Latin America the fundamentalist sects have won millions of people away from the Church of Rome. But the inner struggle that his new-found faith imposed on him both intrigued and touched me. "Here at home," he said, "there are not many bad people. But in Orange Walk and Belize City there is so much sin, mon, you just can't believe how much! I worked in Orange Walk for a year, and the Devil tempted me every day I was there. Me, I want to live in the Holy Spirit, but it's hard in Orange Walk! That's why I wish I didn't have to leave here, mon."

At the time I had no idea how unusual this sentiment was in Belize, where almost everyone seems to have a hankering to be somewhere they are not, preferably the United States.

I asked him the obvious question: What was the problem? Why couldn't he stay in Crooked Tree?

He shook his head gloomily. "There just isn't enough animals left to hunt. And now that it's illegal, the people at the market don't pay you so much. I used to get maybe $4 Belize [$2 U.S.] for a paca. Now I get two. I can't make enough from what I sell now." He leaned forward, hunching his shoulders. "There are no jobs around here, so I guess I got to go back to Orange Walk, or maybe Belize City. I just don't know. I don't know what to do about Helena either. She don't want to go away, unless maybe to New York. I want to marry her, mon, but I can't make it here anymore. And I don't want to go to New York even if I had the money!"

It was in this incidental way that I learned that Roland was a commercial hunter. Which also meant that he was a great sinner according to the tenets of my own unofficial faith. But even that faith has room for charity. There is no way I could dislike this worried youth in whose soul the Holy Spirit, Helena, and the Devil of Necessity were fighting it out among themselves.

Partly to rouse him from his moodiness, partly because I wanted to know, I asked him to expand further on the status of local wildlife populations. For all his gentle niceness, Roland shared with every other poacher I have met the tendency to disclaim responsibility for the scarcity of game. He acknowledged that he and his cohorts hunted far and wide for at least six months of every year, at night with jacklights, by day with dogs. They couldn't afford a Land Rover like their detestable counterpart in Chetumal, but when the water was high they used boats. Nevertheless, he insisted that most of the deer and collared peccary had migrated. The white-lipped peccary that he hunted as a boy, surely not more than three or four years earlier, had entirely vanished. They had moved, he explained, to Guatemala.

He did offer me some good news. The local population of crocodiles seemed to be increasing. He doubted that this had anything to do with the fact that the lagoons at Crooked Tree were now a sanctuary. Indeed, he complained, somewhat ironically, that the warden, a good friend of his, couldn't do his job. "They don't give him nothing, not even a horse, so he can move around." The crocodile comeback, he said, could be better attributed to the reduced demand for the creatures' hides.

Roland also said that jaguars still came through the area. One had killed a calf only a couple of months earlier. "The man asked one of my brothers who has dogs to come hunt it, but my brother had to work that day, so the jaguar got away."

I made a stab at implanting a conservation concept: "It's only fair," I said. "You and your friends kill all the deer, so the jaguar has to kill the cows." Roland laughed at this. "Ha! That's right," he exclaimed, "we eat his food so he says, 'I fix you. I eat yours!'"

When I dropped him off at his parents' house, a ramshackle but homey wooden bungalow much like all the other houses in Crooked Tree, I offered him a bit of money for having given me a personal tour. "Oh, no, mon," he said. "You gave me a ride. I don't want your money. I wanted to do that."

I asked him if he were still going to pray for me. "Oh, yeah!" he said, "for sure."

"Okay," I told him, "in that case I will pray for you too."

He looked nonplused. "You? Pray for me?"

"I'll pray that you can find a job here so you can stay and marry Helena, and not have to kill any more wildlife for money."

"Oh, well," he started to say, "like I told you, the animals are already about gone—"

But then he caught on. "Oh, look, mon," he protested, his young voice earnest, "you got to believe me. I like nature, too!"

I nodded. I did believe him.

A little sadly, feeling the distance between us, we shook hands and wished each other well.

The ferry at Bermuda Landing was a stumpy little barge, propelled back and forth by means of cable and winch, with two sweaty men turning the drum by hand. Unlike some other primitive ferries I've made nervous use of, this one posed no danger of capsizing or just plain falling apart while making the river crossing. The adventure here was in getting on and off. To accomplish the getting on, it was necessary to dip the van down the steep riverbank, run it through the river shallows and gun it up a sharply angled ramp, then brake quickly at the top so as not to bump one of the other two cars—the ferry could only carry three— into the drink. Hitting that ramp was like hitting a high curb; the van's front end scraping alarmingly as it not quite cleared the metal lip. I don't see how the sagging, antique Oldsmobile in front of me could have made it if it had not already lost its muffler and tailpipe.

Bermuda Landing, a one-time logging center, looked to be even smaller and more run-down than Crooked Tree, but was aswarm with people. The tiny cement block store at the top of the landing was packed to the windowsills with folks drinking beer and soft drinks. On the wall near the door hung a blackboard bearing the admonitory epitaph: "Poor Toolous dead. Make bad payment." Outside, a steady stream of people meandered back and forth along the dirt road that followed the river downstream, not paying much attention to the lively sounds of a reggae band that came from that direction. Suddenly remembering what day it was, I wondered if maybe this was the way people celebrated their Sundays hereabouts. But when I asked an elderly gent in a bright blue shirt what was going on, he nodded in the direction of the music and grunted, "The new bridge. They finally got it done."

Sure enough, after I'd gone with the flow of the crowd for a couple of hundred yards, there it was: a brand-new bridge spanned by an arch made of palm fronds, with the flags of Belize and the United States on either side hanging limp in the warm air. On the far side the band was playing to rows of mostly empty folding chairs. Maybe the speeches hadn't begun yet, but to judge from the jaded expressions on the faces of people milling around it was more likely they were just over. I think now that the reason no one seemed in a very festive mood was because this *wasn't* the way they usually spent their Sundays.

But I hadn't driven twelve dirt miles inland from the Northern Highway and risked the underpinnings of my van on Bermuda Landing's soon-to-be abandoned ferry just to observe a bridge. I had come here to see monkeys.

I asked a couple of young fellows for directions. "The Baboon Sanctuary?" one of them grinned. He waved generously at the riverside trees. "Hell, mon," he said, "you in it."

And I was. I had only to wander into a roughly cleared pasture, pick up a footpath that stuck close to the steep muddy bank, and put a little distance between myself and the amplified reggae music in order to hear an amplified music of a quite other kind. A lone howler monkey was sounding off.

It was one thing to hear him; getting close enough to see him was something else again. He was in a small clump of trees at no great distance, but between the trees and me rose a wall of some kind of bamboo that gave new meaning to the word *impenetrable*. There was never a chance of getting through the stuff upright; but even when I tried to belly-crawl my way under it, the canes, equipped with long, savage thorns, raked me over like razor-sharp barbed wire. I had given up any hope of getting closer to the grove when, a little further on, I found a shoulder-wide path cutting off at right angles from the riverside trail. After following it a short distance, the cane thinned out enough to allow me to come at the trees from their far side. The "baboon," as howlers are known in Belize, had continued roaring and bellowing his head off all this time, and once I had a clear view of the trees, I had no trouble seeing him. Howlers are apt to sound off at the drop of a fig, but this one was obviously seriously upset about something. He bounded back and forth from one branch to another, belting out roar after roar, pausing now and then long enough to peer this way and that while nervously scratching his behind. I dunno. Maybe he was responding to the faintly audible hollering of another howler on the river's opposite bank. Or delivering a critical commentary on the reggae music. Or simply complaining because he was all alone. The one sure thing was that *I* hadn't stirred him up. I stood there watching him for ten minutes without his giving me so much as a dirty look. It might have been different, however, if I had been right under his tree, for howlers are notoriously given to defecating on people who impinge on their space too closely.

Howlers are the largest of the New World monkeys, weighing in at up to twenty pounds. Among their anatomical idiosyncrasies is a curious set of structures in their throats that enables them to make a racket that carries for miles, and at their other end, a leathery traction pad on their tails that helps anchor them to tree limbs when they reach out for fruit or get a little carried away with their hollering. I don't know what the story was with my lone bachelor, but ordinarily they travel in family groups of three to ten, headed by a dominant male. Here at the Baboon Sanctuary, at any rate, each troupe lays claim to a home territory of anywhere from five to fifty acres, depending on the abundance of favorite food trees such as wild fig, hog plums, and sapodillas. Within each territory, there are specially favored trees where the resident troupe regularly gets together for a nice group howl.

Of the six species of howlers that inhabit various parts of Central and South America, the Mexican black, which can be found in southern

Mexico, Belize, and some areas of Guatemala, has the most northerly range. Its recent sad history is similar to that of most other Central American wildlife: overhunting and the destruction of forests have eliminated it from most of its former haunts. Ironically, in southern Belize, where the monkeys still have adequate habitat to maintain their numbers, they have never fully recovered—so I am told—from, of all things, an epidemic of yellow fever that decimated them in the 1950s.

All of which makes the Baboon Sanctuary at Bermuda Landing that much more important as an experiment in wildlife management. Impoverished little country though it is, Belize realizes that ecotourism can be an important factor in its economic future, and, to its great credit, it is taking steps to protect some of its spectacular wildlife resources while there is still time to do so. But the remarkable thing about this particular little refuge is that it has come into being without benefit of a government initiative, and not an acre of it is publicly owned. In 1985, at the prompting of a far-sighted conservationist named Dr. Rob Horwich, local landowners voluntarily agreed to protect the riparian forest edges on their property as a means of preserving the monkeys' habitat while at the same time protecting their land from the erosive force of the river in flood. More than ninety landowners in seven river villages now participate in the program, and the number of cooperators—and the size of the refuge—continues to grow. At present a narrow, 20-mile stretch of forest on both sides of the river is protected, with about a thousand howlers in residence. There is talk now of relocating some of them to areas of the Maya Mountains in the south, to build up populations there.

Everybody and everything benefits from this arrangement. High densities of monkeys coexist amicably with high densities of humans, and other wildlife, like the paca and the rare Central American river turtle, come in for protection too. At the same time agricultural lands are protected from erosion, and local people benefit economically from a steady trickle of ecotourists, some of whom stay overnight at the small visitor center or in guest houses run by the villagers themselves. If it hadn't been for all that to-do at the new bridge, I would have stayed the night myself.

Heading back to the van, I could still hear, above the bridge music, my lone howler bellowing away, being answered now by a whole chorus of hoots and hollers from across the river. How great it would be, I thought, if there were thousands of grassroots wildlife sanctuaries along hundreds of tropical rivers in scores of Third World countries. And then I asked myself, "Well, why the hell weren't there? Why *shouldn't* there be?" For the first time in a long time, I heard the clarion bugle's call, and felt myself fairly vibrating with resurgent ecological militancy.

Belize City is not a nice place to visit, and you certainly wouldn't want to live there. But in its own Gin Alley sort of way it teems with colorful, eccentric life. Now that I know my way around there, something theatrical and sleazy in my temperament surrenders to it as uncritically as a young sailor to a motherly whore. Of course, another, more order-loving part of me remains primly scandalized—and wears a money belt.

The whole place—and it is not very large—looks like *Porgy and Bess's* Catfish Row, except that instead of moldering Charlestonian brick there is sagging tropical pine in varying shades of faded pastel and just plain weathered board. Since the ill-chosen setting is a mangrove swamp, the only solid land was, is, and always will be, a midden composed mostly of mahogany logs, shells, and trash—including several centuries' worth of broken rum bottles. With dry land at a premium, all the houses are two-storied and packed together, the porches hanging over narrow, crowded streets. The whole place looks as though it were made of cardboard and might fall down at any moment like the set in *Blazing Saddles.* And in fact, it *has* fallen down on occasion, most notably in 1931, and again in 1961, when hurricanes laid the town flat. With each rebuilding, it has come out looking much as it did before, only a little more frazzled and thrown-together. The general effect is Bahamian Decadent, by no means unpleasant to look at if you squint your eyes a little.

Unfortunately, it's not so easy to squint one's nose. Poverty in Belize City is more intensely tropical than it is in peninsular Mexico: wet, soft, and overripe, rather than stony, dry, and desiccated. Garbage competes with flowering shrubs to scent the air, and the canals and the deep, trenchlike gutters along the side streets reek like the open sewers they are. On the positive side, Haulover Creek, the delta branch of the Belize River that bisects the city, can boast a natural water purification system that puts to shame the more ambitious schemes of environmental engineers: In places, especially near the market, the river roils like the piranha pool in a James Bond movie, only here the fish in question are hundreds of thousands of saltwater catfish—"shittifish," as the natives aptly call them—greedily devouring the city's otherwise untreated wastes.

Actually, one's first impression of Belize City depends a lot on timing, although the timing can no more be scheduled than anything else around here. Some days, nothing much is going on. On others, like the one on which I first arrived, it seems as though all the inmates at the local funny farm have been turned loose in the streets. A sense of civic abandonment prevails that would gladden the soul of even the most hard-to-please anarchist. Its unfocused center is the Swing Bridge, an antiquated engineering marvel that really does swing—manually winched by four men using poles and capstan—on its pivot pier twice a day, allowing boats to pass between the river and the sea. All the city's traffic, vehicular and pedestrian, is channeled to this crossing, where Queen, Albert, and Regent—streets rather less grand than their grand-sounding names—converge. There is a pretty view from the bridge of the fishing fleet parked at the river's mouth, with patient flocks of gulls and vultures lounging on the bank; but on my first crossing I was much too preoccupied with not bumping into the cars and people pressing around me to pay it much attention. Once I reached the south side, I pulled over to the curb as soon as I could to get my bearings.

What I got instead was a thin young man with staring zombie eyes, poking his small, dark head and spindly arms through the window on the passenger side of the van even before it had come to a full stop.

"Can I help you, sir?" he breathed.

"Well, yes," I said. "I'd like to find a bookstore where I can buy a map and a book about Belize."

"Oh, I'll show you where one is. I know a good place."

He made to open the door, but by then I was taking in the scene around me. "Hold on a minute," I told him. "The shops are all closed." They were not only closed, but sealed with metal shutters or grills. A guard holding something that looked like a machine gun stood in front of one of them. Suddenly remembering, I said, "It's Sunday."

"That's right, sir," said the young man. He still hadn't blinked his scary eyes. "Can I have one of your cookies?" A long, thin finger pointed to the box of Oreos on the passenger seat.

I handed him several, which he stuffed in the pockets of his red shirt.

Giving up on the bookstore idea, I named a guest house I had heard about that was supposed to be a little more reasonable than the city's two or three exorbitantly priced tourist hotels. I asked him if he knew where it was.

"Oh, yes, sir," he said. "Are you going to stay here?"

"Well, for the night, anyway."

"I'll show you."

"No, no, just tell me."

"Do you want some grass? A nice girl?"

"No, just a place to sleep."

He withdrew his head from the window. At last his eyes blinked. "Turn right here," he said in a silken, unpleasant way. "Then go straight ahead."

I had already concluded that Belize City was innocent of traffic lights, traffic cops, or directional signs. But judging from the way cars, moving and parked, were pointed, the narrow street the young man had indicated was one way the wrong way. I remarked on this.

"Oh no," he said, "it's both ways. Can I have some money?"

"I don't have any small change," I said, truthfully enough. "But have some more cookies."

He took a handful more, then backed away, giving me a coldly sullen look. At a little distance, he also gave me the finger for good measure.

Catty-corner from where I had pulled over was a small, grassless park. In the middle of the teeming street in front of it, indifferent to the indifferent people and vehicles streaming by, an ancient, skinny crone stood stiff and still. She was wearing a ragged gray dress. An untidy rope of gray hair hung down her back. She stared at absolutely nothing, evidently hating what she saw. Closer by, an elderly man strode along, punctuating an unintelligible chant with sudden loud, keening wails. The passersby ignored the old woman, but they gave the wailer a wide berth.

I got out of the van and approached a pair of men who looked reasonably sane. One was about 30, sandy-haired and smooth-faced. The other was middle-aged, wearing a Panama hat and a trim mustache. When I asked them the location of the guest house, the younger fellow gave me an aghast look, as though I had just stepped out of a nightmare. Then, to my dismay, his face became all squinched up, and he began to cry! His companion, with a blaming look at me, took him firmly by the elbow and led him away.

Now, no one should suppose from all this that everyone in Belize City is certifiable. Only a moment later, a kind old gentleman, no doubt noticing that I was beginning to look a bit around the bend myself, asked if he could be of help; and he soon had me heading in the right direction toward the elusive guest house, which was about a block and a half away. Subsequently I would meet many other nice people who call Belize City home. But taken all in all, there's no denying that, in its colorful, raffish way, the place is a civic mess.

It probably always was. From the very first, it was an anomaly among England's colonial outposts, largely because its modern history did not begin in the customary way, with the subjugation of native peoples by representatives of the Crown acting in the interests of English imperialism. For one thing, there were few if any native peoples living along Belize's malarial coasts when white men first settled here in the early seventeenth century. The ancient Maya who once called this region home had, like their counterparts in Guatemala and Campeche, abandoned their ceremonial centers by the tenth century for reasons still not altogether clear. Although Maya tribes still occupied what are now the Corozal and Cayo districts of Belize, the forebears of most of the Maya Indians that inhabit the country today—Mopan and Kekchi—immigrated from Guatemala about one hundred years ago.

Another reason for Belize's eccentric colonial background is the fact that the first whites to settle here were privateers who were given license by England to prey on the merchant vessels of unfriendly countries, which in the Caribbean usually meant Spain. However, by 1670, most of the settlers were discovering that Belize's forests offered a more dependable way to make a financial killing than did the shipping lanes off its coasts. Those forests were wonderfully rich in logwood, the source of a fixing dye that was bringing very high prices in Europe. The Baymen, as they were called, were all the more motivated to try a new line of work when England, during a peaceful interval in its usually hostile relations with Spain, decided, as a diplomatic gesture, to hunt down all the pirates in the Caribbean, whether it had earlier authorized their activities or not.

Cutting logwood might have been slightly more respectable than privateering in theory, but in practice it was brutal, killing work. The precious trees had to be extracted from steaming jungles in the blazing hot dry season, and then, when the rains came, floated down swollen rivers and through malarial swamps to the raggedy little settlement that was to become Belize City, full of grog shops, itinerant whores, and thieves. Inevitably, the Baymen were a tough, hard-drinking, independent lot, with no strong predilection for law and order. Smuggling, for example, has always been a fact of Belizean life: in the nineteenth century, a lot of people made fortunes running guns for the rebelling Maya in Yucatán and the Confederates in the States, and some still do, running dope. The people of the Bay Settlement were apt to be "takers," willing to try anything to make a quick profit rather than settle down to more staid business and agricultural pursuits like settlers in most other areas. And in Belize City today, that mind-set still prevails.

Early on, the governors of Jamaica, England's main stronghold in the predominantly Spanish West Indies, recognized the economic importance of Belize as a source of the valuable logwood, and they did what they could to keep the area within Britain's sphere of influence. However, it was two hundred years before England, rather reluctantly, officially took the area under its protection as a Crown colony. During the long interim, the Baymen evolved their own democratic public meeting system of government, and that tradition of self-government remained strong even after Crown rule was established in 1862. For decades before Belize became independent in 1981, it was accustomed to managing most its internal affairs with much guidance, but little actual interference, from England, which is one reason why the transition to independence was relatively painless, and the two countries remain on friendly terms.

Another reason has to do with the Bay Settlement's peculiar way of dealing with that "peculiar institution," slavery. Large numbers of blacks were imported as manpower to fell and process logwood, and later, in the eighteenth century, mahogany. But this was never a planter society; blacks and whites worked side by side in the jungles and on the rivers, miscegenation was socially acceptable, and slaves could, and frequently did, earn their freedom by working overtime for wages. The injustices built into the system should not be glossed over, of course. In the eighteenth century, for example, there were several instances of slaves rebelling against their overseers. But in general, there does seem to have been a shared realization on the part of the two races that, like it or not, they had their backs against the same wall. Repeatedly throughout the 1700s, whenever England and Spain's on-again, off-again wars were on again, Spanish troops stationed in the Yucatán attacked, and on several occasions burned, the Bay Settlement; and during these often bloody encounters, the Baymen, black and white, fought together against their common enemy. For that matter, not all blacks who came to the colony arrived as slaves. When an all-black West India regiment was disbanded in 1817, hundreds of its men and their families were transported to Belize as independent woodcutters. And in just one year, 1836, more than five hundred blacks were rescued from slave ships and allowed to settle in the Bay Colony as free citizens. When slavery was abolished in all of England's colonies two years later, the Baymen accepted the declaration without much fuss. By that time, two-thirds of Belize's inhabitants were of pure African or mixed descent. Originally, the latter reserved for themselves the term "Creole"; and it is an ironic fact that the strongest bias in this racially mixed country seems to have been between these two groups. Some of it is still around, but nowadays the term "Creole" covers every shade of black from practically white to plum-dark.

Except, that is, for the black Caribs, the Garifuna. These ethnically unique people are in part descendants of a fierce tribe of South American Indians who invaded the Lesser Antilles at about the time Columbus was discovering the New World. They were cannibals, and more or less literally ate up the Arawak tribes that got in their way, not to mention any shipwrecked Caucasians hapless enough to fall into their hands. By the seventeenth century, however, white men's weapons and diseases had weakened, though not defeated, them. When two Spanish slave ships ran aground on St. Vincent's Island in 1635, the slaves understandably resisted the efforts of the Indians to pop them in their cooking pots. They gave such a good account of themselves that they and the Caribs ended by making love, not war. From this union, in which the black genetic line was predominant, the Garifuna were born. After suffering many cruel privations, inflicted chiefly by the English, some of them settled along the southern coast of Belize early in the nineteenth century. Their numbers were augmented in 1832 when the

Garifuna in the republic of Honduras, having backed the wrong side in an attempted political coup, were driven from that country. Most of their descendants can still be found in the southern towns of Dangriga and Punta Gorda and the small fishing villages in between. They are fiercely proud of their Indian ancestors, who were never slaves; and some still resent the black component in their bloodlines. Although nowadays they are much less ethnocentric than in the past, and coexist peacefully with Creoles, they are apt to hold themselves superior and rarely intermarry with them. They still speak their own Carib-based language, preserve their unique cultural mishmash of superstitions, customs, and religious beliefs, and observe their own commemorative holidays.

Black Creoles constitute the majority of Belize's multiracial citizenry, but not by the margin they enjoyed two hundred years ago. The Garifuna are only one of many ethnic groups that have come to Belize since then, most of them refugees or deportees from somewhere else. By far, the single largest influx came in 1848, when thousands of Yucatecan mestizos fled across the Río Hondo during the War of the Castes. Their "Spanish" descendants are now the second largest ethnic group in the country. Like the Creoles, they are a ubiquitous presence everywhere in Belize, but most are concentrated in the northern and western districts of Corozal, Cayo, and Orange Walk. Living side by side with these numerically dominant groups are the offspring of East Indians deported after the Sepoy Mutiny, imported Chinese laborers, Lebanese peddlers, and the aforementioned Kekchi and Mopan Maya. More recent arrivals have been Canadian-German Mennonites, a great flood of refugees from Honduras and Guatemala, and, last but not least, a considerable number of Americans who are drawn here both by this little country's laid-back lifestyle and the real and imagined opportunities it affords for making a fast buck.

While I was easing the van along the street toward the guest house, I spied two young Caucasian males, the only whites in sight, walking toward me through the Sunday crowds. Their white shirts were soaked with sweat, and they carried their suit jackets under their arms; but their ties were bravely knotted under their chins, their hair was combed, and they were managing, against the odds, to look impressively neat.

You could tell, though, that they were pretty unstrung. They had to be newly arrived Mormon missionaries, and they were obviously in the throes of culture shock. To judge from the stunned expressions of their nice, clean-cut faces you would have thought some sadistic church elder had dumped them in the middle of Harlem with night coming on and not even a subway token in their pockets. One of the local panhandlers had fallen into step beside them, and they were trying politely but desperately to shoo him away.

Poor guys, I thought. But I couldn't help grinning as I passed them. I felt that I had already survived my initiation. They still had a ways to go.

"It looks sort of like a walrus," said the middle-aged lady from California, peering nervously over the side, as though it might jump out of the water and snap at her.

"People must feed it fish or something," her husband said. He chuckled. "It's looking for a handout like everybody else around here."

"They don't eat fish," muttered Bruce, offering the lady a hit on his joint, which she flutteringly refused. "They eat seaweed, kelp, stuff like that."

Everyone except me seemed to be taking this extraordinary sight in stride. The Swedish boy went right on reading his pocket Bible. The blonde girl with olive skin, who had accepted a couple of drags from Bruce's joint, gave it one dreamy glance and looked away. As for me, I could hardly believe what I was staring at: Right here within sight of the Swing Bridge, aimlessly muddling about in the polluted, shittifish-crowded waters of Haulover Creek, was a manatee! I had gone looking for them once or twice during visits to Florida, but the timing wasn't right; so this was the first wild one I had ever seen. Like spotting a blue whale from the Brooklyn Bridge.

The sighting was not an unalloyed joy, however. The animal, just a few feet out from the pier and mere inches below the surface, was a youngster, only about four feet long. Much too young to be on its own, which it plainly was. I supposed it must be hungry for mother's milk. It swam about just below the surface in a vague, disoriented way, touching its boxing-glove nose to the pier, gliding under the prow of the motor launch, swinging slowly out into the river's current, then moseying back to the pier again. I wondered aloud if a motorboat like the one we were sitting in, waiting to be taxied out to Caye Caulker, might have done the mother in. "Why, hell, we hit them all the time, mon," said the captain. "It don' hurt them, it hurt the engine!"

Bruce, who used to be a marine biologist and Peace Corps volunteer in Belize before he became an alcoholic and a dopehead and a poet and a searcher for truth and sunken treasure, said in a slurred but authoritative voice, "Belize is the only place in Central America where there's still a pretty good supply of manatees left. Mostly in the bays and rivers south of the city. But you can spot 'em sometimes on the flight to San Pedro. The old-time sailors thought they were mermaids; which just goes to show how horny they must of been after months at sea."

"They good meat," said the little boat's tall, rather fierce-looking mate. Small deep-set eyes peered out from under his heavy, purple-black brow, a broad upper lip protruded from under a broad, flattened nose, and a rather menacing smile exposed astonishingly wide, white teeth, big as piano keys. "They got four kinds of meat on 'em. One part tastes jus' like beef, another jus' like chicken, another sorta like pork." He smacked his lips with comic exaggeration. "Like buyin' the whole damn butcher shop in one package."

The several hangers-on lounging about the pier laughed appreciatively. In between their sporadic efforts to persuade us passengers to send them on errands to pick up beer ("One for me, one for you, mon") or a lid of grass ("Cost you twice as much on Caye Caulker, mon"), the mate had been regaling them with apparently very funny anecdotes that only one of us, the olive-skinned girl with dyed yellow hair, was able to understand. She was sitting next to me, and once—when I had caught a loud, exclamatory "What!"—I asked her to translate. She giggled. "He says, 'I went to the Chinese to buy two cigarettes, and mon, he thinked I want chicken or something. He ask me if I want ketchup or sauce or something. So I say, WHAT? You crazy Chinese put ketchup on your cigarettes!'"

The mate had been speaking Creole. Most Belizeans are trilingual. English is still the official language, although Spanish is now almost as frequently heard in some districts. But Creole is the *lingua franca* everywhere. It is a marvelously garbled pidgin English that evolved among the slave population ages ago. Phonetically spelled out, it sometimes becomes intelligible—"I went to Belize and it was great," for example, is "I gawn da Belize and e me good"—but it is always delivered in such a jabbered, rapid-fire way that a visitor to the country might as well be hearing Greek. Unlike the foreign languages he would encounter elsewhere, this one is the private property of all the displaced peoples who have made Belize their home for generations. It is deliberately intended to separate them from those of us who come and go without time or motivation to learn a patois we don't need while we are here and could never use anywhere else. Still, I wished I could understand it. By now I was really liking Belize. I had the feeling that the little country would keep surprising me. I wanted not to feel so overwhelmingly like the tourist I was.

Bruce, whose face wore a couple of bruises (from a recent fight, as I later learned), was bargaining with one of the hangers-on in his toughest Hemingway voice, making it clear that *he* was not some tourist who could be easily gulled. He warned the fellow that he'd better be back by the time the boat left or else. The hanger-on grinned, cajoled, and said, "Yeh, mon," twenty times before Bruce finally handed him the money to fetch a half-lid of grass and a couple of beers.

After the fellow had hied himself off, the mate said something to the other hangers-on that made them and the captain and the girl next to me laugh. When I asked the girl what had been said, she glanced at Bruce, who was slipping into a stoned and drunken doze. Even though she had accepted the hits from his joint, you could tell she didn't like him. She leaned close and whispered in a slow, carefully enunciated Creole, "Da bawly tink e adright bute da wa fuckin' ass." I nodded, pleased that I had got the drift, and we exchanged a conspiratorial smile.

Fifteen, twenty minutes passed. The boat looked to be about full. Besides the Swedish boy, the California couple, Bruce, the girl, and myself, there were now three young men ranged on the padded benches— British soldiers on a two-day leave from the base that England maintains at Ladyville as a safeguard against Guatemala's periodic attempts to annex Belize. But it wasn't four-thirty yet, when the boat was scheduled to leave, and so we waited, none of us having much to say now, not even the mate, all of us growing torpid in the heat of the tropical afternoon. The Swedish boy scratched at his ulcerated toes. While living with a family at Teakettle he had acquired a case of jungle rot so hurtful he couldn't wear shoes or sandals; but he was sure the sun and salt water at Caye Caulker would clear the problem up. Bruce dozed, the California couple stared blankly at a crowd of children departing the Holy Redeemer Cathedral on Front Street, the British soldiers drank beer and read the pasted-up legends on the luggage compartment. Sentiments like "IF I DON'T GET LAID SOON I'M GOING TO KILL SOMEBODY."

It hurt me now to watch the little manatee still swimming forlornly back and forth along the pier. I shut my eyes. My jaw was so heavy I could hardly keep my sagging mouth closed. In another minute I would be asleep . . . Which was when the captain decided it was time to push off. The motor revved up, the hangers-on threw the ropes to the mate, and then we were all ducking our heads as the boat moved under the low Swing Bridge. I supposed the baby manatee hadn't gotten in the way of the propeller blades, since I hadn't felt a bump.

Bruce was wide awake now, aware that his beer and lid of grass hadn't been delivered. Above the roar of the motor, he raved, "The sonuvabitch, I knew I shouldn't 'uv trusted him. I'll kill him if I ever get my hands on him." He went on like that for some minutes. The rest of us pretended we couldn't hear a thing, our faces expressionless. But it was as though there were a wicked, secret grin being passed around from the captain to the mate to each of us in turn. Except maybe the Swedish boy, who seemed to be listening to some very different voice the rest of us couldn't hear. Presently the girl beside me turned her face to the sea, gazing at the lovely mangrove islands that lay ahead of us, her olive cheek brushing my shoulder. Above the roar of the engine and the hard slap of the waves, I could hear her tittering like a little bird.

All the world of deep-sea divers knows that the 176-mile barrier reef extending the length of Belize's coast is second only to Australia's Great Barrier Reef in size, and second to none in the crystalline clarity of its waters, the glory of its rose, yellow, lavender coral gardens, the myriad of its glittering fish more colorful than butterflies, the wonders of its mysterious Blue Hole and cavern dormitories full of sleeping sharks, the blue dells where lie its hidden troves of sunken treasure ships.

But alas and, again, alas; the rapture of the deep does not enrapture me. Although I am a fair swimmer, and I like to snorkel now and then,

I will never qualify as an underwater sort of person. Serious diving makes me feel even more insecure and disoriented than I actually am; but that aside, even the most gorgeously tinted formations of coelenterates, the most kaleidoscopic and effervescent throngs of fishes large and small, do not thrill me near as much as land-based beasts and birds and reptiles do.

There are hundreds of cays, or in Belizean, cayes (pronounced "keys"), lined up behind the ridge of Belize's great barrier reef, sporting names like Dog Flea, Baby Roach, Wee Wee, and Bread and Butter. They range in size from little nubbins of coral barely large enough to accommodate a few orange-blossomed *ziricote*, wish willy iguanas, and nesting seabirds, to sizable watery forests of green mangroves sheltering herons, spoonbills, frigate birds, and millions of juvenile fish, to long, narrow, dry islands where palms grow, fisherfolk make their homes, and tourists come to roost.

Of these latter, Ambergris Caye is by far the largest and most developed. The one-time sleepy fishing village of San Pedro at its southern end, settled in the long ago by pirates and, later, refugees from the War of the Castes, is now a boomy little place with an air strip, shops and restaurants, mopeds, and miles of fancy hotels and resorts that offer all the pricey amenities one requires for above- and underwater life on a tropic isle. On some of the other cayes—Chapel, Goff's, way-out-in-the-blue Glover's Reef, and the Turneffe atoll—there are other more isolated and exclusive places for the deep-sea diving and swimming set, all requiring reservations and special transportation arrangements.

And then there is Caye Caulker. It began its tourist history as a way station on the Gringo Trail, frequented by students, dropouts, posthippie hippies, or just plain druggies who were taking off a semester or the rest of their lives to drift about, sopping up sun and local color on the cheap. Nowadays, the tourists who come here are a much more mixed, and generally more upscale, bag. But Caye Caulker is still, far and away, the funkiest, most easygoing, and least expensive of Belize's pleasure islands.

Also, the most interesting and entertaining. One imagines that Key Largo might have been like this place in the good old Humphrey Bogart days of fifty years ago. There are two sandy main streets, one along the island's central spine, the other hugging the sea front. Most of the houses are pure West Indian: tin-roofed wooden boxes on piers, with jalousies and plank shutters, and gauzy curtains waving out the windows, and cisterns to catch rainwater under the eaves. Some, including a number of new cinder block uglies, are small hotels. At most of them, the no-frills rooms are dirt cheap.

No sandy beach separates land from sea; just groves of coconut palms and then a coral curb dropping into the kelpy shallows. Scores of narrow little piers extend out to the deeper water, with small fishing launches rocking up against them. Pelicans dive in the usually calm seas, little blue herons patrol the docks, gulls and terns ride the glittering Caribbean air. Even when the breeze lags and the mosquitoes and sand flies assert themselves, this is still a lovely scene.

On the surface, anyway. For some of the residents, and the occasional unlucky visitor, Caye Caulker can be a long way down the road from paradise. It is, in fact, a mixed and mixed-up little world. Unlike mostly Spanish San Pedro, the people here are a typical Belizean blend of whites, Creoles, and mestizos. Nowadays most of them rely on the tourist trade to make a living; but the swashbuckling days when the islanders were pirates and salvagers as well as fishermen are, though gone, not forgotten. In those days people worked dangerously and hard when they worked, and either prayed a lot or stayed drunk and stoned when they didn't.

The stark contrasts are still there. I remember walking past the little Templo Evangélico with Bruce one evening. Inside, the islanders, mostly Spanish women, were joining with the preacher in singing hymns. "Disgusting," Bruce snorted. "I hate to see the minds of young girls being twisted with all that crap."

When I remarked that there were worse ways that people could get their minds twisted, Bruce didn't ask what I meant.

Since practically forever, marijuana has been the opiate of the masses in Belize. You could, and still can, buy it anywhere, any time, from practically anyone. Whatever the consequences of its use in terms of missed appointments and work left undone, if you wanted the stuff you didn't have to rob or murder someone in order to get it. But times have changed. Belize, land of cannabis, has now also become the Land of Cocaine. A lot of people down here blame the United States for this development. They argue that, in exchange for importing Belizean sugar, we have pressured the government into at least making an effort—granted, not a very successful one—to crack down on marijuana production. But the real explanation is that, in recent years, cocaine smugglers have been using Belize as a refueling stop between Colombia and the States. It is nothing unusual for aircraft loaded with coke to land on public roads around Orange Walk—or even the Northern Highway—while their on-the-ground confederates politely hold up traffic and the local cops look the other way. In exchange for services rendered, the smugglers pay off their Belizean accomplices in crack, to be sold locally. The widespread addiction that has resulted accounts for much of the crime that goes on in Orange Walk and Belize City. And now, sad to say, on Caye Caulker. Some tourists support the habit by buying the stuff themselves; others by being robbed or hustled. Either way, it makes for occasional bad scenes in this coral-and-palm-tree Eden.

I don't want to overstate the problem, though. For almost all tourists who come here, Caye Caulker is a trip in the best sense of the word. Like the natives, the visitors are a mixed lot: middle-income, middle-aged couples on a budget vacation, slumming cosmopolites, posthippies, bright-eyed West Coast yuppies, Peace Corps workers, British soldiers, and an assortment of stray mavericks like Bruce, who wants to find sunken treasure and lose himself, and the Swedish boy, who is even more concerned with the well-being of his soul than his feet. You can see them all, as well as a few locals, every evening at the Reef Bar, swilling down rum Cokes or Belican, the excellent Belizean beer. The scene is an update on a setting in a Conrad novel: the beat-up wooden porch with a couple of rickety benches and a view of the moonlit sea; the coconut palms clattering like old fans in the stiff breeze; the grubby interior with a floor of thin sand covering long-dead coral; the convivial bar; the jukebox with its good selection. All told, maybe thirty or forty people milling around. Except for a few Lord Jims keeping poetically to themselves, everyone seems to know at least half the other people who have happily stranded themselves in this snug little den.

My second night on the island, my first in the bar, I was of half a mind to join the outcast-of-the-islands minority. The way I saw it, Caye Caulker's charms were of a romantic sort that fairly cried out to be shared with someone one cared a lot about. Since that option wasn't in the cards, keeping to myself seemed to be the next best alternative.

But my shipmates of the previous afternoon had other ideas. They were all present and accounted for, except the olive-skinned girl, and they took turns seeing to it that I didn't feel left out of things. Like all travelers whose paths recross in out-of-the-way places, they and I reengaged with a familiarity no less sincere for being superficial. We were, after all, voyagers who had been, and in a sense still were, in the same boat.

The three British soldiers were the first to settle at the small table, their bare knees setting it to rocking on the uneven floor, jeopardizing all our beers. "Had a rough time finding bunks last night, mate," said the tallest and most blonde of the trio. "None of the buggers wanted to take us in. Had to practically bribe one of them."

They were the first British soldiers to show up on Caye Caulker in the last six months. During that period, the island had been declared off limits to army personnel. "As far as most of the bastards what run the hotels are concerned," said the blonde, "it's still off limits. They're afraid of us now."

"Good!" grunted one of his chums, short and dark, perhaps a Welshman, who talked from the side of his mouth.

"It wouldn't 'uv been so good if we'd had to sleep with the sand flies," the third soldier, older than the other two, chimed in.

What happened was that a Scots infantryman on liberty had been beaten up and robbed on the island by a couple of local hoods. When no arrests were immediately forthcoming, a bunch of his compatriots had staged an unauthorized invasion, laying waste the Reef and a couple of other bars, and roughing up some of the natives. "They did tear the place up a bit," the blonde conceded.

"Good for them," said the short, dark fellow. "We're supposed to be protecting these jokers, and they skin us any chance they get."

"Well," said the third soldier, "even if he was drunk, that Scots bloke should 'uv known better than to head back for his room by himself, late as it was."

"In B.C. [Belize City]," the blonde explained to me, "they won't let us off the base at night except in threes. It's a lot riskier there, but some of the places are a good bit of fun."

"More than here," growled short-and-dark, who kept looking over his shoulder at a couple of young women leaning through the bar window. The women seemed willing to flirt with anyone but him.

"You got to be careful about AIDS, though," said the older soldier. "They say a lot of the girls in B.C. have it now."

They filled me in on the places to go in Ladyville and Belize City—Legend's, where the music was a bastardized reggae-rap; Rosie's and the Upstairs Café, where you could meet really pretty Creole women; the Miami Nights and the Lumberyard. The blonde said they were heading back next day, and if I wanted to come along, they'd make the rounds with me, show me the sights. I was tempted. It all sounded a lot more lively than the cocktail lounge at the ritzy St. George Hotel, the only night spot in Belize City that I'd been to. But my more prudent self got the better of me. I told them I'd stay on at Caye Caulker a little longer, that the Reef and the nearby Pirate's Disco were all the nightlife I could handle right now.

"Suit yourself," said the blonde.

"Where you going after?" asked the older fellow.

"San Ignacio, I guess. Then maybe try to see some jungle. The Cockscomb Range."

"Let me tell you about the Cockscomb," said short-and-dark. "Some mates of mine tried to climb Victoria Peak in there, and they come back with half their hides skinned off. We catch some of that on maneuvers too. It's that bloody bamboo cane. Cuts like knives."

"I know," I said.

"Well," said the blonde, "I don't know what you want the jungle for, but San Ignacio can be a bit of fun."

Before they moved on, we talked a little about the Guatemala-Belize hassle, which I'd read about but half-forgotten. The older soldier knew the story by heart: How in the first half of the nineteenth century, the newly created Republic of Guatemala had laid claim to Belize, which at that time had no official boundaries or status as an independent state. How England, eager to protect its interest in the still flourishing logwood and mahogany industry, entered into an agreement with Guatemala stipulating that the English would build a road from the Bay Settlement to the Guatemalan capital—thus enhancing trade possibilities for both countries—in exchange for Guatemala's recognition of Belize's existence as a separate state. How, having surveyed the route, the English found the proposed road too costly to construct and reneged on the agreement. And how that set the stage for an ongoing border

dispute among Belize, England, and Guatemala that, twice during the
1970s, had the latter country mustering troops on the Belizean border.
An invasion would quite probably have occurred if international pressure, and the English military presence, had not forced Guatemala to
back off.

"On Guatemalan maps, they still show Belize as part of Guatemala,"
said the blonde.

"Well, it's all over now," said the older soldier. "Looks like Guatemala's given up on the idea of a takeover. I don't understand why they
still keep us stationed here."

"What I don't understand," said short-and-dark, "is why Guatemala
would *want* this bloody place."

The middle-aged California couple were next to descend, with a
younger California couple in tow whom they had met while snorkeling
that afternoon. They stayed just long enough to kindly buy me a fresh
beer and assure me they were having a glorious time. I could see they
were. They looked toasty-red, bright-eyed, younger. "It's so—so—,"
burbled the female half of the older couple. She knew that "atmospheric" or "picturesque" were words too obvious to use, but she couldn't
think of a substitute.

"Atmospheric?" I said.

"Yes!" she exclaimed, looking relieved.

With a stupid little pang, I noticed that she and her husband were
holding hands under the table.

"I don't really give a shit about the scuba diving and all that," said
the male half of the younger couple. "What I like is the lying around.
I've never been to such a laid-back place. It's great. It's the exact opposite of San Francisco."

We all nodded our agreement to that.

The Swedish boy said his feet already felt a little better. He extended
one of them out into the amber light flowing from the bar so I could see.
His surprisingly deep voice carried the right heavy accent, but in appearance he didn't match up with the stereotypical idea of what a Scandinavian youth is supposed to look like. He was about twenty, and
handsome, but not at all in a tow-headed, apple-cheeked way. In the
murk of the bar, his hair and eyes were mahogany dark, and his skin was
very pale. Which seemed strange, considering where he'd been spend-

ing his time lately. Fact was, he would have looked equally out of place in the tropical boondocks or an icy fjord.

As if to confirm this impression, he said, "I want to go to Israel."

When I asked him why, he seemed surprised. The answer was so obvious: "Because it's the center of the world."

He wasn't a Jew or a Palestinian. Nor did he belong to any Christian denomination, orthodox or otherwise. What he was was a mystic, with very powerful nihilistic tendencies that he had tailored to suit himself. Even at the Reef, he had his pocket Bible with him. He showed it to me after he had finished showing me his foot. He explained that he read it, day in, day out; that it was God's voice speaking to him in a very direct and private way; that he had never allowed himself to be corrupted by what other men had to say about that voice. "Whenever my soul is coming close to a purified state," he explained, "I am not just reading anymore, you understand? The words are not any longer just words on paper. I hear His voice talking directly to me. When that happens, I move deeper and deeper toward a true understanding of what He is trying to tell me. What He tells me is that I must wipe my soul absolutely clean. I am not talking about virtue, you understand. There is no such thing as that. I mean I must erase it clean the way you would erase a song on a diskette tape. Create a perfect blankness. That is what God means by purity."

By quoting his comments like that, I might seem to be suggesting that the young fellow had some circuits disconnected. But I'm not; and I'm sure he didn't. He was strange, maybe. Too much alone inside himself. But not at all goofy. In fact, I felt at ease with him and really liked him. He reminded me a little of Roland, the young poacher at Crooked Tree. Both young men were a little lost; and they were both hung up on the idea of purity. True, their notions of that blessed state could hardly have been more opposed. I can't imagine what Roland would have thought about the square-jawed young man from Minnesota who was buying the Swedish boy beers. While we talked he came over, set a fresh beer on the table, and walked back to the bar without saying a word. The boy wiggled his toes at me again. "Corruption of the flesh is nothing. I want my feet to heal, yes, but if they don't, it's not important. What matters is to achieve inside a perfect whiteness, an emptiness filled with white light. That way, one need never care about anything, not really. Except that pure inner state of being beyond caring. You understand? Even when one feels hunger, or passion, or love, it doesn't touch the soul anymore. People don't realize how everything we think and feel is as much a part of the body as blood and bones. They don't understand that grief and pain are just as physical as the tears we shed. The same is true of the love of someone, even the love of God. It's not what is important, you see? It doesn't matter how we use or abuse that physical side of us, as long as the soul is absolutely separate and untouched." He stared at me with his great dark eyes. "God doesn't want us to love Him. To Him, that is all part of the bodily unimportance. He doesn't want anything. But if He did, He would want our souls to be free of *everything.*"

He said he had come a step closer to that beatific state—which, presumably, not even the joy of beatitude could taint—while living with a rustic Creole family at Teakettle. He had baby-sat the several children ("When they are very little they have no souls, which is the next closest thing to having a soul that is truly pure"), caught edible mud fish—"poopsie" and "crana"—in roadside ditches, and ridden the family's runty little horse in the fields behind the simple house on stilts. And for hours every day he had read his Bible and often heard the voice of God. "Belize is a good place to work toward purity. Everything is 'body' here, but people make a joke of it. They are like wise animals; they know none of it really matters, although, of course, they don't know why." He shook his head solemnly. "But wherever you are, even in a good place like Belize, it takes a long time. When I know I am almost ready, then I will go to Israel."

I gave him a supportive nod or two. God knows, there had been times during the last year when I could have wished for a pure, dry whiteness as devoid of "bodily" feeling as unleavened bread is devoid of taste. But now in the presence of this Swedish boy I just felt sad and oddly moved, and a little worried for him. I'm not much on instant psychoanalysis, but, extrapolating from my own experience, I guessed that he must have been terribly hurt at some point, to find solace in the kind of salvation he envisioned. Only in his case the damage must have been done when he was still too young to have discovered that love and grief, though all too often linked, are not the same thing. He had drawn a false syllogism somewhere along the line, equating them with jungle rot.

We talked for a little while longer. Then the Swedish boy finished his beer and got up.

I said, "Even if they aren't all that important, I hope your feet get better soon."

He smiled gravely, like the lost child he was. "Thank you," he said. "And I hope that whatever is bothering you gets better soon too."

I had been careful not to catch Bruce's eye when I noticed him at the bar, but he joined me anyway. I had nothing against him. In fact, we got along well enough. The previous evening, when we were both headed in the same direction through the southern end of the village, he had been a real help in advising me about an inexpensive place to stay. And along the way he introduced me to a good little restaurant where we had a quick supper. True, when it was over, he had announced that he didn't have any more cash on him; so I had to lend him five bucks that I figured I might as well write off.

He had fooled me, though. This morning, while I was passing by the little cement building where he kept a room rented, he had waved me over and offered me a beer and a hit from the inevitable joint. When I declined both of those, he macheted the top off a coconut, and while I drank the milk he recited some of his poetry:

> Lamely prattle vocalizes
> Every thought that still surprises
> So laugh and jeer a short life here
> Some are beckoned and do not fear
> The darkening of a sunswept sky
> Feeling just a bit too high.

"I wouldn't think of writing unless I'm good and stoned," he explained. When I said that that was pretty obvious, he frowned rather dangerously for a second, then broke into a coughing laugh. "You're right about that," he said. As punishment or reward, he gave me a piece of his prose to read, a short story. The hero was an ultramacho Mickey Spillane type who returns to Honduras—alias the Mosquito Coast— where he is *persona non grata,* and becomes gorily involved with a local cult leader who still celebrates the good old Carib rites of human sacrifice and cannibalism. At the end the hero is about to be sacrificed, but he breaks loose and regretfully kills the cult leader, who is basically his sort of people even though they are enemies.

When I had finished it, I told Bruce, honestly enough, that the story idea was interesting, but he needed to do some rewriting. Again the angry scowl. "I never rewrite," he said. "It takes away the spontaneity, the innocence. I write from the gut."

After that he showed me his diving equipment, insisting that I try out his brand new 1280× metal detector to detect metal objects on the bed, in his luggage, wherever. Then, as he readied himself to go out treasure hunting and I made for the door, he reached into his pocket and peeled a $5 bill from a pretty thick roll. He said, "Thought I'd forgot, didn't you? Well, if you'd asked for it, I wouldn't have paid you back."

As I say, I really had nothing against Bruce. Except his poetry. But he had a bellicose way about him that did make me uneasy. The waitress at the restaurant the previous evening had almost refused to serve him when he came on to her in a pretty crude, aggressive way; and he had had an ugly quarrel with the island youth who had wheelbarrowed his gear, including the new metal detector, to his quarters. True enough, the fellow, a slim mestizo with a hustler's smile, had doubled the agreed-on price for his services between the main pier and Bruce's room; but in the argument that followed, Bruce was the one who seemed ready to settle things with his fists if the youth didn't back down, which he halfway did.

And now here he was sitting across from me, more drunk and stoned than ever. I noticed that the mestizo youth was in the bar too. Bruce exchanged a long sullen look with him. "Bastards," he muttered, "they'll steal you blind if you let 'em." But then, to my relief, he subsided, leaned his thick arms on the table, and, without much prompting, began telling me the story of his life.

While he talked, I reflected that, although I'd met quite a few people like Bruce over the years, I still found it difficult to relate to them. Alcoholism was their obvious problem—with a round-the-clock drug habit, in a case like Bruce's, thrown in for bad measure. But that wasn't what bothered me. I could understand addiction; I could also understand the urge to self-destruct. No; what I couldn't understand was all the other stuff that went with the Bruce syndrome: the bullying and bragging and the propensity for violence, the fake heartiness, the weird mood shifts from tough guy cynicism to maudlin sentimentality. I just couldn't figure it out. Self-destructive people were supposed to hate themselves. But if Bruce was seriously unhappy with himself, he didn't seem aware of it; and he was by no means a stupid or imperceptive person. He knew he was supposed to feel things. So he assumed all these stylized roles, pretending that he did. But it was all posturing. It was as though real feeling had gone dead inside him somewhere along the line; as though, without trying, he had somehow acquired that perfect inner emptiness the Swedish boy was searching for.

For a while he talked about his beautiful ex-wife, who had divorced him because he drank too much, and their beautiful daughter whom he thought a lot about, but hadn't been in touch with for years. Then he began telling me about his stint in the Peace Corps, almost a decade earlier, when he had no doubt been more in charge of himself than he was now. "I censused the fish and everything else out here," he said. "Not that I know what goddamned good it's ever done. Sometimes I'd mark the young conches—their carapaces are real thin compared to the older ones—and then see if they'd turn up later. Mostly though, I'd pick one spot on the reef and kill all the fish there with my spear gun, hundreds of 'em, and then see how fast it would fill up with fish again. Used to teem with fish out there—huge groupers, snappers, jacks, hog fish. And lobsters! They were so thick you could just wade out from the beach and scoop them up for dinner." He swigged his rum. "I'll tell you this. There's a lot less of all that stuff now. The people out here started getting too goddamned greedy." Another swig. "I'll tell you something else. The fish may be thinning out, but there's still a lot of gold down there. While I was censusing fish, I located dozens of old wrecks outside the reef, right where the Spanish galleons used to come past every year from Portobello. I know where every one of them is at. I've been planning this a long time. Now I got all the gear, I'm going fishing for gold!"

I don't know about the gold. But Bruce's opinion about the fish thinning out and people getting greedy is supported by the facts. During the 1960s, fishing cooperatives were established on the cayes, and the fishermen were provided with improved lobster traps, refrigeration units, and the means of exporting their catches—without, at the same time, being subjected to enforceable regulations that would have preserved the seafood resource. The result should have been predictable: as in Quintana Roo, populations of conch, spiny lobsters, and sea turtles have plummeted, and the fish being brought to market have been getting smaller and smaller. The sad thing is that overharvesting continues, legally and otherwise, even though a good many of the fishermen are now hauling tourists, rather than lobster traps, out to the reefs. . . . And that's another thing: the reef itself, especially off San Pedro, is being barnacled with white "dead zones" where the coral has taken a beating from divers and boatmen alike.

I've already remarked that Belize is making a serious effort to preserve sizable chunks of its natural environments while there is still time. But the country is poor, poor, poor, without the means, on its own, to protect conservation areas even when they are set aside. There are a couple of small reef reserves, but as of now, the main thing protecting Belize's extraordinary marine ecosystem is the sheer size of the barrier reef itself and the uninhabitable smallness of so many of the cayes. But if our species has learned anything, it must be that there is no ecosystem in the world too vast or too small for us to mess up once we start noticing it. And every year, more and more people are taking notice of Belize's magnificent coral reef and delicate little cayes.

Small as Caye Caulker is, I didn't see much of my fellow boat passengers after that. I went out to the reef a couple of times. During the afternoons I either sat for hours at the southern tip of the island where there were a lot of shorebirds and not many people, or swam across the narrow hurricane-made cut that divides the caye in two, to explore the uninhabited northern half. Acutus crocodiles are said to hang out in the mangrove swamps there, but I had no luck spotting them.

In between these unurgent activities, I napped a lot. At about five, I would drink a couple of beers at the Reef, then have dinner in one of the little restaurants, and get back to my cubicle of a room at an unnaturally early hour to write and read. A few times I did run into the Californians, still relishing the laid-backness of it all. Once I saw the Swedish boy going into one of the little stilted houses with a blonde girl; and from a distance, we waved at each other. As they said they would, the British soldiers had headed back to B.C. the morning after they and I had shared a table.

As for Bruce, I helped him, the third morning, to carry some of his gear to the little skiff he part-owned, but I declined his not very enthusiastic invitation to come along on his first hunt for sunken treasure. Actually, I wanted to avoid him. That was one of the reasons I stopped going to the Reef at night.

When it was my turn to leave the island, the man from Minnesota was a fellow passenger on the boat trip back to Belize City. He gave me a wry smile when I asked about the Swedish boy. "It was bad luck," he said, "at least for me. I mean, there can't be that many Swedes that come to Caye Caulker, right? But damned if a couple of Swedish girls didn't show up yesterday—and *they* started buying him beers. And talking existential philosophy, which I don't know shit about." He shrugged. "Who could compete with that?"

I watched the green islands of mangroves sailing past us. The stalk-like roots gleamed like polished red gold in the lovely golden light. A fine spray peeling off the boat's prow fell on us like a golden rain. It was a perfect Caribbean day, and I felt sad to be leaving Caye Caulker behind.

"Oh, by the way," said the Michigan man, shouting above the engine's roar, "did you hear about that friend of yours?"

"What friend?"

"Don't know his name, but I noticed him sitting with you one night at the Reef. He looked like he'd had a few too many."

"Bruce."

"Well, him. He deliberately picked a fight with some local guys who were in the bar last night. He was drunk out of his head. They weren't doing anything, but he kept on insulting them, calling one of them a crook. It all happened so fast! Be glad you weren't there. It was awful! They were all using broken bottles, and there was a lot of blood. I cleared out, along with most everybody else, but I heard this morning that your friend was in a bad way, all cut up. They got him off the island as fast as they could; but I don't know whether he made it or not."

I thought seriously about going to the hospital in Belize City to find out. But I never did.

You could film a dandy spaghetti Western in San Ignacio. The little town, only a few miles from the Guatemalan border, has a genuine

Dodge City ambiance about it, what with its clapboard houses, ramshackle storefronts, and smattering of latter-day saloons indifferently
aligned on the steep hills above the Macal River. Then too, there is its
beguiling cast of characters—a frontier mix of wheeler-dealers, evan-
gelicals, merchants, pioneering farmers, part-time whores, dreamers,
conmen and conned men, drifters, and as fine a collection of burnt-out
cases as you could hope to find anywhere. Ten minutes after I drove
across the one-lane Hawkesworth Bridge, where the first traffic light in
Belize will have been installed by now, I loved the place. If only it would
promise not to change, I wouldn't mind dead-ending here someday. If I
did, I would have a lot of company.

San Ignacio is no tourist mecca—I wouldn't like it if it were—but it
has an unpretentious flaky-quaint look about it that is very easy on the
eye. And on closer acquaintance, it lives up to that first amiable impression. There is plenty of barefoot poverty, to be sure; but there is very
little serious crime, and no crazies standing on the corners, no gangs of
abandoned youngsters running wild, no one who looks hungry. In fact,
although the recent advent of television will probably change things,
no one seems to resent being poor overmuch since almost everyone is.
It helps, of course, that here as elsewhere in Belize, half the population—that's no exaggeration—has relatives working in the States who
send money home. Indeed, this unofficial and unacknowledged foreign
aid probably has more to do with the survival of the country's economy,
and the remarkable absence of revolutionary movements, than any
other single factor. But it doesn't necessarily explain why San Ignacians,
in particular, are so civil to each other, and to strangers. I don't know
what does, unless it is the fact that they have never learned to feel sorry
for themselves.

By any but Belizean standards, San Ignacio's racial and ethnic mix
would give a conscientious demographer a nervous breakdown. The
Spanish have the edge in terms of numbers here, but they are composed
of several subgroups, mostly mestizos of Yucatecan descent, but also
Hondurans, Salvadorans, a few Guatemalans, and some folks who look
just plain Maya. The Creoles, in all possible shades between "white"
and "African," are the next largest contingent; and in their corner, I
suppose, you could classify a good many people who are of quite recent
Creole-mestizo descent. There is also a pretty sizable white colony, its

members deriving from England, the States, and half a dozen West European countries. Sprinkle that ethnic concoction with Chinese, Lebanese, and even a few Sri Lankans and you get—what? Well, for one thing, the appearance—which is all that any sensible person can hope for—of racial-ethnic harmony. If you ask Bob Jones, the proprietor of Eva's bar and restaurant, what he thinks of race relations hereabouts, he'll say, "Ha! On the surface, it's all right. But get a few drinks in people and then hear 'em talk. The blacks and the Spanish don't like each other a bit, and the whites don't like anybody." Bob is married to a Spanish Belizean, by the way, but never mind that. He's right about the subsurface tensions in this little country. Indeed, in some places, notably Belize City, they aren't always that subsurface. Creole males returning from the United States have been bringing back with them—along with what amounts in Belize to considerable sums of money—the oppression-oriented rhetoric of the American ghettos; with the result that some of them now wear a permanent chip on their shoulder when dealing with whites.

But here in San Ignacio, no matter what little toads may pop out of people's mouths when they are getting loaded, almost everyone mixes anywhere, everywhere, in a polite and easy way. Except for the Mennonites, who choose to live apart, there are no ghettos. Everyone knows they have to get along with each other whether they like it or not. Compared to the sort of mutual prejudice and bitterness—and fear—that are festering nowadays in most American cities, the live-and-let-live attitude around here is a joy to contemplate.

The night of the day I arrived in San Ignacio, it looked like everyone for miles around was on the streets. The usual Saturday night turnout was augmented by the fact that a school fund-raiser was in progress. The sticky scent of barbecued chicken and pork rose from the ragged little park below the bus depot, where people were selling food from pickups and stands to raise money for the school. Live music poured out of the dance halls. Coveys of girls sashayed up and down the steep streets in short, glitzy dresses. A big crowd of young people, unable to afford the cover charge, stood and sat around outside the Blue Angel, listening to what sounded like American rock. The swinging doors at R.B.'s bar never stopped swinging for the customers coming in and out, and down at the river's edge, the Western's dance pavilion, an unfinished and unsightly concrete fantasy by day, glowed like a pleasure boat at its moorings now. It was an altogether pleasant, almost sedate block party, everybody having a nice time, nobody being very rowdy, some older people standing on a corner talking, mothers and kids eating greasy barbecue from newspaper napkins.

I enjoyed the scene. I felt comfortable being part of it, but I just wasn't in a festive mood. So after I'd done my share of parading the streets, listening to the music, eating a charred chicken breast, I wandered down to the Macal. I followed it a ways, along the edge of the soccer field that the river sometimes covers when it is in flood. The music and light came from a distance now, along with an occasional loud belly-laugh or the lawnmower roar of an old car starting up. I sat down on the bank and lit a cigarette.

I had almost finished it and was thinking of heading back when I saw them, only a few yards away, coming straight toward me. Three black men, silhouetted by the orangy glow from the Western dance hall. I don't know why I didn't freeze, or get to my feet, ready to fight or run. In any comparable situation almost anywhere in the States, that's how I would have reacted. Here though, I just kept my seat, feeling cool and languid as the river itself.

"Hey, mon," said one of the young men, "you got a light?" I gave him one, with which he lit a joint. When he offered me a hit, I told him thanks but I wasn't in the mood.

He nodded. It was too dark to see his face distinctly, but I could see the smile. "Yeh, mon," he said, "I know that feelin'. Where it'll just put you further down. You just visitin'?"

They plunked themselves down beside me, and we talked for a while. They were interested in New Orleans—not the music, but the way people lived there, so I told them about that. They in turn advised me about what to see and do while I was in San Ignacio. "Which ain' much, mon," said one of them, and we all laughed. After a while I said it had been a long day and I had better get some sleep. They got up when I did. The one who had asked for a light patted my shoulder. "Go easy, mon," he said. "I can't see you too good in this dark, but I can tell you tired."

Mention Eva's to any Peace Corps worker who has done some time in Belize and he will know the place the way big-time financiers in New

York City once knew the Oak Room at the Plaza. Even more than Mom's Triangle Restaurant in Belize City, or the Watering Hole midway between there and Belmopan, or the Pelican Hotel in Dangriga, it is *the* hangout, the club house, for gringos in this country. Not that it's exclusive by any means; the clientele is multiracial. But the Creoles and Spanish don't need Eva's the way the white folks do. Here they can leave messages or forwarding addresses for friends who don't otherwise know how to contact them, post advertisements for the small businesses they are trying to get started, learn the latest local gossip, arrange for a canoe trip on the river or a journey to Pine Ridge, drown their homesickness or existential gloom in the company of acquaintances or strangers who are doing the same thing, or just order one of the unmemorable but filling specials that are offered each day at a reasonable price. For some of the lone males who are trying to make it here in San Ignacio, or who are just hanging around waiting for something to happen to them, Eva's is the only place in the world that feels like home.

The owner, Bob Jones, was a career soldier in the British army. He married a local girl while stationed in Belize, and for that reason as much as any other, settled here when he retired. He is bantam-sized, with tattoos, thinning black hair, and the impersonal but good-natured air appropriate to a bartender who has heard it all but is willing—if he isn't too busy—to listen to it all again. On the mustard-yellow wall behind the bar, among the hundreds of postcards sent to him by customers who have moved on, is the legend "Don't Worry About the Dog; Beware of Owner." No doubt he would be someone to beware of if anyone ever crossed him, but no one ever does. On the contrary, you don't sit around here long without hearing unsolicited testimonials about the way he let the tab run up for weeks while some down-and-outer was waiting for a check that never came, or how he brought a portable television set to the hospital when one of his regulars got sick, or how he lent a stranded drifter he barely knew the money to get back home.

Bob himself brushes all this off. He suffers fools gladly, but only up to a certain point. "I may not have much education," he says, "but I've got common sense. Sure, I help people out sometimes; but I'm not like some of these guys who put a lot of money into something and lose their shirt. I lend out what I can afford to lose. Some of these people who come down here with a hundred thousand and invest it are crazy. Unless they got a market in the States for what they're sellin', they're goin' to go broke—which is exactly how most of them end up." He shakes his terrier head incredulously. "Hell, if I had a hundred thousand, you better believe I'd put it in the bank, not some get-rich-quick scheme."

One of the gone-broke ones is at the bar now. He is hunched on a stool, reading Smokey Joe's column in *Amandala,* the most popular of Belize's eccentric little newspapers. People who spend much time in Belize often become addicted to Smokey Joe, following him, or trying to, with various admixtures of fascination, amusement, and dismay. Whether or not his sobriquet is a veiled reference to the stimulus he needs when writing, his clouded insights, though never dull, leave something to be desired in the way of coherence. A column that begins by stating: "We, as Belizeans, must learn the true meaning of *racism.* This word and *monopoly* are the same, leaving out black and white," will end by asking, "Parent, it is now I A.M. Do you know where your children are?" In between may be a stream of consciousness that goes like this: "As long as we continue to act stupid, the middle class will take advantage of us. This is to their benefit. Again, as they say, a bridle is for the mouth of an ass, and a whip is for the back of a fool. A curfew in any country is for the well-being of the children; it is not punishment." A little later, he will randomly but colorfully note that "most of us are so backward that we do not even know there are two sides to any story. We hear one side of a story, and we carry it like a duck with loose bowels. No bad intent here, but that is just the way most of us are."

When he has finished with Smokey Joe, the fellow at the bar half turns and peers at me through rimless sunglasses perched on a thin, beaked nose. He is in need of a shave, and looks unwell. "Jeez," he says, "the guy is spacier than I am." He shakes his head.

We will call this one of Eva's habitués Jeff. In the time it takes me to eat two overfried eggs and drink three cups of coffee, I have learned as much of his life story as he sees fit to tell. Which is quite a bit.

He is a Vietnam vet and a reformed heroin addict. After the war he worked for a time in a service business for hotels on the East Coast, but then he switched to California and dealing drugs in a pretty big way. He and his partners had their own pilot making flights from Colombia, and they kept the cocaine he imported stashed in a luxurious house not far from Reagan's ranch. For a while they all lived high, which meant among other things beautiful girls and cars and clothes. Unfortunately, the pilot became careless and got himself caught. "He said if we didn't get him off, he'd spill everything he knew about us. The lawyers took everything my partners and me had, about $36 million. And when they were sure they'd got every dime, they let him walk on some technicality."

After that, Jeff had a dream. "I'd never even heard of Belize before, but in this dream the name came to me out of nowhere. So I came down here. Why not, right? I didn't have anywhere else to go."

At Caye Caulker he went partners with a friend on a 30-foot sailboat. But then he came down with a mysterious illness—weight loss, fevers, a general malaise—so he put himself in the B.C. hospital. The doctors tried one thing and another without much success. (When I asked him if he'd been tested for AIDS, he said yes, but the test was negative.) After several weeks, still ill, he returned to the island. The house he had rented was stripped of his belongings, even the mattress on the bed, and was now occupied by a gang of cokeheads. As for his friend and partner, also a coke addict, he had disappeared with the sloop.

All this had happened some months earlier. Jeff was sure that sooner or later the ship would be spotted, his ex-friend caught. "He's down around Dangriga someplace," he said. "Where else can he go? You got to have a license, papers." Meantime, Jeff has drifted to San Ignacio, where he sits around at Eva's for an hour every morning, reading Smokey Joe and waiting.

Jeff and Buddy Worm might as well be from different planets. Buddy is as fresh of face and nice to look at as spring in Kansas—Kansas being where he's from. He and his wife and three daughters have been down here for two years, pioneering several hundred thickety acres, raising chickens, corn, soybeans, and most importantly, citrus. He too has a partner—an absent one—who has been footing the bills while Buddy does the work. Buddy is full of enthusiasm and bright-eyed agricultural idealism ("intelligent management is the key"), and he knows his subject. While we sip coffee, he reels off a textbook's worth of information about the fertile soil here in the Cayo District, the weather, the cost of maintaining an acre of orange trees, the time it takes (four years if everything goes right) before each tree produces five or six crates of oranges, and so on.

Buddy has nothing good to say about the Mennonites, who have a huge agribusiness going at nearby Spanish Lookout. It and their other large operations in northern Belize pretty much keep the country supplied with all the farm produce it can use. "They make a big thing of their religion," says Buddy bitterly, "but the truth is, they're a tight-fisted people, without generosity or charity."

On the other hand, he is up-beat about Belizean workers—the only person I ever spoke with who was. "If you treat them right, they'll work for you. Of course, they don't see anything wrong with stealing if you're foolish enough to let them do it, but I get along with them just fine."

When I mumble something about hating to see Belize deforested like most of the rest of Central America, Buddy says that only 40 percent of the country is fit for agriculture, the rest of it being too steep or too wet. And although he couldn't care less about wildlife, he assures me there is still a good bit of it on his farm, which is only a few miles from town. His daughters have recently seen a tapir, and he himself has twice spotted jaguars—nope, not ocelots, jaguars—near the chicken pens. He acknowledges, though, that he has killed hordes of the melodious blackbirds that raid his milo, and, less forgivably, the parrots that eat his corn.

Buddy has been sounding so optimistic about his farm's potential yield, both in produce and profit, that it comes as a real shock when he suddenly remarks that his partner is pulling out on him. It seems that, so far, the farm had been operating at a loss of more than $30,000 a year. Now, without the partner backing him, Buddy will have to pull up stakes. His young Tom Sawyer face takes on a grimly determined look. "I'm not worried," he says, although he plainly is. "We've found another place; and this time I'll have a partner who has more patience, someone who knows how to take the long view."

Robby is one of the most regular of the regulars at Eva's, and one of the most gregarious. Even before I have a chance to ask him anything about himself, he tells me that he is "just hanging in there, y'know. Just waiting for a proper break."

While he is waiting, Robby serves as the off-and-on manager of the Central Hotel-*cum*-jumping house (lumpy mattresses and one light bulb per room) next door to Eva's. Since it is not a demanding job, he starts hitting the bottle the minute he wakes up and doesn't quit until he passes out in his closet-sized room at midnight. In between, he is an ap-

pealing sort of person, a small, debauched Cockney leprechaun full of
opinions, hopes, and fitful energy. In spite of the evidence to the contrary, he still believes in himself, which, in San Ignacio, makes him a
minority of one. He is well liked by everybody, he assures me; and if
only he owned the Central Hotel, he would give it a little class and
make a success both of it and himself. As for his adopted country,
"Well," he says, "I'll tell you the truth as I see it. This is for the record.
Do I like Belize? Damn right I like Belize! Best little country I've ever
been in. I run off from Mexico where I was an oil explorer, y'know, and
came to Belize with fifty dollars in my pocket. Had to sleep under the
bar at San Pedro for a week. But who cares, right? I'm giving it to you
straight: this is a good country. They don't care who you are. But I'll tell
you what"—he looks around warningly—"them they don't want,
they'll make it hard for 'em. There's no law here, you know. If you don't
drive the police to the scene of the crime, they don't come. In a Third
World country, you got to know how to take care of yourself! Me, I understand the people, right? Ask me who I was talkin' to five minutes ago
and I can't remember if they was black or white. That's just the way I
am. Isn't that the way I am, Bob?"

From behind the cash register Bob looks up. "You're so drunk all the
time," he says with a wink at me, "you wouldn't remember if they was
purple."

One of the successes among San Ignacio's expatriate community, albeit in a modest, rather off-beat way, is Rosita Arvigo. She is an attractive, gypsy-looking woman in her middle years who sometimes comes
to Eva's, accompanied by her young husband, for dinner and a change
of pace. She is the first woman I have ever met who has an honest-to-
God Mona Lisa smile. For years she apprenticed herself to an ancient
Maya shaman, learning from him the secret medicinal and health-
preserving properties of Belizean herbs and plants—secrets that among
his own people were rapidly being lost. Rosita has dedicated her own life
to this occult and perhaps important study. She lives outside of town at
a pleasant place on the Macal where visitors can buy her herb remedies
and, for a small fee, walk along a nature trail where many of the medicinal plants are growing. I like her, among other reasons, because she
seems so profoundly calm and imperturbable; and also because she
doesn't want to see San Ignacio and its environs change too much. She

comforts me by saying, "This country is not to everyone's taste. For one thing, Belize City serves as a wonderful buffer." I had never thought of Belize City in quite that constructive way, and resolve to like it all the better for scaring at least some outsiders off.

Of all the people who frequent Eva's, the one who moves me most is Andy, though I'm not sure why. He was wary of me at first. Later he would admit that when I introduced myself he suspected I was from the CIA.

Andy is one of those legions of blue-collar Americans, no longer young, who were left culturally stranded two decades ago in the ebbing tide of the Aquarian Age and the Vietnam War. Without benefit of affluent parents, a heightened social consciousness, or a college education, he grew up doing all the hippie things, wearing long hair and earrings and smoking dope; but he was not much affected by the ideals that had once given the counterculture its ephemeral vitality. Before he knew it, he was slipping into early middle age without ever having discovered any sense of purpose in himself or the world around him. Tired of pumping gas and starting cars in the midwestern snow, he hankered for some place warm to live, and by hit-and-miss he wound up here. Behind him he left a couple of ex-wives, and a son and daughter. "The boy's doing all right, but the girl's no good. She's on heroin, and she's got this little kid." Andy refuses to accept any responsibility for the way his daughter has turned out. The grandchild, whom he has never seen, is the one he worries about. "It really bugs me, what's going to happen to him. With a mother like that, the kid don't have a chance. If I could just get set up here, maybe he could come down here sometimes. Get outdoors. He's old enough now. When my son was his age, I used to take him canoeing in the Ozarks, stuff like that. Maybe that's one reason he hasn't turned out too bad."

Andy owns some canoes. He didn't come to Belize with $100,000 to invest in a get-rich-quick scheme; and—fortunately—he doesn't have a partner. But he has sunk all the little money he had in the canoes and the beat-up pickup he needs to haul them around.

His idea, to build up a canoe rental and takeout service for outdoor-minded tourists, with himself available as guide, would seem to make a lot of sense. Belize is blessed with a number of beautiful rivers and streams that twist and turn their way down from the Maya Mountains to the sea. The Macal, one of the two main tributaries of the Belize River, is probably the loveliest of them all. It rises deep in the all-but-inaccessible jungle wilderness of the Vaca plateau, not very far from the ruins of Caracol, the largest Maya ceremonial center in Belize, where glyphs have been discovered that commemorate the conquest of neighboring Tikal in the sixth century.

Descending the Vaca, the Macal flows clear, cold, and swift, through the Mountain Pine Ridge Forest Reserve, past miles of tropical pine forests and rocky ledges riddled with caves. At Negroman, it becomes navigable to a canoe, and from there it is a day's paddling, with some white water, to San Ignacio. Just below the town, it joins with the Mopan tributary to form the Belize River. And from there, one can canoe all the way to Belize City if one wishes to—a trip that takes about a week.

Andy's idea makes sense. But perhaps not common sense. There are problems. For one thing, it can be murder getting into Negroman or one of the other put-in spots, especially in a pickup that has seen better days. Under the best of circumstances, the ride can shake your teeth loose; and after a heavy rain the logging roads, the only access, may be altogether impassable. Far more serious, though, is the fact that eco-tourism, though it holds great promise in terms of Belize's future economy, still has a long way to go before it has much impact in the San Ignacio area.

So the pickings have been pretty slim for Andy. Still, he somehow manages, making his home in a defunct school bus, painting "Canoes for Rent" signs, waiting around Eva's on the chance a prospective customer may turn up. "This is all I got," he says moodily. "I don't have nowhere else to go." Then he brightens momentarily. "Anyway, I like it here. Of course everything is getting built up—the West Branch of the Belize River has a lot of farms along it now—but this little country's still got everything; swamps, mountains, barrier reefs, jungles. There's still a lot of bush left once you get away from the roads. And so far there ain't that many of them."

It is early evening. We have left Eva's where our conversation began, and wandered down to the now all-but-deserted Western bar. In its way, the Western tells us what happens to the dreams of many of the people—not all—who have found their way here from somewhere else. The place was ambitiously conceived. The pavilion-like dance hall (though not the folk arts shop underneath) is raised safely above the river's flood stage by an arcade of quasi-baroque concrete columns. And the wide balcony, decorated with ornamental brackets and a balustrade of elaborately patterned cinder block, allows a fine view of the river. But the blue interior is bare and rather gloomy; and inside and out, nothing is finished. The fancy balustrade ends in a makeshift plank barricade, iron braces poke out where the concrete casting has left off, and unconnected electric wires hang limp from the walls. The place has remained in this state for years, the conception half realized, half abandoned. No one notices, no one minds. Only if someone ever finishes work on it will anyone be surprised.

From the balcony where Andy and I sit, we can watch half-naked Creole men washing the trucks they have backed into the river shallows. On the opposite side, under billowing trees, small Hispanic children splash about. Closer by, a crowd is watching a soccer game being played on the field I had walked across two nights earlier, when I first arrived in San Ignacio. I feel as though I have been living here for much longer than that.

Andy orders another double shot of rum. In the two hours we've been talking, he has already put away at least four. He does not look as unwell as Jeff, but he doesn't look in the best of health either. What with his earring and ponytail of lank brown hair, his sunk-in eyes and gaunt face, he could pass for a pirate who has had to cope with one bout of malaria too many.

"I dunno," he is saying. "I wish it could be enough for me—nature and all that. I like being outdoors. But to tell the truth, I don't like going with the tourists and Peace Corps kids that much. They're so fuckin' cheery, and they want to know the names of the birds and all that, and I feel like an ignorant asshole for not knowing the answers. Anyway, they don't usually need someone along. It's not like you're going to get lost or anything. What I'd like to do more of is go fishing. There's good fishing around here, you know. They got catfish, snook, tuba. The tuba is good eating. Sort of a perch with a bump on its head like a dolphin. . . . And another thing they got is these giant crawdads, river lobsters they call them. Hardly anybody knows about them because the guys who catch them cook and eat them on the spot. They'd make some good money if they had the sense to sell them at the market. They're a real delicacy." He reaches behind him, trying to rub his back.

"I dunno. Maybe if I could get the boy down here, I'd do that kind of thing more."

Unexpectedly, he spits out his dentures. When they come to a skidding stop on the table between us, he gives me a sunken smile, amused to have startled me. "I hate them," he explains. "They hurt. I got enough else hurting without them bugging me too."

I don't ask what else is hurting, and for a while we fall silent. The trees across the river are turning a velvety blue. The air has a pretty lavender glow. The soccer game is over, and we watch the unexcited crowd disperse.

Inside the empty dance hall, a single yellow neon light comes on, throwing just enough of a pallid glow around to make the gloom more visible. Suddenly the whole world seems down-at-the-heels and a little sad. Andy sinks deeper by the minute into an alcoholic melancholy. Trying to nudge him out of it, I ask him what he thinks of them—the San Ignacians, the Belizeans.

After a long pause, he gives out a little, grunting laugh and answers, "You want to know what the highest aspiration of a Belizean is? It's to have a little store. If you go down the street, you'll see a half-dozen little stores that've all got the same damn thing. They go to the United States—they got more Belizeans in the States than in Belize, you know—and they send home forty bucks a month. So they get their store, and whatta they do? They stock it with the same stuff that's in all the other little stores. And even if they make a little money, instead of restocking, they spend it. . . . People down here just don't have the business mind."

He drains off the last of the rum, and then gives me a long dead-sober stare. "I know what you're thinking," he says. "You're thinking, Hell, who am I to talk, right? Well, the answer is, I'm Nobody, that's who. I know a lotta guys I went to school with who are really making it right now. And here I am, just scrounging around." He turns away, looking out across the empty field. "I just wish . . ."

He decides not to finish the thought, but I can guess what it is. We sit there a while longer. I try to come up with something helpful to say. But then I think, Hell, who am I to talk?

A few months ago, I returned to San Ignacio. A year and a half had passed since my first visit. As soon as I stepped into Eva's, Bob, knowing

I had liked Andy, gave me the news that he was dead. The pain in his back had been the symptom of a spreading cancer that had killed him about ten months after I had left. But before Andy himself had realized what was happening to him, he had learned that his daughter had been jailed on a drug charge, so he had brought his grandson to San Ignacio.

A very nice, quiet German named Chris Heckert filled me in on what had happened after that. Chris had showed up in San Ignacio about a year earlier with his Daimler-Benz Unimog, an all-terrain truck that can plow its way through almost anything: desert sand, snow and ice—even jungle mud five feet deep. He had invested his life savings in the vehicle and was now trying to start a tour business, transporting tourists—I was an eager candidate—to Caracol, which was virtually inaccessible to ordinary four-wheel drives. During the last months of Andy's life, he and Chris had become buddies, spending a lot of evening hours talking and drinking together at Eva's.

"But it wasn't a good setup for the kid," Chris told me. "Andy was living in this broken-down bus up the hill. It was a pretty crumby place to live; so the two of them were here at Eva's all the time. The kid would be sitting at the table, trying to do his homework, and there was Andy sitting next to him, getting drunk." He shook his head sadly. "It wasn't good. And then Andy got really sick, and he headed back to the States to try and get treatment there. But he didn't make it. He died on the way."

In the lovely pine forests above San Ignacio live a man from South Africa and his American wife. They are among the fortunate ones who have done well in Belize, operating a small luxury resort on the banks of the Macal. Like all the other expatriates in the Cayo District, they come to Eva's from time to time to have a dinner out and visit with their neighbors. So they often ran into Andy and got to know his grandson. They have four daughters, but no son. When Andy headed back to the States, they took the boy into their home and made him part of their family. And that is where he lives now.

That same evening, while Chris and I were talking about the planned trip into the jungle near Caracol, Chris interrupted himself to say, "That's them."

The family had come to Eva's for dinner and were arranging themselves around a table in a corner of the room. Even if I hadn't known a thing about them, I would have found it agreeable just to look at them. They were the sort of family one might imagine being featured in a Belizean version of *Little House on the Prairie*—this is still pioneer country, remember—what with the handsome, steady-looking father, the smiling, officiating mother, the pretty daughters in their teens. And, holding the chairs for two of his adoptive sisters, before sitting down between them, a young boy, maybe 10 or 11 years old. He had fine, clean-cut features, neatly combed blond hair, a scrubbed, cared-for look about him. He was on his best behavior—eating out at Eva's was an occasion, after all—but his bright eyes swept the room with an alert, smiling interest, resting briefly on one face and another, including mine. He was having a good time.

"Nice-looking kid, uh?" said Chris.

I had to turn away. I was thinking of poor Andy, of course, wishing he could see his grandson now. .

As for Andy's canoe rental business, it has been taken over by a former Hollywood set designer. The set designer originally came to Belize because he had invested all his savings in a can't-lose lumber export business down here. When he arrived, however, he discovered that his partner in the enterprise had simply vanished with his money. After that, joined by his nephew who had nothing better to do, he had just sort of drifted to San Ignacio where he heard about some canoes for sale. Now, he and the nephew are just hanging in there, trying hard to make it, hoping tourists will notice the flyers they've posted above the bar at Eva's.

From Belize City the only road access to Dangriga is via a dog-leg route that takes one fifty-five miles inland to bleak, deserted-looking Belmopan, Belize's new capital city, then another fifty-five miles to the southern coast.

The second lap of this detour is called the Hummingbird Highway. Belize is wonderfully rich in geographic names that sound as though they were borrowed from Truman Capote's *House of Flowers:* Orange Walk, Burrel Boom, Double Head Cabbage, Pull Trouser Swamp. But for all their whimsicality, such names are usually based on something

actual. "Hummingbird Highway," in its own witty way, is no exception
to the rule. There is an abundance of hummingbirds resident in the
area—barbthroats, hermits, and sabrewings, among others—but the
highway takes its name, not from the birds themselves, but from their
frenetic mode of flight, which it does its best to emulate as it zigs and
zags through the Maya Mountains.

My jaded van has seen many roads worse than this one; but still, at
anything over forty mph, some stretches of the Hummingbird make for
an adventurous ride. Aside from a few unpaved stretches and potholes,
the going isn't bad at all until you get past the Blue Hole—a lovely, easily missed place about eight miles out of Belmopan, where an underground river surfaces for a few dozen yards before ducking out of sight
again. But from there on to Middlesex, some thirty miles as the Hummingbird flies, the tarmac is as full of holes as a Swiss cheese; between
them and the sharp dips and turns and one-lane bridges, a driver has no
choice but to keep his eyes on the road full time.

Which is too bad, since the Hummingbird makes its way through
some perfectly stunning jungle scenery, all of it perpendicular. The
Maya Mountains are not especially high as mountains go. At 3,675 feet,
Victoria Peak in the Cockscomb Range is as tall as they get. But their
slopes are a challenge to a climber, being not only steep but covered by
a tropical forest that guards the peaks like a miles-wide barbed wire
barricade.

Nevertheless, even these impenetrable mountains are being pene-
trated. The process is just beginning along the Hummingbird Highway,
but already a good many of the knolls and lower slopes look as though
they had been given a roundhead's haircut.

"It's crazy to clear those slopes," I grumble. "They're way too steep
for farming."

"Yeh, mon," says Lincoln, "but they good for herbs."

"Herbs?"

"Yeh, mon; you know, marijuana. They good for growin' that."

Sarita says, "Ha. Ha."

I had stopped at a narrow bridge a ways back to allow a truck to cross
from the other side. The two of them were just standing there at the
road edge, in the middle of nowhere, waiting for God or Godot or somebody. They had started at me through the van window with blank,
unexpectant eyes. When I invited them aboard, Lincoln had loaded

several cloth bags and cardboard boxes, as well as his machete and him-self, into the back. Saying, "Thank you, sir. Ha. Ha," Sarita struggled into the front seat beside me.

Now, a few minutes later, a part of me is still glad I am doing my good deed for the day; but Lincoln is making another part of me uneasy.

Lincoln is maybe 35, from Dangriga. Tall, black, gaunt, with a deep, dreamy voice. Sarita is considerably younger, short, and would be plump even if she were not pregnant, which she obviously is. She does not trust the seat belt, so whenever we hit a pothole, which is every few seconds, she bounces like a rubber ball. She has a tiny snub nose and an oriental cast to her eyes. She tells me she was born and raised in Punta Gorda. She is her own round little melting pot. Red, white, and black are visibly joined in her.

She and Lincoln are both tired. They are also pretty stoned.

"You take grass, mon?" Lincoln asks in his slurred baritone. "Co-caine? Everybody does it here."

Through the rearview mirror I can see him slouched on the cot, ma-chete in his lap, examining the camera he has extracted from my open bag.

"Government is really cracking down on growers," says Sarita. "It's hard. Ha. Ha."

"Yeh, if they are catching you with one stick in the city streets, that's $100 fine. But they don't care if you're smoking in the village or the fields. That's all right."

They tell me they have occupied a five-acre tract on the Humming-bird not far from where I picked them up. "But times are hard," Sarita says. "No jobs. We go to Dangriga, maybe get work picking oranges. He picks; I follow him, help stack and bag. It's quicker. More bags, more money." If they do get work, they can earn perhaps $15 or $20 Belize— $8 or $10 U.S.—in a nine-hour day.

Lincoln is now fiddling with my binoculars. "The El Salvadorans and Guatemalans are the ones that make the money, mon. They come in to buy the drugs, then they are taking them to Mexico in their tires."

Sarita tells me she has seven children, not counting the one on the way. When I remark that it must be hard to raise that many, she looks unhappy. "Yes," she says, chewing on her lower lip. "It's not good. I have to leave them back there by themselves."

I remember what I have read: that because Belize is one-third inhospitable mangrove swamp and one-third precipitous mountain, it is the only country in Central America that has thus far escaped the curse of overpopulation. Unfortunately, with almost 80 percent of its inhabitants under 18, and a very high birthrate, that state of grace is not destined to last. The government, incredibly, welcomes a population boom even though more than half of the country's citizens presently have no jobs or are underemployed.

"Excuse me, sir," says Sarita. "You got something to eat?"

I open the glove compartment and extract a half-empty box of Oreo cookies. She finishes it off in no time at all. I offer her a bag of lemon drops, and she quickly eats those too.

"Good," she says. "Ha. Ha."

The "Ha. Ha." isn't a laugh, not even a mirthless one. Just two nervous, disconnected sounds. During the drive, the only time Sarita really laughs is when I tell her she has a pretty name.

Somewhere along the way she politely asks where I am headed. "The Cockscomb Jaguar Preserve," I tell her, "south of Dangriga."

She looks bemused, as though jaguar preserves might be something that comes in jars. But she wants to be helpful, so she says, "Oh, south of Dangriga. Down there the road is not so good."

When we reach Middlesex, we have left the mountains behind. The settlement is a profoundly depressing little place: a few rows of look-alike board shacks housing the seasonal laborers who work the citrus groves. On the gate of one roadside shanty is a sign saying, "Quarantined. Stay Out!"

We have entered the Stann Creek Valley. The road levels out, but traffic is heavier, and there is one narrow one-way bridge after another spanning deep, eroded gullies. Under the circumstances, it is not a good idea to keep looking in the rearview mirror just to see what Lincoln is up to. But I can't help it. Right now he is carefully setting the tape recorder on the cot next to the binocs, the camera, and a Panama hat I had picked up in Mérida.

Sarita asks, "You know Chicago? My sister is in Chicago. She wants to come home because it's so cold there. But she has a job. I want to go there. Is it a lot of money to get there?"

I tell her yes. I also tell her it's not the promised land.

"I know," she says, nibbling her lower lip.

Lincoln mutters, "You have to pay the government or they won't let you have the papers to leave. Even then they are giving you a hard time. I don't know why. They should be glad to be getting us out."

"Someday we get there," Sarita says, giving me an uncertain little smile.

It is almost dark. In the middle of fields of sugarcane, still miles from Dangriga, Sarita tells me this is where they get off. A dirt road leads away to the right. A sign promises an agricultural station, but according to Lincoln the road also leads to the Stann Creek penitentiary. They unload their belongings. My belongings, I notice, are all still on the cot.

When I ask them how far they have to go, Sarita says maybe a couple of miles. Lincoln hefts his machete. "That's why I bring this, mon. I know we are walking this road at night."

Inwardly sighing, I tell them to get back in.

They are too tired and hungry and stoned to seem pleased that I am saving them a hike. I am too tired to care whether they are pleased or not.

Four or five washboard miles later, Sarita again tells me to stop. We are at a forlorn country crossroads. There is just enough light left to make out a small vacant-looking house standing on a scrubby rise. It looks like the sort of place a poorer-than-average Georgia sharecropper might have lived in fifty years ago. Except there isn't even a porch.

When they unload again at the side of the road—it is hardly more than a track—Lincoln says, "Hey mon, you want to sell this?" He has found an unopened box of Oreos in my suitcase. "Keep them," I tell him. As I drive away, he is just standing there in the road, looking as vacant as the house behind him. Sarita has opened the box and is cramming cookies into her mouth as fast as she can.

Later, when I am gratefully unloading my own bags at Dangriga's Pelican Beach Hotel, a dull gleam at the rear of the van catches my eye. It is Lincoln's machete. . . . For people like him and Sarita, it is an expensive and indispensable weapon and tool they can ill afford to lose. I groan, remembering that when they had first disembarked, Lincoln had the machete in his hand. If I hadn't taken them those extra few miles . . .

An hour later I am back at the crossroads. No light, not even a candle, shines in the little shack. I walk through knee-high weeds to the door, pound on it, yell their names, but I already know the place is deserted. Furiously, I wonder why they had asked me to leave them at this place when there is absolutely nothing around except the empty house. Where the hell have they gone? What has happened to them?

For a moment I almost hate them—for making me feel as helpless to help them as they are helpless to help themselves.

Not knowing what else to do with it, I leave the machete on the sagging doorstep. Then, angry and guilt-ridden, I head back toward Dangriga as fast as the road and the darkness will allow.

A couple of Maya workers would later find the tracks in the sand and confirm my story; but Dan Taylor, a young biologist and Peace Corps volunteer, didn't know that when I drove up to the headquarters building of the Cockscomb Jaguar Preserve and practically fell out of the van. Nevertheless, when he was finally able to make sense of my jabbering, he believed me right away. Obviously, no one could get *that* excited about something he had just made up. He gave me a congratulatory smile and a pat on the back, but he couldn't help shaking his head a bit ruefully. "I've been here fourteen months," he said, "and just once I've caught a glimpse of the tail end of one of them."

He did a quick calculation, dividing the number of people who had visited the reserve during the few years of its existence by the three recorded visitor sightings. "Boy, talk about luck!" he said. "Do you realize the odds against your actually seeing a jaguar were about a thousand to one?"

I just stood there and jiggled around inside my skin, nodding and grinning like an idiot. But privately I was thinking that there was more to it than luck. There had to be.

The 102,000-acre Cockscomb Jaguar Preserve lies in the lap of the Maya Mountains southwest of Dangriga. The Cockscomb Range, which flanks the basin on the northern side, could not be more aptly named: its serrated ridges and jagged pinnacles, very like a fighting cock's comb, rise precipitously from the jungle in a series of contorted geological spasms, reaching an elevation of 3,675 feet at the summit of Victoria Peak. From high up on these steep slopes, clear, bright streams, patrolled by otters and tapirs, tumble down through a maze of forested ravines to the basin's floor. There, they variously converge to form all or part of the headwaters of three of the Stann Creek District's major rivers. The abundant rainfall that replenishes them also accounts for the "tropical moist" jungle that drapes itself like a heavy pelt over all but the most vertical ups and downs of this rough terrain.

Remote and difficult of access though it is, even this wild enclave was not safe from the mahogany cutters. They were already up here, chopping away, more than a hundred years ago. Maps still indicate the overgrown sites of the old lumber camps, and some of their names—"Go to Hell" and "*Sale Si Se Puede*" (Leave If You Can)—are succinct comments on what the loggers thought of life in these parts. What with their activities and the pummeling administered by several hurricanes, most recently Hattie in 1961, much of the basin's forest that one sees nowadays is second growth. But terms like "virgin wilderness" are academic in a place such as this. Virgin or not, the jungle here is as much a wilderness as anyone could wish for.

The Cockscomb is the first refuge to be set aside anywhere in Central or South America for the specific purpose of protecting jaguars. It owes its existence to the research, tenacity, and sheer fortitude of a single person, Alan Rabinowitz, who comes as close as anyone I can think of to being my idea of a hero. For that reason, I have made a point of not reading his book, *Jaguar*, which recounts his efforts to track and census the great cats he loved so much. Nor have I asked probing questions of the several people I have met who knew him. Heroes deserve better of their admirers than to have their lives too closely scrutinized. What I have already heard about him is enough. He grew up a tough, withdrawn Jewish kid in a Bronx that was already well on its way to becoming the model of all our urban jungles. The only wild animals he knew anything about were the two-legged kind that stalked his neighborhood. But he did know a lot about underdogs (he being one of them), and when, later on, he chanced on the connection between the one category and the other, the preservation of wildlife became the driving passion of his life. When he was in graduate school, the great naturalist George Schaller must have recognized that passion for what it was. At any rate, he arranged for the untried young man to study the ecology of jaguars in Belize. A couple of years and a couple of close calls with death later, Rabinowitz was able to conclude that the Cockscomb basin probably contained a higher concentration of jaguars—about one for every four or five square miles—than any other place in Central America.

Rabinowitz's findings led to the establishment of a small (3,900 acre) sanctuary in 1986; but the international attention that his adventurous study generated, and the government's own growing awareness of the value of ecotourism (plus, according to one former official, the prospect of a state visit by that indefatigable and much publicized conservationist, Britain's Prince Philip), led to the setting aside of the entire basin as a jaguar refuge in 1990. By then, Rabinowitz was off in Thailand, trying to save that country's leopards and their vanishing habitat; but he did take time out to send a wire on the occasion of the ceremony dedicating the expanded preserve. In it he congratulated the government on its enlightened decision. And he also congratulated "the jaguars of Cockscomb, who are truly fortunate to have the people of Belize as their guardians."

Amen to that. Since it became independent, little Belize has demonstrated a versatile, open-minded approach to protecting its natural resources, one that I wish its neighbors, Mexico and Guatemala, would do a better job of emulating. Too broke to do much of the managing or research itself, the government, instead of jealously guarding its prerogatives, has wisely allowed the country's own (autonomous) Audubon Society and various combinations of international organizations and local people to run what is becoming an impressive assortment of forest reserves and wildlife refuges—from the jungly Río Bravo Conservation Area near Gallon Jug, and the lagoon-laced Shipstern Reserve on the northern coast, to the Mountain Pine Ridge and Caracol Natural Monument in the Cayo District. Plans to link the reserves in the southern part of the country are in the works even as this book goes to press.

All these ecologically diverse reserves are more than worth the considerable inconvenience (and/or expense) involved in getting to them. But for me, the Cockscomb will always be a place apart, the home of a heart's desire, a wish fulfilled.

Because I saw a jaguar there, of course. But also, I think, because it was the right place for a jaguar to allow itself to be seen by me.

I had already decided by the time I reached Dangriga that the Cockscomb would be the southernmost point I would try for on my outbound journey. Even before braving the potholes of the Hummingbird Highway and the washboard dirt of the Southern Highway, my van had been losing a half a quart of oil a day. It had also developed a cough and a noticeable list to starboard. With nary a Toyota spare part to be had between southern Belize and south Texas, it would be touch and go to get the poor old crate back home again.

But I had to actually arrive at Cockscomb before I realized that was not the important thing. The important thing was that I was ready to head home.

"You got to go on," Anita had adjured me in her irresistibly gallant way. When she had said that, we had both understood that "going on" would eventually mean going back—back to New Orleans, to where I had left off, to where I could start the process of starting over again. Only, it had been impossible, sitting with bright-eyed Anita in that little kitchen in Samula—God, it seemed an age ago!—to imagine the moment in the future when I would actually be ready to do that.

Now the moment had come. Or more exactly, I had come to it. It, the moment, was a destination like any other. It had been waiting for me, fixed in place—the Cockscomb—as surely as it was in time.

A few hours after I so excitedly introduced myself to him, Dan Taylor had left for Dangriga on his little Honda. At dusk, the new director of the sanctuary, Ernesto Saqui, and his assistant, Margarito, had also departed, driving the jeep down the steep seven miles of stony trail to their homes in Maya Center. I was the only visitor at the sanctuary, which meant that, until dawn, I had the whole of the Cockscomb basin to myself. Sitting there in the large, screened enclosure that was the headquarters building, eating canned tuna by the light of a kerosene lamp, listening to the cheeps, squeaks, and chirring choruses sounding from the next-door jungle, I was seized by one of those epiphanic surges of well-being when one knows with absolute certainty that one's cup runneth over. I loved this place; I rejoiced that I had come here; yet at the same time, with no sense of paradox, I felt suddenly, gladly homesick.

Dazed by the remembered vision of the jaguar, I had spent much of the day aimlessly following the well-maintained trails that wander off in all directions from the presently deserted campground. I had climbed a little way in the direction of Victoria Peak, sidestepping columns of carpenter ants bearing leaf fragments back to their sprawling hills. I had followed a tributary of South Stann Creek as it rippled around boulders and enormous buttressed roots; and I had taken a dip in the chilly, clear waters of the creek itself. On sandbars I had discovered the tracks of "mountain cow" (tapir), "antelope" (deer), and a "red tiger" (puma). And, for an hour, I had sat beside a hauntingly lovely tropical version of a cypress slough, where long rays of misty, filtered sunlight fell among the trunks of enormous trees. Some of that time I had for company a collared forest falcon, sublimely indifferent to its own beauty, posed on a branch among bromeliads and giant tree ferns.

In the late afternoon, I had settled down on the agreeably cluttered screen porch of the headquarters building with Ernesto Saqui. Along with everything else that was just right about the ending of my long outbound journey, this final interview was just right too. I had been traveling through the land of the Maya, after all. But everywhere along the way, most of the articulate and educated people I had met had been mestizos or whites or, in Belize, upper-class Creoles. They all had a lot to say about the Maya—much of it amiably patronizing. Most were agreed that they were backward; and that, in any case, "pure" Maya Indians, as a racial type, were as hard to find as jaguars, at least in the Yucatán peninsula. (In Chiapas, that is not so true.) The more-or-less Maya campesinos I had talked with had not contradicted this external view. They had struck me as a shy, patient people, trapped in a cultural time warp, drawn in on themselves. When they did try to face the onslaught of a modernism more annihilating than anything the Toltecs or the Spaniards could have dreamed of, they were likely to become changelings, like Cristino in Cancún: displaced persons waiting tables in a world that moved forward too swiftly to allow them ever to catch up.

Yet now, here was Ernesto Saqui, the exception who might or might not prove the rule. He was indisputably a pure-blooded Mopan Maya, and proud of it; and in his quiet, mild-mannered way, he was trying hard to be a leader of his people in this heterogeneous little country where the Maya are very much a minority.

"I am different," he acknowledged, by way of disposing of the obvious. "When I was a little boy, I saw what happened to these people who were Maya people when they came to Punta Gorda to sell their maize and rice. I saw how the Creoles would play a game with them.

The Maya people didn't know the difference between two dollars and five dollars. So I saw them being cheated. I saw my own father being cheated. . . . My father was only a simple man, but he never told me not to go to school. And so I went through high school and got something like a college degree. I did that because I have always decided to help my people. I guess I will continue to struggle for that as long as I have life in me."

Ernesto is largely responsible for the survival of Maya Center Village, a small thatched-roof community on the Southern Highway that lies directly below the Cockscomb basin. He is himself unmarried, but when his extended family clan were displaced by "a few rich people" who were buying Indian lands around Punta Gorda in order to raise cattle, he and they chose to settle here, "like pioneers." At first the government supported and subsidized the move; but in the mid-1980s there was a change in the country's leadership, and the Maya settlers were threatened with eviction for not meeting payments on a government loan. "So there was a fight," says Ernesto with a grim little smile. "We were very outspoken for ourselves; and also the church people helped us. And finally, because we stood up for ourselves, it was established that no one should have this land but us."

Ernesto became an elementary school teacher. When the jaguar refuge was established, he was "not too conscious of what was happening back here." When he was offered the job of director, it took him several months to make up his mind to accept. "But then I said to myself, 'This is a challenge for my life, a new thing, so I will give it a try.' Now I see that it is more of a job than I thought it would be. It is up to us to show it can be a success." Almost as an afterthought, he adds, "Also I understand now that conservation is important, not just to protect jaguars but to protect people. Belizeans are not a conservation-directed people. This is a new idea for us. We are surrounded by communities that used to hunt and fish here, and it is important they understand why the sanctuary is here. I don't think we are going to change the minds of the older folks. But I am related to the schools—I was considered one of the few teachers who were dedicated to keeping up the standard—so I have been successful in bringing the schoolchildren here, and also the local leaders. A lot of important people respect the way I do things."

Margarito, Ernesto's young assistant and close friend, joins us on the porch for a few minutes. To judge from his looks, he is a mestizo; and one of the few residents of Maya Center Village who is not related to everyone else. The idea of wildlife conservation is as new to him as to everyone else in these parts, and he speaks his piece about it as though it were a lesson learned by rote: "Well, at first I don't get to understand about not hunting here anymore, and I don't like it. But after, when I really understand, I get very involved in how we should keep the wildlife. Not just for tourists but for our younger children, to see something in their own country. So this is very important to me now."

When Margarito must deal with poachers, sweet reason is apparently the only available deterrent. "I talk to them very nicely," he says. "I try to educate them like I was educated." He glances at his friend. "I was really happy for Ernesto, who is a local Maya, to have this job. To explain to his people the reason for this wildlife. I believe he will do his very best to educate them."

Ernesto, still very much the schoolteacher, smiles and nods.

It saddens me a little that I cannot fully express to Ernesto and Margarito what it has meant to me to see a jaguar at Cockscomb. But I have learned by now that it is pointless to regret the almost total absence in the consciousness of economically hard-pressed Third World peoples of an altruistic or imaginative love of wildlife. God knows, that sort of elitist enthusiasm is not exactly commonplace even in far more privileged countries like my own. What matters, I remind myself, is that, for whatever pragmatic reasons, this sanctuary exists.

And there is only one road into it! Even without the threat of fines or jail, it is quite possible that poachers, knowing they may be intercepted by Ernesto or Margarito and obliged to listen to their lectures, prefer to do their illegal hunting somewhere else.

Ernesto is now speaking of the future of Maya Center, and of Belize. "When we first came here there were only six or seven families on the reservation. Now there are fifteen or twenty. Overpopulation? Yes, there is that problem but at least we are aware of it. I am looking into cash crops, into mechanized farming. We are going to do citrus farming, maybe, and raise cacao if the soil here is right. People say I must be crazy. They have this cultural problem; they don't want to change, so we are not always in tune with the agricultural system. But at least we are looking into these things very closely."

Ernesto is looking into other things as well. It may be that Maya

Center and the Cockscomb sanctuary will eventually prove too small a world for him. He is the spokesman for the Maya of the Toledo District and a member of the District Board. "My people are going further in education now, but they are not so educated that they can explain their problems, which is why I am wanting to defend their needs. Politics is something I always have on my mind. I want to sit where I can make decisions like anyone else. The dominant group in the country are the Creoles, so there is perhaps some discrimination because they will help their own people first. The second biggest group are the Spanish—the mestizos—and they and the Creoles don't like each other. But we and the Spanish get along much better." He pauses, thinking ahead. "As long as no one group outnumbers all the others by too much, there will not be real oppression or racial discrimination in Belize. We Maya are only 17 percent, which is not much. But"—he smiles faintly—"I think that our 17 percent can be very important if we go further with education. And if we have good leadership."

While Margarito goes off to get the jeep, Ernesto and I stand at the screen door, watching the swift onset of the luridly beautiful tropical evening. Tomorrow there will be a bunch of schoolchildren arriving, and the day after that, the country's prime minister will make his first visit to the sanctuary. Ernesto already has the walking tours and the talks all planned out. For now, his careful Maya thoughts are free to roam as they will.

"Some of the Creoles say that they have been deprived of their identity. I guess they mean because they were slaves. Which is why they fight for their identity now. Well, I think we Maya must fight too." He pauses, staring at the sunset. Then he resumes, "Education means a lot to me. I know I must change. But I will never let go of the root of me. If that is taken away, I am not the same person that was me. I will have to struggle, I guess, but no matter how I change I will still maintain myself."

By now Ernesto and Margarito will have almost reached Maya Center, where Margarito's wife and Ernesto's mother will have their suppers waiting. They will have long since eased the jeep through the Cabbage Haul Gap at the basin's low easterly rim, passing the spot where, early this morning, the jaguar had kept his appointment with me.

It had been a real ordeal for the van, skidding and scraping its way up through the jungle along a track that only a four-wheel drive could be reasonably expected to tackle—especially after a pretty heavy rain. The rocky spots and the shallow streams spilling across the trail were worrisome enough, but it was the muddy stretches, where the van had to balance on slippery ridges between deep ruts, that had almost turned a slow drive into a long hike.

I didn't care, though. By now I had become enough of a connoisseur of all-but-impassable roads to take this one in stride. Also, I was already loving the Cockscomb basin, even though I hadn't yet properly reached its borders. Gray, broad-leaved trees, only a few of which I could iden- tify, formed thick walls along the way. The little streams ran clear and sweet. Up ahead, bright green parrots (were they yellow-lored? or red- lored?) flew across the trail. A toucan waited until I was almost abreast of it before it surrendered its roadside perch. Even though it was frus- trating to have to keep my eyes so much on the track in front of me, I was glad to be in this place, glad I had come this far.

But I was unexpectant. The van was moving slowly, with a lot of noise. Any sizable something on the trail would have more than enough time to move out of sight.

Until, that is, I got over the gap and into the basin proper. Then, unexpectedly, there was a longish fairly level stretch where the lane was sandy and reasonably firm. Low, dense scrub rather than jungle crowded in on either side. I accelerated, zoomed forward, came around a sharp curve—

And there he was.

There are moments in all our lives that we remember in slow motion; and that is the way I remember this one. At exactly the right instant, not twelve feet ahead of me, he came bounding out of the wall of un- derbrush on the left side of the road, landed in the middle of the track with his tail curving upward, his outstretched legs seeming to fold, to collect under him; so that for a long second he appeared to pause, the sunlight glowing on his arched, exquisitely dappled back, his white muzzle and golden eyes turned toward me. Then, momentum gathered, he lunged forward as I braked, vanishing effortlessly into the thickets on my right.

There was a comic aftermath to this stunning moment. At almost the exact spot where the jaguar had disappeared, a skinny little gray fox darted into view, tail a-bristle, and ran frantically down the trail. Possibly the jaguar had been pursuing it; but I think it more likely that the cat, his attention focused on me, had almost landed on top of the poor creature unawares, scaring it out of its wits.

I was thrilled out of mine. It took me several minutes to collect myself, to begin to breathe normally, to remember which pedal in the van was the accelerator and which the brake. I didn't need the benefit of Dan Taylor's calculations a little while later to know how slim the chances were that I should actually see a jaguar in the wild.

Yet I also knew, even while my heart was still throbbing like a kettle drum and my brain practically short-circuiting with excitement, that there was more to this encounter than random chance could explain. Later, alone in the Cockscomb's restless night, I did try to make some rational sense of this irrational certainty. I didn't get very far, however. The best I could come up with was the fact that I had, so to speak, got in the way of traffic. I had brought myself to a place where there was a chance—a thousand-to-one chance—that an encounter with a jaguar could occur.

I have returned to that moment a thousand times since. And logic always takes me that far and no further. Always I end up where I began, with the unshakable conviction that my own longing, my dire need, loaded the dice that morning in my favor.

I had set out on a journey, hopelessly hoping that I might somehow find the means to make myself whole again. In due course that muddled quest had been paralleled by another: the not quite acknowledged search for an animal that was to me as mysterious and magical as a unicorn, the incarnation of everything in the world that was still beautiful and wild. Neither quest had seemed to have much chance of success. Yet I had found my elusive and magical beast. And in doing so I had recovered a measure of joy in my life that I had thought was lost for good.   .

I say I "found" the jaguar. But it would be more exact to say that the jaguar found me. He had been waiting there, I am absolutely sure of it, at that turning in the trail.